# GROW

## JOURNEY TO A TRANSFORMED LIFE

### BRAD BRUCKER

*For Mimi –*
*One of the dearest people we have ever known.*
*A true friend, a surrogate grandma to my kids.*
*We love you and will see you again!*

# Endorsements

---

"GROW is a discipleship emphasis that is desperately needed today. Brad Brucker's book is a clear and encouraging plan to lead a follower of Jesus to become a mature believer. This book has major potential to change a life, a church and the world."

Mark Batterson
New York Times Best-Selling author – *The Circle Maker*
Lead Pastor of National Community Church

"Brad Brucker maps a course to the abundant life for followers of Christ. There are some rest stops along the way, but it's not for slackers. It's a practical, demanding, church-centered plan to change the world, one transformed life at a time."

Robert E. Coleman
Best-Selling author – *The Master Plan of Evangelism*
Distinguished Senior Professor of Evangelism and Discipleship
Gordon Conwell Theological Seminary

"Brad Brucker provides an excellent step-by-step guide to spiritual transformation and discipleship— Steps he's developed after years of training and experience. Practice what you discover in this book and your life will be changed and so will those you love."

> Bill Perkins
> Best-Selling Author – *Six Battles Every Man Must Win* and *When Good Men Are Tempted*
> Contributing Editor – The Journey Bible and The Leadership Bible

"If you are just a leader in the church trying to make it 'run', then this isn't the book for you. Brad Brucker takes Jesus' command to "make disciples" very seriously. He has developed an ordered plan toward that goal. The wise reader will use this book as a template to develop a disciple making plan for his or her congregation."

> Matt Hannan–Senior Pastor
> New Heights Church
> Vancouver, WA

# Acknowledgements

The insights and experiences found in these pages are first and foremost a result of the grace of God and him putting many amazing people into my GROW Journey. I am constantly amazed that God first drew me to University Presbyterian Church in Seattle in my early Christian journey. So many people there have help shaped in me a healthy view of Christ and His church. When I was there, I went on a retreat and met a monk named Father Francis. Francis, early on you brought spiritual and emotional healing that were vital to my journey.

From Seattle, we moved to Chicago and spent five years at Willow Creek Community Church, where Bill Hybels totally rocked my boat and infused in me a deep love for the lost. So many leaders and fellow ministry partners there were instrumental in equipping Ann and me to come back to Oregon to plant a church. Once back in the Pacific Northwest, Matt Hannan of New Heights Church took a big risk on me. It was through New Heights and Dave Reynolds and NW Church Planting that we were able to launch Woodhaven Community Church in Sherwood, OR. Many people at Woodhaven were instrumental in my own growth, too many to share here. The Transformeter was the early version of GROW way back when at Woodhaven. Andrea, Bob, Mike, Armando and others were so key in creating that original tool that would become GROW.

I'd also like to give special thanks to my pastor and friend, Stan Russell, who kept the dream of GROW alive in me once Woodhaven merged with Horizon Community Church. Your leadership and encouragement as well as the rest of the Horizon leaders and staff at all our campuses were absolutely essential in making GROW happen.

Natalie, you have been nothing short of remarkable in helping to put this book together. Thank you so much. Jayson you've been like a son to me and such a great partner to journey with who, with me, are living out the truths of GROW. Bob and Sue, without you, both Ann and I would be toast by now. When we got hit hard, you were always there to scrape us off the pavement, pick us up and keep us in the game. We are so blessed to have you in our lives.

Thanks to Phil Disney and David Conlee for your contributions to the graphics found in GROW. Thanks also to my incredibly creative daughter, Sarah Otteson, for leading the way in birthing the vision for all the graphics for GROW. Makes all the difference!

Willie, Sarah, Nathan and Elliot, my kids…what can I say? God has used you perhaps more than anyone to help me grow. Fact is, without you, I wouldn't have many sermon illustrations, for better and for worse, some of which are shared in these pages. You're amazing and I love you desperately.

Lastly, and most importantly, thank you to Ann, my bride and true life and ministry partner. I've said it before and I'll say it again, I could have never started a church, done ministry, planted churches without your amazing help, sermon editing, book editing and devotion. You are my one and only. I love you all the time and all the time!

# Foreword

B rad Brucker has been my friend for many years. I can tell you with great enthusiasm that he is genuine, authentic and a true disciple of Christ. Brad is the real deal and everything he says in this book he endeavors to live out with his whole heart. I have observed his life close up and have seen firsthand that he is a person who is in the Word every day, a hard-working servant of the Lord and a soul winner. I have seen Brad work through some difficult circumstances in his life and apply the principles of forgiveness and reconciliation emphasized in this plan. As his pastor, I can also say most assuredly that Brad is a generous and gracious man of God.

He has not only endeavored to live the principles in this book, but he has tried and tested this plan through years of being a pastor.

Most importantly, I want you to know that Brad has been great at making disciples and that those he has taught have grown strong and vibrant in their faith. He has taken biblical values and created a discipleship plan that works for the local church. I believe this so much that our local body, Horizon Community Church, has adapted GROW as our discipleship model. Whether an individual or a church, reading and applying the biblical values in GROW will change your life for the better!

Pastor Stan Russell
Lead Pastor, Horizon Community Church
Tualatin, Oregon, USA

# Content

# Introduction

I f you were offered a miracle elixir that was proven to totally change your life for the better, would you take it? No? Me neither. But what if there was something you might already have or something very close to you, that would help, and millions of credible folks over two millennia attest to its transformative power in their lives? Would you buy it? What if God himself told you in writing about a plan he has for your life to truly give you sustained joy and an amazing future? Well, that's exactly where this book is headed.

In this book, I share a biblical plan to transform your life. It works, if you embrace it. However, this is likely not your typical book. In it, I share several of my mess ups. Oh yeah, I have made mistakes—big ones! Many are in here. Funny how we Christ-followers are always trying to put a perfect face on our faith. Why do we do that? The Holy Spirit didn't when he inspired forty plus flawed human authors to write the Bible. We are messy people, but God is good in spite of us. So, I will share a little dirt about myself for the sake of transparency. I want to show how any willing soul can have their messy life transformed by a holy God and be used to transform others. This book is a real, time-tested plan. If you use and apply the plan in this book to your life, I believe God will take your mess and make it a message for his glory.

Over the course of my spiritual journey as a Christ-follower and pastor, I have been to many excellent conferences and have had the privilege of being pastored by some amazing, world-class pastors and leaders. The one thing they all have in common is a desire to fulfill The Great Commission. Now, that said, here's the big question: Do you have a plan? Do you have a clear plan and path to "Make Disciples?" Be honest! Is it happening in your church? If you are a church attender, is it happening to you? The truth is, some surveys state that only one percent of all churches in America have a definitive clear plan to make disciples. Other surveys indicate that perhaps up to 30 percent of churches are doing an okay job at making disciples. Still, that's not a number to get too excited about. The crazy thing is, every pastor and Christian leader wants to make disciples, but very few have a plan do so. Some want a plan, others don't. But that's what this book is all about. It's a plan! It's a proven plan to radically transform people's lives. All church leaders should want to do that!

### Turning Pagans into Missionaries

When I was living in Chicago, getting a Masters in Divinity at Trinity Evangelical Divinity School and doing my internship at Willow Creek Community Church, I remember my pastor at the time, Bill Hybels, telling the story of a visit he made to the Harvard Business School. This is how I recall the story: After giving a presentation of what Willow was all about, Hybels began to field questions. One student asked, "So, let me get this straight, what you're trying to do is turn pagans into missionaries?" Hybels replied, "Exactly!" And, after being at Willow Creek for five years and starting a parenting ministry there, I can say without a doubt, Bill Hybels' greatest and most sincere intention was to do just that. His mission was to "Turn unchurched people into fully devoted followers of Christ." The problem was that after their own (very bold) "Reveal" study, their plan was lopsidedly seeker-targeted and didn't work out as well as they hoped.

Now, that said, I have nothing but the highest admiration for Bill Hybels and Willow Creek. They gave it their best shot. And what leader is humble enough to re-evaluate what they're doing, after 30 years of doing it, and actually publish that they got some things wrong?

On another occasion, during my five-year stint at Willow, I heard Bill give a leadership talk to the staff about discipleship, and he said, "We really need to crack the code on this." I love that! I love his heart and, knowing Bill from afar, I think he's a little too hard on himself. I'm convinced he has made more disciples than most. For one, his leadership produced an amazing Christian author in Lee Strobel—from atheist to missionary—one of the greatest apologists of our time!

Fast forward a few years. In 1999, my wife Ann and I left Willow for Oregon, where we sensed God calling us to plant a church. I thought, "We've got the goods. We've been trained!" So, we started a church, and people actually came. It was amazing! More than that, people were coming to Christ. It was so good! But, if I'm honest, I was more concerned with building a megachurch like Willow Creek than making disciples. We saw many people come and go, but about six years into it, I just wasn't seeing huge fruit in the form of people sold out to Jesus. So, I went up into the Oregon mountains by myself to my favorite lake to pray and fast. It was October of 2005, at 4700 feet, no one else was in the campground but me.

There I was in my little tent: me, my sleeping bag, my lantern, and my Bible. I read Luke chapter four, where Jesus is led by the Holy Spirit out into the wilderness. The Devil tempts Jesus in multiple ways, but Jesus isn't buying. At one point, the Devil takes Jesus to a high place and shows him all the kingdoms of the world. And then, preying on Jesus' ego, he promises, "If you bow down and worship me, I will give you all of these." When I read that, God squarely landed a wrecking ball on my heart and I realized that, in my desire for a mega-church, I was seeking to build my own kingdom and not his. I bought something Jesus never tried to sell, but the devil has been selling to men and women for centuries to stroke their egos. I realized that Jesus didn't have an ego to stroke, but I sure did. E.G.O. = Edge God Out. That's what I was doing—edging God out! So, I repented right there and then. And I asked him, "Lord, what do you want me to do?" The words of Jesus to Peter immediately came to mind, "Feed my sheep." In other words, "Make disciples and teach them to obey everything I commanded them." "Everything?" "Everything!" "Okay," I said, and I felt the weight of the world fall off my shoulders and the love and favor of God flood back into my soul.

That was a defining moment for me and our church. Make disciples! It was, and is, *the* command! Most Christ-followers and Christian leaders have heard it a million times. We know it as The Great Commission. We believe it. The problem is that very few churches are actually doing it. So, how? How do you do that? How do you make disciples? How do we turn pagans into missionaries? Great question! It's been said, "People don't plan to fail, they just fail to plan." Without a plan to follow, not much is going to happen.

What you have in your hands is a proven plan. It's a map to help you and others become fully devoted followers of Jesus. It will help you, and the people in your church, start from exactly where you're at and move on a spiritual continuum to *grow* and achieve key milestones on your spiritual journey, and to become fruit-bearing disciples. I often say, "We've got a plan, but we're making it up as we go, too." We always want to be teachable and be led by the Holy Spirit to tweak the plan as we go. So, if you've got some good input, please feel free to share it by visiting us at thegrowjourney.com.

# Understanding
# The Spiritual Journey Map

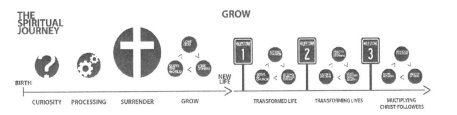

When taking a road trip to an exciting new destination, it only makes sense to take a good look at a map that shows you how to get there. The above graphic is such a map to spiritual transformation. It's not a legalistic formula to make you "better than" someone else. It's not a set of rules to impress God or other Christ-followers. This is simply a guide that encourages proven biblical spiritual exercises to help you grow closer to Jesus Christ. What follows is an explanation of the icons on the above map, to help you journey well.

The goal of this book—and all spiritual growth—is to enable you to grow in your ability to love God more, love people more, and increasingly seek to serve the world more!

## The Prime Hermeneutic

Jesus was asked, "What's the most important commandment?" He responded, "Love the Lord your God with all your heart, all your soul and all your mind. And a second one is like it. Love your neighbor as yourself." And then he said, and I paraphrase, "The whole Bible was written for these two primary purposes!" (Matt. 22:36-40). I call this the PRIME Hermeneutic. Don't let that word scare you. The word hermeneutic is simply the science of interpretation. Meaning, according to Jesus, the entire Bible should be interpreted through the lenses of loving God and loving people. If we miss on this, we are in danger of using God's word wrongly—like beating someone with a Bible verse or two.

Another time when Jesus' disciples were jockeying for position and wanting to be somebody—looking for others to serve them and yes, have their egos stroked, Jesus said, *"The Son of Man did not come to be served, but to serve, and give his life as a ransom for many"* (Matt. 20:28 NIV). His primary purpose was to serve this world's greatest need—dying on the cross for our sins. If Jesus came to serve, then shouldn't we, his followers, be intentionally serving his world and his kingdom as well? Developing a servant heart does amazing things to diminish our egos. A few years back, we had a nationally recognized consulting group come in and survey our congregation. While they had some great suggestions for improvement, they stated—unequivocally—that in all the churches they surveyed, they'd never seen a church with a larger percentage of servants. And not just servants who might help move the single mom on the weekend, but committed, Christ-centered servants who are actually leading or serving in a ministry in which they are gifted by the Holy Spirit to serve.

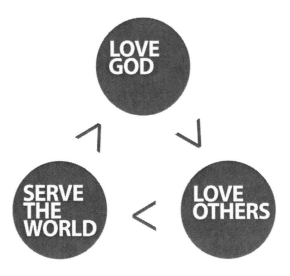

Love God. Love Others. Serve the World. The above icon is the lens to understand and read the entire map as we embark on The Spiritual Journey.

As we GROW in these three areas, our lives are transformed and God uses us to transform other people's lives too—from pagans to missionaries! And when that happens, watch out! We then find more purpose, satisfaction, and fulfillment than we ever dreamed. This book is a plan and a path to do just that.

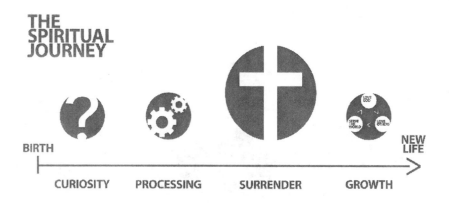

THE SPIRITUAL JOURNEY

BIRTH

NEW LIFE

CURIOSITY     PROCESSING     SURRENDER     GROWTH

**Adapted from New Heights Church**

### The Spiritual Journey—
### "There's gotta be more to life than this!"

We are all born, and at some point, we will all die. Got that? Many anthropologists have studied humanity for centuries and, in virtually every culture and ethnicity, it's clear we are spiritual beings. For right or wrong, all seek some sort of deity, god, spiritual being or beings. Therefore, we are all spiritual beings and on a spiritual journey as illustrated above. Some people are far to the left, some are on the right. Many are somewhere in between.

 **Spiritual Curiosity**—At some point in life most people begin to have deeply spiritual thoughts like, "Why am I here?" or "What is my purpose in life?" or "There's gotta be more to life than this." Ever had any of those kinds of thoughts? Good! You're not the only one. The fact is, if it were just you or me who had those thoughts, that would indicate perhaps those thoughts are peculiar to us, but I've thrown this out while speaking at large gatherings and when speaking in different countries, and many, many people all

over the planet have had those thoughts. That tells me that those thoughts did not originate with you or me. I believe God put those thoughts into your brain and they are a key indication that God is trying to get your attention. Pretty cool, huh? He loves you so much that he prompts those thoughts in you, so you might begin to seek him in earnest. Those thoughts are called Spiritual Curiosity.

***Star Trek Theology?*** I have a good friend, named Jim, who happens to be my plumber. When Jim and I met ten years ago, he had a somewhat bizarre answer to the "Why are we here?" question. He said he knew. Now keep in mind, this was ten years ago and I had just met him. Jim said, "Brad, I believe in Star Trek theology" as he held his hand up with the Spock "V" hand gesture. "We are here because aliens from other planets put us here millions of years ago!" Jim boldly proclaimed. "'*Spock to Jim?' Really? That's highly illogical*," I thought. Then I said, "That's interesting Jim," After a short pause I continued, "So, Jim, let's just go with that for now. But, you gotta ask, if aliens put us here millions of years ago, how did the aliens get started on their planet?" And I just let it sit without any argument whatsoever. Jim, I discerned, was spiritually curious and we began to engage in a spiritual journey that would last many years. More on Jim later—it's pretty cool really!

Spiritual Curiosity is a great place to be, especially when you've identified the fact that you are there. So, what then? Well, the best thing to do is to begin to ask spiritual questions and process those questions. You're moving along The Spiritual Journey! Way to go! Keep going!

 **Processing**—At this stage along The Spiritual Journey, we begin to ask sincere questions and seek good thoughtful answers to those questions. I believe, and *all* healthy pastors and spiritual leaders believe, that asking questions about God and the spiritual life is

a very good thing. Some of the most basic questions are as follows:

**Is there a God? Really?** Great question! There have been many attempts in the realm of the scientific community to disprove the existence of God and they have not really made much headway. There have been and are countries and ideologies like the Soviet Union and North Korea who strong arm their people into atheism. Ironically, both countries using such tactics have failed miserably in virtually every aspect of life. The conditions of a majority of the people are terrible. The environment under these regimes suffers horribly. I could go on and on. Then there is the Neo-Darwinist movement, which says because evolution is now a fact, it's obvious we have no need for God.

Charles Darwin posited the theory of macroevolution—one species evolving into another species, such as fish into birds and monkeys into humans—based on his observations of microevolution (variation within a species i.e. different kinds of birds and dogs and human races). Charles Darwin did state that it was highly likely that many transitionary fossils would be found (fossils showing one species evolving into another), but if they aren't found, the theory must be abandoned.

Alas, after over 150 years since Darwin's statement, we have none, nada, not one real macroevolutionary transitionary fossil. The truth is the fossil record shows species suddenly appearing—as stated in chapter one of the Bible, the book of Genesis—and then, at a given period, some becoming extinct. Suffice to say, Julie Andrews in *The Sound of Music* got it right when she sang, "Nothing comes from nothing, nothing ever could." Now, there is a great movement among scientists that says the whole natural world wreaks of design—plants, rocks, animals—you name it. Therefore, they say, if there is design, there must be a Grand Designer. Pretty solid proof there is indeed a God!

There are many great books written that answer this question with amazing clarity. Here are a few—*Darwin on Trial* by Phillip

Johnson, *Darwin's Black Box* by Michael Behe, *Reasonable Faith* by William Lane Craig, and *The Case for Faith* by Lee Strobel. Or here's a great option: Google: "*The Case for a Creator*" and you can listen to this great book by Lee Strobel online for free. Fair? We *cannot* prove the existence of God beyond a shadow of a doubt, but we *can* prove God's existence beyond a reasonable doubt. All that is needed in a court of law for a conviction is proof beyond a reasonable doubt. So, yes, there most certainly is a God. To believe otherwise, as visiting speaker at my seminary, Dallas Willard stated, "Would be a worse mistake than saying the moon is made of Swiss cheese."

**Is the Bible true?** This is another great question. I mean, the Bible is so old. For crying out loud, how can it be true when it's been translated over and over and over again for centuries? There is no way it can be accurate to what they wrote back two or three thousand years ago, right? Well... wrong! Here's why; I believe after much study on this subject, the Bible was written over a period of about 1500 years by around 40 human authors, inspired by the Holy Spirit. Good translations of the Bible are not "retranslated or paraphrased over and over again." The best translations are done in a very systematic and scholarly fashion. Teams of translators go back to the oldest and most difficult readings of the original fragments and manuscripts and translate directly from those ancient documents.

The Bible is, by far, the most scrutinized body of literature in human history. The Bible has stood the test of time. Year after year, for centuries now, The Bible has stood alone on top of the best sellers list. In fact, it's way, way above all the Number Ones on the *New York Times* best seller list. Nothing in the Bible has ever been overturned by an archaeological find. On the contrary, archeology continues to affirm facts and coinage and historical aspects that are written in the Bible. In fact, I had a professor in seminary that went to the holy land on archeological digs say this about the Bible: "*They didn't make it up, they dug it up!*"

**If God is good, why is there pain and suffering?** Wow! That is a big question. Short answer: *Star Wars!* Yeah, good and evil. If God didn't allow a dark side to be a possibility, then the side of light and good would only be a robotic response imposed by God. It really wouldn't be truly good at all—it would be fabricated by God. To be sure, there is an overwhelming amount of pain and suffering on planet earth. Why? Isn't that the question we cry out to God when something bad happens to us or someone we love? Why, God? Why? Certainly, natural catastrophic events like hurricanes, earthquakes, tornados, and tsunamis inflict much pain and suffering. I cannot begin to give an adequate answer in this book for why all these natural disasters happen. The short answer from the Bible is that *sin* entered the world and infected every aspect of the natural order. I encourage you to type this question into your browser and do a Google search. Look for thoughtful answers. There are many. But here's something very interesting to consider; natural disasters constitute a small percentage of human pain and suffering. Cancer and sickness count for more, but by far the greatest percentage of human pain and suffering is inflicted by one person or group on another as a result of human sin and self-centeredness. Ever had it happen to you? Been rejected? Lied to? Left behind or left out? Been slandered? Been physically or emotionally abused? Hurts, doesn't it! Why God, why? We ask that question often. Why? The deep answer is love! It's all because of *love!* And real love can only be had via *free will.* As C.S. Lewis put it, God wanted us to have the real ability to truly love and be loved. But in order for love to really happen, we also need to have the freedom to choose to hate. If God just *made* us love each other, it wouldn't be real love at all. We'd all simply be robots. Love and hate and good and evil go hand in hand—it's the basis of free will and choice. Now, God wants us to choose love and good—he gives us the ability to make that choice, but he also gives us the ability to choose to hate and enact evil. It's our choice. Oh, and again, that's ultimately what this book is all about; to help us to learn to choose to love, even when we don't feel the love, just like Jesus did when he passionately and lovingly went to the cross—even for those who hated him, which leads to our next question.

**Is Jesus who he said he was?** Jesus really made no bones about it. He makes it clear he was God come to earth in the form of a human being. Bizarre, huh? Some religions attempt to make gods out of human beings, Mormonism and some forms of Buddhism are a few examples. True Christianity from both the Old and the New Testaments teaches one God exists in three divine *Persons*—The Father, The Son and The Holy Spirit, who are distinct yet are 100 percent unified—totally on the same page with each other. True Christianity calls that the Holy Trinity. Three, yet one. These divine persons have existed for all eternity in perfect unity with each other. Theologians can only explain it so far before the Trinity becomes mystery. We need to be okay with that. I'm convinced even when we die and go to heaven we will never know everything about God because he is infinite and we are finite. This is the single most important doctrine (teaching) of the Christian faith. Everything Christians believe flows from this doctrine. Christians believe that The Son who is the second *person* of the Holy Trinity was sent by the Father to deal with humanity's greatest problem—sin. Jesus became a human being for one primary purpose—to offer himself to pay for your sins and mine. The Bible teaches *"The wages of sin is death"* (Rom. 6:23 NIV). Death in the Bible is often more than just physical death—it's spiritual death, separation from God. God is the author of all life. And sin, our sins separate us from God. The closer we get to God, the more we experience life. The further away we get from God, the more we die. It's just that simple. In that same verse, Romans 6:23 it says, *"But the free gift of God is eternal life through Jesus Christ our Lord"* (NIV) Some say Jesus was just a great teacher and he was certainly that, but he was way more than that. He, with the

Father and the Holy Spirit, was the author of life and the life giver. Jesus said, *"I have come that they may have life, and have it to the full"* (John 10:10b NIV) Here's a question for you? Have you ever sinned? Be honest! Sure! We all have. The Bible says, *"All have sinned and fall short of the Glory of God"* (Rom. 3:23 NIV). All fall short, you, me, everyone! God, the Father knew this so he sent his Son, precisely because he loves us so, so much! Jesus said, *"For God so loved the world that he gave his one and only son, that whoever believes in him shall not perish, but have eternal life"* (John 3:16 NIV). Jesus really said it and he really is the real deal who offers the life you've always wanted. The way to get that life is to surrender to Jesus and commit to an eternal, ever deepening relationship with the person of Jesus Christ. I say "surrender" because to simply "commit" means we maintain control. To surrender is giving up control. You see, with God, when you give up you win!

That brings us to the next stop on The Spiritual Journey, but before we get there, it's important to ask questions. Process those questions. There are plenty more questions. Good questions and seeking answers to faith issues deepens our faith and just because I've put processing here on The Spiritual Journey doesn't mean you won't have questions in the future. We all do, but what I've shared here should enable you to move to the next stage. Ready?

**Surrender**–The reality is this: based on our own good deeds, good looks, or good whatever, we will never make it to heaven. Remember, all have sinned and fallen short. A lot of people think and a lot of religions teach, "If the good outweighs the bad—you're in!" But that's a lie! No one is good enough. And how do you know? Here are some questions to consider: Do you believe God is good? I hope so. Do you believe a good God would want to keep us guessing whether or not we, his children, would make it home to heaven?

What good parent would say to their son as they send them off to school, "Charlie, if you're good in school today and pay attention, you might be able to eat dinner and sleep in your bed in the house tonight? If not, you are out on the street tonight, hungry and cold!" What good mom or dad would then let Charlie worry all day whether he's been good enough to have a meal that night? That would be a terrible parent who should be reported to Child Protective Services. That's certainly not the good God of the Bible. Jesus constantly spoke of how good his Father is. He said, "*You parents—if your children ask for a loaf of bread, do you give them a stone instead? Or if they ask for a fish, do you give them a snake? Of course not! So if you sinful people know how to give good gifts to your children, how much more will your heavenly Father give good gifts to those who ask him*" (Matt. 7:9-11 NLT). How much more indeed? See, if it's up to us to rely on our own goodness, then all we can do is hope we're good enough—and we'll never know for sure. However, if we commit to rely on God and trust him we can be absolutely sure! God is so good that he offers us *grace*. That word grace literally means *undeserved favor*. You can never earn it, you can never pay for it. And the only way to receive it is to humbly admit your need for it. You, me, we utterly need grace! And our good Father offers it to anyone who wants it. The Bible says, "*By grace you are saved, through faith—and this is not from yourselves, it is a gift of God—not by works, so that no one can boast*" (Eph. 2:8, 9 NIV). I shared that verse with my friend Paul, who grew up Catholic. He said, "My Catholic Bible doesn't say that." I said, "I bet it does!" So, he ran next door to his house, grabbed his big old flower-pressing Catholic Bible, brought it over and we opened that baby up to these verses and guess what? It said this almost exactly to the word! He said, "They didn't teach me this growing up and I was an altar boy!" And shortly after that, he made a focused commitment to surrender to Christ and receive God's grace.

So, how do you get this grace? Glad you asked! It's a gift and, like any gift, we need to receive it. But here's the key, we need to realize our need for it. Jesus said, "*Blessed are the poor in spirit, for theirs in the kingdom of heaven*" (Matt. 5:3 NIV). Being poor in spirit means we realize we are spiritually bankrupt and we have nothing to offer God. We also need to realize in his love for us, he offered everything to us on the cross. God offered his one and only Son, Jesus Christ, to pay for all of our sins on that cross. By doing so, he filled our spiritual bank up to the brim. He reconciled the books on our behalf. That's really what the cross is a symbol of, reconciliation. The vertical member symbolizes our reconciliation to God and the horizontal member symbolizes being reconciled to one another in Christ.

Are you ready to receive God's grace and make a focused commitment to Christ? Are you ready to surrender? You can do that by humbly going before God and saying a simple prayer like this:

> "*Lord, I surrender my life to you. I realize I'm a sinner and I'm spiritually bankrupt, but I believe you sent your son, Jesus, to die on the cross to pay for all my sins, I receive your gift of grace right now and promise, with the help of the Holy Spirit to make Jesus my Savior and Lord now and into eternity. In Jesus' name, Amen.*"

That's *the* key part of The Spiritual Journey. If you've made it that far, wow! You are good to go! But there is so much more! That's what the rest of this book is all about.

**Filling the Void**

It wasn't long after I put my faith in Christ for the first time that I realized something was wrong with me. Once a party animal, I continued to party for the next month, even after I put my faith in Christ. In hindsight, I now realize it was the Holy Spirit telling me that drugs and alcohol would never suffice. In fact, on December 26, 1986 I was at my brother's house partying. I had a whole bottle of fine single malt scotch and my brother was drinking vodka. After I had finished that bottle off and smoked some really fine marijuana, I was in a room all by myself and God spoke to me. *"Brad, is that filling the void in your soul? Only I can fill the void in your soul."* That was it! And that was the last time I ever touched the stuff. With the help of AA, the Church and great Christian fellowship, I have been clean and sober for over 30 years. By the grace of God. I share that story only because often new Christians bring old bad habits and hang-ups into their new life with Jesus. It really doesn't work. He wants so much more for you. He wants us free. What used to enslave us is always best let go completely. If need be, find a recovery group or some sort of support to help you break free.

In the late 4th or early 5th century, a redeemed womanizer named Augustine of Hippo wrote, "Our hearts are restless, O Lord, until they rest in thee." Every human being has a deep need to fill the void in their soul and we attempt to do it with sex, drugs, alcohol, gambling, food, or just about anything else imaginable other than God. But the truth is only God will suffice. Jesus shared this with the woman at the well who was trying to fill the void in her soul with men, when he told her, *"Whoever drinks the water I give them will never thirst. Indeed, the water I give them will become in them a spring of water welling up to eternal life"* (John 4:14 NIV). We have a new Master who only wants the best for us, who truly does fill the void in our souls to overflowing. And he teaches us what's best.

**Teach them to obey...** If you prayed the prayer above and have truly put your faith in Christ, now that you have received the gift of salvation, Jesus said, ***"Teach these new disciples to obey all the commands I have given you"*** (Matt. 28:20 NLT). The Apostle Paul got this when he wrote: *"Continue to work out your salvation with fear and trembling"* (Phil. 2:12 NIV).

Notice it says, "Continue" meaning don't stop now, it just gets better and better. This is so key: it says, work *out* your salvation *not* work *for* your salvation. See the difference? Paul also wrote *"Physical training is good, but training for godliness is much better, promising benefits in this life and the life to come"* (1 Tim. 4:8 NLT). We get the word "gym" from that word "training" in the original language. Now that you have been saved, like going to gym and getting in great shape, you can begin to really work out to become stronger and stronger in your faith. It's like God paid for our eternal lifetime membership to the YMCA. All you and I have to do is start showing up and working out. And this book is all about that, getting you to and through three milestones so you can be a very strong mature Christ-follower where your life will be totally transformed and God will use you to transform other peoples' lives more and more as you *grow*! Jesus called it being one of his disciples.

# THE SPIRITUAL JOURNEY

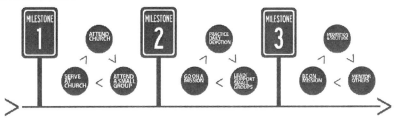

GROW

**Grow**–Remember, this book is all about growing in your ability to Love God, Love Others, and Serve the World. It's what we do after the cross. Grow–it's a key word in the New Testament. Peter, one of Jesus' closest disciples wrote, *"May God give you more and more grace and peace as you **grow** in your knowledge of God and Jesus our Lord"* (2 Pet. 1:2 NLT). Then he says, *"Make every effort to respond to God's promises"* (2 Pet. 1:5 NLT). And to paraphrase verses 6 and 7, he says, *"**Grow** in moral excellence, in knowledge, in self-control, in endurance, in patience, in godliness, in brotherly affection and in love!"* Then he says, *"The more you **grow** like this, the more productive and useful you will be in your knowledge of our Lord Jesus Christ. But those who fail to develop in this way are shortsighted or blind, forgetting they have been cleansed from their old sins"* (2 Pet. 1:8-9 NLT). The more you and I grow the more productive and useful you will be to God and to others. Isn't that great? The last verse in 2 Peter says, *"Rather, you must **grow** in the grace and knowledge of our Lord and Savior Jesus Christ"* (2 Pet. 3:18 NLT). ***Grow, Grow, Grow!*** Journey intentionally from Milestone 1 to Milestone 2 and onto Milestone 3. Moving from one milestone to the next doesn't mean we stop doing things we learn in the previous milestone. No, we just keep growing. In this life, we're either intentionally growing closer to God or moving away. There is no status quo in the kingdom of God. So, grow with intention and you will have increased grace, peace, and love. You will live life to the fullest. It's a promise from God!

### *An overview of doing your own spiritual inventory at each milestone*

Remember the *Love God, Love Others, and Serve the World* icon? At each milestone there are eight mile points—tangible ways to take action and grow.

Here's the deal: At the end of each milestone, there are statements. What you need to do is score yourself between 1 and 5 on how well you agree with those statements—1 is weak, 5 is strong. For example on bar below, score yourself on the truth of following statement as it applies to you:

I have read and understood just about everything to this point in this book.

( WEAK    **1**     **2**     **3**     **4**     **5**    STRONG )

## Measuring Spiritual Growth?

Some say, "You can't measure your spiritual growth." I beg to differ. We measure everything else that we deem important: our blood sugar, our heart rates, our cholesterol, our finances, our hard drive space. You name it, we measure it. Jesus told stories and parables of the fruitfulness of peoples' lives all the time and related to people's spiritual journeys. Just one example is when three guys had been given different amounts of money to invest. They were all held accountable for how they invested it (Matt. 25:14-30). Two were commended and praised, one was punished. In the end, we will all stand before God and be held accountable. So, between now and then, it simply is prudent to do a little self-evaluation of our spiritual progress. The Bible says, *"Be honest in your evaluation of yourselves, measuring yourselves by the faith God has given us"* (Rom. 12:3b NLT). Measure yourselves it says, but be honest about it.

**How to score yourself:** Read each statement and assess where you are currently. If you rate yourself weak on any of the statements, look up the passage(s) of scripture noted and use the SOAP method in the appendix C to further study and grow and apply it to your life. Just work on your own growth and then take the test again in six months or a year and I'll bet you will have grown significantly. **There are two complete surveys at the back of this book in Appendix A in order for you to periodically check your own spiritual progress.** You'll be amazed!

*Allergic Reaction:* When we first presented this to our church we had a few allergic reactions, Mike was one. He did not want to do it. But, after a few months, he was honest. He said, "I knew this would expose me as a spiritual poser, so I naturally reacted against it." That's honesty. That right there is huge spiritual growth. Remember, this is a self-evaluation tool. Refrain from measuring yourself against others—for better or for worse. Fair?

**Enjoy the Journey**

Many years ago, my wife and I went to Maui for our honeymoon. It was awesome. We stayed in Lahaina which was on the other side of the island from Hana. One day we decided to "Take the Road to Hana." Just beyond Hana are the Seven Sacred Pools. I was excited to go with Ann, my new awesome bride, but on that little excursion I learned more than ever that I'm a very destination-oriented, fast-paced guy and my wife is simply not. As we jumped into the car, I surveyed the map and saw it was a very winding road, but Lahaina was only about 70 miles from Hana, yet people told us it took about three hours. I thought, "No way! I'm going to obliterate that record!" On the way, we were making great time. We were about half way there and we'd only been gone for 45 minutes. "I'm killing it," I thought. Along the way, Ann asked me to stop at certain points to take in some of the roadside wonders. Mostly, I wouldn't listen or I'd say, "Honey, can't stop, it will destroy the great time we're making." Well, that lasted until she saw this beautiful old church out next to a rocky ocean side black beach lava flow. It was stunning! She quietly says, "Brad, please stop at that little church." "Honey," I retort, "No way, we are making great time, can't!" She looks at me and with firm conviction says, "Brad, we are stopping here, now!" "Okay, but hurry up!" Alas, she took about an hour. My record time was now all but lost. So, off we go, she sees a roadside Hawaiian basket weaver, "Stop, Brad." "Okay, might as well." And we stopped a few more times before we finally got to Hana... in about three hours.

The irony is Hana was not that impressive; just a simple small town with not much there. It was the "Road to Hana," enjoying the journey and all that it held that was what it was all about. It made me wonder about our spiritual journey. Unlike Hana, I think heaven is going to be exceedingly impressive. However, I'm now absolutely sure God wants us to enjoy the journey between now and then. Jesus said, 'The kingdom of heaven is at hand." Once we have Jesus in the car, heaven is both now and not yet. We would do well to pause to enjoy the roadside marvels of this life's spiritual journey with Jesus.

**Rest Area**—What follows are three milestones along The Spiritual Journey that have nine stops each. Take some time to enjoy each stop. But make sure you pause at the Rest Areas for rest, reflection and recording. It's vital! This is not a book simply to "get through." It's a journey to experience. Enjoy and apply each point to your life and go back and re-explore points that need further growth. Once we put our faith in Jesus, heaven begins now. Enjoy it and grow.

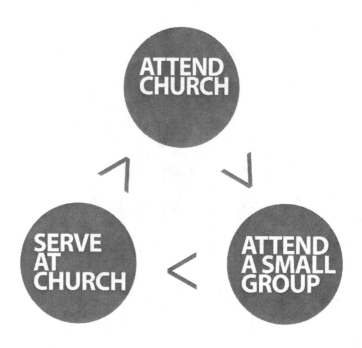

*Milestone 1 Goal—Your Life is Transformed!*

*At Milestone 1, the way we love God is to attend church regularly. The way we love people is to attend a small group that meets weekly. The way we serve the world is to serve in our local church. If you do that consistently, your life will be transformed. In addition, there are five other significant stops that will enable you to grow in Milestone 1. At Milestone 1.9 make sure you pull over for to the Rest Area and reflect on where you're at and record your journey.*

# 1.1 Attend Church Regularly

Have you ever gone to a concert? Ever gone to a NFL or college football game? Ever gone to a convention or conference? I'm a huge baseball fan and love to go to Major League baseball games as well as all my kids' games. All these games and places have one thing in common; people. People naturally assemble in large groups for many purposes. Some of them, like concerts or football games, are often attended by thousands of people. For many people, they freely admit, to root for their team is a religious ritual. Something in our human nature loves to assemble with other people to admire, applaud, and even worship those performing. It's actually how God made us.

The Apostle Paul addressed this propensity when he observed all sorts of statues that were made to honor the Greek gods in Athens. When he saw a statue that was dedicated "to an Unknown God," Paul seized the moment, pointing people to the One True God, he said, I know him. *"His purpose was for the nations to seek after God and perhaps feel their way toward him and find him—though he is not far from any one of us. For in him we live and move and exist. As some of your poets have said, "'We are his offspring.'"* (Acts 17:27-29 NLT). And then after quoting the Greek poets, Paul proclaimed, "And since this is true!" Paul affirmed what the Greek poets stated was true–that we are God's offspring and therefore have an innate desire to seek him out to worship him. Now, where that went wrong is back in Genesis chapter 3, when the first human couple corrupted our spiritual DNA by disobeying God. After that, instead of assembling to worship God, often we assemble to worship a sports team or a rock star or movie celebrity—something other than our Creator. For many people, it really is a religious experience. Don't get me wrong, I love sports, music, and movies, but it's imperative that I keep them a distant second and never worship them. See, the very best reason to assemble is to worship and pay homage to our Creator.

And guess what? More people assemble together to worship God by attending church services on a weekly basis than all of the categories above combined. Yeah! But that's less than 20 percent of the population in the United States and that number is dropping yearly.

It's been said that showing up is 90 percent of the grade. Now, showing up for church is a different story. I was a senior pastor at a church for sixteen years and we made it our mission to connect with people who generally didn't do church. I saw so many people come with big time issues—marriages in shambles, finances in disarray, severe medical problems, family members dying. You name the issue, people had or have it and they often come to church for one reason—hope! Hope that there really is a God who can and will do something about their issues, who will comfort them and give them wisdom and help them in dealing with whatever is going on. What's amazing is he does do something! I have seen marriages healed, finances restored, relationships reconciled and even people healed of debilitating sicknesses.

I love the church! But make no mistake, the church is messy. You know why? Sinners like me start them! I've heard it a number of times out on the street, "Church is full of nothing but a bunch of hypocrites." To people who say that, I reply, "You know, you are right, and if you're honest with yourself, you'll fit right in!"

Now, there are many ways to love God, but attending church regularly shows him that you want to hear from him. You want to worship him. You want to be with people who love him too. Showing up for church regularly is absolutely essential to your spiritual growth. I have surveyed many lives of committed attenders and then the lives of those who simply stop in for a service from time to time. I can honestly tell you that there is a significant increase in maturity and joy for those who attend regularly. Being part of a vibrant church community brings so much to a person's life. There was a recent twenty-year Harvard study of churchgoers that showed huge benefits of simply going to church—people lived longer, healthier lives compared to those who don't go to church (Harvard study led by Professor Tyler VanderWeele).

On the flip side, I have seen people come to church, marriage a wreck. They commit their lives to Christ and things get way better. Then, after a few years, some begin to drift and pretty soon they are nowhere to be found. I wonder if they've found another church to attend and I'd be thrilled if they did. Most often, however, they haven't. And then, a year, maybe two or three later, I hear they've gotten divorced or their family is a train wreck. I've seen this scenario way too many times for it to be a coincidence. It's avoidable! Just make it a habit to come to church regularly. Hebrews 10:25 says, *"And let us not neglect our meeting together, as some are in the habit of doing, but encourage one another."* Most would agree, neglecting physical exercise becomes a bad habit that leads to an unhealthy life. Not going to church is actually worse. Making church attendance a priority is a really good habit. It's a spiritual discipline that has a huge lifelong and eternal payoff.

You and I, we were made for worship! Did you know that? All cultures have sought to worship God—a power greater than themselves—in one form or another since time began. Some have done it in a healthy fashion, some not so much. But, it is intrinsic to our humanity to worship an almighty God.

There is something God put inside our souls that longs to worship him. It's part of how he created us. *"In the image of God he created them"* (Genesis 1:27 NIV). An image is a reflection. If I show you a picture of yourself and I ask, "Is that you?" You will likely say, "Yes, that's me!" I will say, "No, it's not, it's a reflection of you. It's an image of you, but that's not you. It's just a picture of you!" That's how it is with us and God. We are much more than paper or cellphone pictures, we are images of God. And when we reflect his image in us most clearly, that's when our lives take on so much more meaning. When we worship God regularly together, through song, his word in the Bible and a life application message, we begin to reflect the good God he is more and more.

Jesus told a parable of four soils that relates to going to church and too much of what follows in this book. To paraphrase, a farmer went to plant seed. He scattered it and some fell on the hard pan path, some fell on rocky soil, some fell on thorny soil and some fell on fertile soil. The hard pan soil is a person who simply refuses to hear much of anything about God, let alone go to church. The rocky soil is a person who will listen at first, come to church and be excited, but then they *fall away fairly soon because they haven't developed deep roots.*

The same can be said about the thorny soil person. Jesus said *the cares of this world and the lure of wealth chokes out* this person's desire for the spiritual life.

So, both the rocky soil person and the thorny soil person simply have not gone any further than to the beginning of Milestone 1 in their spiritual journey and they're done.

I learned in seminary generally all of Jesus' parables have one main point he was making, just one. For the parable of the soils this is it: Only one soil produced a crop, the fertile soil. All three of the others produced nothing. I'm convinced the key difference between the fertile soil person and all three of the other soils people is the fertile soil person tilled the soil of their soul by continuing to go to church, even when they didn't feel like it. And they grew in practicing many of the other spiritual exercises in this book, while the others simply stopped. Jesus said, *"The seed that fell on good soil represents those who truly hear and understand God's word and produce a harvest of thirty, sixty or even a hundred times as much as had been planted"* (Matt. 13:23 NLT).

Now, I also am convinced all three of the other soils represent people who are not only spiritually immature, but they are emotionally immature as well because our emotions often drive much that is messed up about our lives. Generally, people stop going to church for two reasons, both are emotional reasons: 1) They just don't feel like it anymore, or, 2) they have an issue with someone in the church. I've learned that when I don't feel like going, that's exactly when I need to go to church most. Remember this; emotions make great cars for the train, but terrible engines. Don't let your emotions train wreck your pursuit of God in attending church regularly. Attending church is so key to having a fruitful, joy-filled life.

*"Remember the Sabbath and keep it holy"* (Exod. 20:8). It's the fourth of the Ten Commandments. There is something vital about taking one day a week to pause, worship God and rest. It's just really good for you. Jesus said, *"The Sabbath was made for man, not man for the Sabbath"* (Mark 2:27 NIV). In other words, we don't do it as a duty, but as a need. Just like wise farmers who rest different sections of their fields every seven years to replenish the nutrients in the soil, wise people rest every seven days and worship God to replenish the nutrients in their souls.

One of the reasons many people go to church is to worship God in song. There is something about directing our hearts and minds and voices toward God in worship. The Psalms are a great example of worshipping God; The Psalms are to be read aloud or sung, pouring out our emotions to God. During the week, our spiritual GPS gets out of whack, we become disoriented. Do you ever get drained emotionally? Worshipping God reorients us to our True North and honestly makes us feel better. If for no other reason, that's a great one not to miss church.

One other reason is your showing up may well be more important to someone than them hearing the pastor's message. Back when I was single, I had a pastor friend name Rich. One Sunday morning a new guy showed up named Pete (not his real name). Pastor Rich was really busy, but wanted to make sure Pete got connected, so he asked me to take Pete out for coffee after church. I said no problem. I took him out and bought him breakfast. I didn't get to know Pete much, but a year later Pete was a member of our church and I reconnected with him. I'll never forget it. He said, "Brad, you have no idea what that meant to me when you took me out for breakfast a year ago." Do you think Pete remembered the sermon that Sunday? Doubtful. What he remembered was a guy who had no clue God was using him to connect Pete to his church family. When you don't feel like going, that's exactly when you must go, for Pete's sake!

**A special note to parents**: Parents, your children need church these days more than ever. Again, I love sports. I'm for my kids being involved in sports. However, sports have displaced the intent of the Sabbath in many families. With all the travel that teams do, we find many families gone most weekends. Whole families' Sabbaths have been hijacked by their devotion to a child's sport, instead of God. In fact, it's almost as if many families worship sports more than they do God these days. As much as sports can be a great character builder and social outlet for your child, I am absolutely convinced bringing your child to church and to a youth group will have a far greater long-term impact. Watch the movie Chariots of Fire as a family, please. It's a true story about Eric Liddell who was a great British Olympic runner who refused to violate the Sabbath. Yes, he was ridiculed for it, but God also blessed him. So good! Parents, there is a spiritual impact factor— something about your going to church and worshipping side by side with your child,— that cannot be quantified, but it's huge. Your faithful weekly modeling going to church, worshipping before a holy God, will virtually guarantee your child's continued devotion to God when they leave home. Lastly, parents often say to me, "My child just doesn't want to come to church. What do I do?" I ask, "What if they said that about school? Would you just say, 'Sure, no problem. I wish you would go, though.' "No!" I say, "Who is the parent? Be parents to your kids." *"As for me and my household, we will serve the Lord!"* (Josh. 24:15 NIV). As long as I'm feeding them, clothing them, and giving them a bed to sleep in, missing church is not an option. It's what we do as a family, even if that means getting up early to attend an early service before an event. Next question!

Yes, there is the person who says, "I'm just not into organized religion." I get it and I also know that there have been some very hurtful things done in the name of Christ and religion. It's sad, but know this: for every church out there that has done damage to people's lives, there are many more that have done so much good. The truth is, while that "I'm not into organized religion" statement can be a real indication of being hurt by a church in the past, it is most often a smokescreen for people who want to remain in darkness and are close-minded to God. Just pray for them. Often it takes a cataclysmic event in their lives to be open. Just don't let their negative view on the church dissuade your attendance.

A few keys about church. Find a healthy one. A church that believes in the Holy Trinity. A church who believes the Bible is 100 percent true. A church that preaches from the Bible. A church that believes in a real heaven and a real hell. A church that encourages you to ask faith questions. A church that believes all human beings are sinners and we are saved by grace that Jesus offered us on the cross alone and not by following rules. A church that believes in the resurrection of Jesus Christ and his eternal reign over the universe.

One last thing about church. Never disparage a church. The Bible calls the church the bride of Christ. Now, I love my wife desperately and if someone came up to me and told me how much they didn't like her and started saying negative things about her, they might as well be saying that about me. Somehow, I believe Jesus thinks the same about people who disparage the church. Be careful with that. Is she messy? Yes. Does Jesus still love her/you? Absolutely!

Okay, how are you doing on this milestone?

If you go to church two times a year, give yourself a 1. If you're a twice a month person give yourself a 4. I mean, going to church from two times a year to two times a month is a huge jump. If you're three or more times a month, give yourself a 5. Fair? That's the idea when you score yourself on subsequent statements. We want you to err on the side of grace. Just be honest with yourself!

Read the following statement go ahead and score yourself:

### 1.1–Attend Weekly Church Services
Attending a church service and joining in worship is an essential first step to help me grow in loving God.

| WEAK | 1 | 2 | 3 | 4 | 5 | STRONG |
|------|---|---|---|---|---|--------|

**Memory verse: Hebrews 10:25 (NLT)** *"And let us not neglect our meeting together, as some are in the habit of doing, but encourage one another—and all the more as you see the Day approaching"*

## Questions for Further Reflection and Discussion

1. Why do you go to church?

2. What are some of the reasons you don't go to church when you miss? Are they good ones?

3. Read the above memory verse and discuss it. How can you encourage others, even in your family, not to neglect going to church?

4. Perhaps you've had times in life when you didn't do church or did it less than you do now. Did you observe any difference in how your life went? What was different?

5. How's the soil of your soul? Is it fertile? Does it need some weeding?

6. What, if anything, interferes with your church attendance? How can you change that? Will you?

# 1.2 Attend a Small Group

Do you have a favorite sitcom? One of my all-time favorites is *Seinfeld*. I love all the characters: Jerry, George, Elaine, and Kramer were the mainstays. Kramer! I absolutely loved Kramer! When he'd come sliding into Jerry's apartment with a quick quip and a shake of his head it was hilarious! One unique human being for sure. Guess what? The reason we like Seinfeld, or any other sitcom, is because we all have a need to belong somewhere—to be known. That's what a small group is; a group of unique people gathering on purpose, to grow to reflect Christ more intentionally to a world who needs him desperately—to know and be known, love and be loved.

Hey, I love Seinfeld; I watched it every week for years. As I think about my time spent watching Seinfeld, I know this without a doubt, it was fun, but it didn't really help me grow as a human being, it didn't help me love others and Jerry never came to my house. What's with that? Sometimes I think about spending an hour or more watching TV and how much I grow from it— not much, if at all. But spending that kind of time

49

once a week over the course of a year in a small group, that's life changing! Honestly, I cannot imagine how my life would have gone without being part of small groups since I became a Christ-follower.

Perhaps that's why one of the first things Jesus did when he began his ministry was start a small group. He went down to the fishing boats and snagged Peter, James and John. He went to the tax collectors' booth and invited Matthew. He initially gathered twelve men into a small group that would later transform the world. Imagine, just for a minute, if those guys simply watched their favorite show instead and never spent any time talking with each other about how doing God's will might improve their lives. Here's the truth: spiritual growth happens best in community. Jesus doing it is a great indicator that we should too. Those twelve men's lives and a number of women's lives were totally transformed by doing one key thing: hanging with Jesus. If you could hang with Jesus once a week, would you? That's really what happens in a small group. Jesus said, *"Where two or three gather in my name, there I am with them"* (Matt. 18:20). So, it makes sense that being connected to the small group is a great formula for spiritual growth.

I'm a pastor and teacher. I've been one for years and I'm very passionate about the importance of coming to church on Sundays and feeding the flock with a message. I know it's important that people come and get fed on Sunday. I get that! I believe in that! But here's the deal, if that's all you do, is come to church on the weekend, and not connect with other like-minded believers during the week at some point, you won't grow much. It wouldn't matter if I was the greatest teacher in the world or if you have the greatest preacher in the world at your church. The great pastor and conference speaker, Andy Stanley says, "Life change happens better in circles, not in rows" (YouTube 2015 DTS). So, he says, "Get out of a row [church seats] and into a circle [a small group]. The depth of discussion and dialogue is so much greater in a small group.

I fly a bit to other countries for mission trips. During some flights, I end up sitting next to a fellow Christ-follower. It's amazing the depth of conversation that seems to happen naturally when Christ is the common denominator. Consider this, if I am a Harley Davidson owner, it's a great starting point for a friendship with another Harley owner, but if that's as far as the relationship goes, it remains fairly shallow. But, if it starts there and eventually takes us into a conversation about Jesus and all God has for us, suddenly we've plunged into the depths of meaningful, life giving discussion. Honestly, after sitting on a plane and meeting a new friend who knows Christ as well, at the end of the flight and we need to part ways, I somehow feel like I've known that person all my life. This phenomenon is not peculiar to me. I have shared this with many people over the years and they have experienced similar encounters. Why? Well, when you talk about matters of life from an eternal rather than a temporal perspective, it's far more meaningful. It just matters way more. That's what small groups are all about.

Love develops in small groups, deep love that matters. The recent long-term 75 year Harvard Grant Study confirmed how love, the kind of love found in a small group enables people to live longer, healthier lives. Harvard psychiatrist, George Vaillant, who directed the study for 32 years, said "The two keys for a happy fulfilling life are love and finding a way of coping with life that does not push love away." What I take from that is lean into loving God and others,–it will transform your life. That's what committed small group members do.

When believers gather in a group of six to sixteen people for an hour and a half, there is dialogue around God's eternal word concerning issues that matter deeply. And, questions can be asked about God and faith issues. That can never really happen during a church service. I hate to say it, but all you get in a Sunday worship service is a talking head—a monologue. Albeit, a good monologue in the message and it's very important. But something really powerful happens when people gather together to study God's word and enter into dialogue about it and how to live it out, together. At times, small groups will eat together, have fun together, cry together, and do life together. It's similar to a sitcom, but way better! And you get to be one of the key characters! This was what happened in the early church in the book of Acts; *"They devoted themselves to the apostles' teaching and to fellowship, to the breaking of bread and to prayer"* (Acts 2:42 NIV). *"They broke bread in their homes and ate together with glad and sincere hearts"* (Acts 2:46b NIV). A sitcom? Sitcoms, by nature, are filled with comedy and sarcasm, and the characters' hearts aren't nearly as sincere as a church small group. The truth is, being part of a small group will change your life.

One of my favorite movie trilogies is *The Lord of The Rings.* In the first movie, The Fellowship of the Ring, a Middle Earth saving small group is formed to destroy the evil ring—to take the ring back to Mordor and "Throw it back into the fiery pit from whence it came." What's most amazing about that is the bond of nine unlikely mates. Incredibly, against just about everyone's temperament, each person's devotion was increased, their character was developed and a strong loyalty was forged between them all during their journey together. They actually grew to love one-another, not in spite of each other, but because of each other. That's really how small groups work. Honestly, no one grows much in isolation. Before God made Eve, God said to Adam, *"It's not good for the man to be alone"* (Gen. 1:18 NIV) We are created for community, for love. *"Let us make human beings in our own image, in our likeness"* (Gen. 1:26a NIV). Did you catch that? Us, our, our! God himself exists in a small group community consisting of the Father, the Son, and the Holy Spirit. When we show up for our small group, He is there waiting for us to fellowship with him. It's so good.

A great benefit of being part of a small group is that deep friendships often develop. Some of my very best and longest friendships started in a small group. My wife and I still have friendships with couples we were in a small group with over 25 years ago. They have supported us through thick and thin. My best friend, Bob, and his wife, Sue, were in one of our first small groups when we planted a church 17 years ago. Their kids were young like ours, so it's like we had an extended family in Bob and Sue and their children, Bobby and Anna. I still meet with Bob weekly at Starbucks and talk to him on the phone a few times a week. This year Bobby and Anna are both getting married and I have the honor of officiating both weddings, while Bob and Sue get to pay for them. It's a great deal!

Life is tough at times. That's when being part of a small group really pays off. My daughter Sarah was born with a condition around her eyes that needed plastic surgery when she was 3-years-old. It was through a few small groups, that we were bathed in prayer and supported through the whole ordeal, which included three trips to a special pediatric eye clinic in Utah. Ann and I were in a small group with Anderson and his wife Margaret, while Anderson was studying medicine Seattle when Sarah was born. He went on to Nashville to practice and teach at Vanderbilt. Ann and I went from doctor to doctor, surgeon to surgeon trying find the right one and had no peace about any of them, as it was such a rare condition for most surgeons. Anderson learned about Sarah's problem and tipped us off to the best pediatric plastic surgeon in the country to deal with this particular condition. It was a huge gift! Speaking two minutes to this surgeon on the phone, and then within one minute while taking Sarah in for her initial appointment, we knew, this surgeon was the one. Sarah had two very successful surgeries and she's so beautiful. Only God. A year or so after that, I received a call from Anderson I'll never forget; Margaret was pregnant and their unborn son was diagnosed with Down Syndrome. We both wept and I got the privilege of praying with Anderson. And now, as I think about it, and I'm sure many who know them would agree, I can't imagine God giving a child with Down Syndrome to a more loving, caring, God-fearing couple. That's one lucky child! We are so grateful for Anderson and Margaret and so many people we have been in small groups with over the years.

Really! Begin to develop eternal relationships now based on God's word and God will bless you and those around you. You'll be so glad you did and you will become a more loving person.

One last thing: *you are needed!* Yeah, that's right! Often people think, "I really don't have time for that." And, "I can't see how a small group is going to help me." What I've learned and experienced is that showing up for a small group is often not about you. It's about how God is going to use you to encourage someone else. If you don't show up, you've missed an opportunity to be used of God. So, show up! What if Sam abandoned Frodo, even when Frodo told him to leave? The Ring would never have gotten destroyed and all Middle Earth would be doomed. What if Ann and I never decided to go to that small group where we met Anderson and Margaret? Believe me, there are thousands of stories like Sarah's, where God provided support, love and hope because a small group of people decided to gather in his name.

Are you in a small group? Do you make it a priority? Great! Is this an area of growth for you? Score yourself relating to the following statements:

### 1.2–Attend a Small Group
I regularly attend a small group or Bible study. Attending a small group is an essential first step to help me grow in loving people.

| WEAK | 1 | 2 | 3 | 4 | 5 | STRONG |
|---|---|---|---|---|---|---|

**Memory verse: Acts 2:42 (NIV)** *"They devoted themselves to the apostles' teaching and to fellowship, to the breaking of bread and to prayer."*

**Questions for Further Reflection and Discussion**

1.  Discuss how you feel about attending a small group.

2.  What are some of the benefits you've experienced as a result of being part of a small group?

3.  Discuss a time you really didn't feel like going to your small group, then you did.

4.  Read Acts 2:42 and discuss the values that the early church embraced. What values are similar or different in your small group?

# 1.3 Serve at Church

I f everyone would just do things like I wanted, life would be so good. If everyone would stay off the roads when I decided to go somewhere in my car, especially to the city during rush hour, it would make my life so much easier. If I could eat what and all I wanted every day, without gaining weight—Bliss! Right? Nope! This is one of life's great paradoxes.

Paradox: Word! "A seemingly absurd or self-contradictory statement or proposition that when investigated or explained may prove to be well founded or true" (Google). Jesus was the master of paradox. He said, *"If you try to hang onto your life, you will lose it. But if you give up your life for my sake you will save it"* (Matt. 16:25 NLT). It's a paradox! If you want to serve your best interests, serve others. If you want to really live, be willing to die! Jesus not only mouthed paradoxical statements, He embodied them. He was *the* Paradox! God, yet man! King, yet servant! All powerful, yet the humblest person to ever walk the earth. He said, *"For even the Son of Man did not come to be served, but to serve others, and give his life as a ransom for many"*

(Mark 10:45 NLT). Our paradox: If we demand to get all our needs met constantly, we end up miserable. It never works. If we seek to give ourselves away, we find our lives to be exceedingly meaningful and fulfilled. One of humanity's primary problems and diseases is self-centeredness. Serving others cures the disease.

Tell me, as followers of Jesus, if he was a servant, shouldn't we be servants too? Just like our King, serving God and others should be increasingly part and parcel of who we are.

At Milestone 1.3 we learn to serve God's world. And I believe there are good reasons to begin your life as a servant in the context of your local church. I think of it this way, if I want my kids to be great employees out in the real world someday, first I need to do my best to teach them how to do their chores at home. The same concept is in play in your local church.

In his letter to the church at Corinth, the Apostle Paul used the metaphor of a human body to describe serving in the local church. *"Our bodies have many parts, and God has put each part just where he wants it. How strange a body would be if it had only one part! Yes, there are many parts, but only one body. The eye can never say to the hand, "I don't need you." The head can't say to the feet, "I don't need you"* (1 Cor. 12:19-21 NLT). In a properly functioning home, everyone does their part. The same is true in a biblically functioning local church. You are absolutely needed to make the church function the way God intended it. We, together, are the body of Christ. Most local churches have 20 percent of the people serving to do 100 percent of the tasks to keep it operational. And most often, when that happens, the church is not operating anywhere near it's redemptive potential. So, everyone is needed! You are essential!

### Discover Your Spiritual Gifts

*"When you believed in Christ, he identified you as his own by giving you the Holy Spirit... The Spirit is God's guarantee that he will give us the inheritance he promised"* (Eph. 1:13b, 14a NLT).

In essence, when we believe in Christ, God gives us one really big gift—Salvation—guaranteed by the Holy Spirit. He also gives us a few really amazing smaller gifts.

Paul points out that the Holy Spirit distributes special gifts to each part of the body of Christ. *"There are different kinds of spiritual gifts, but the same Spirit distributes them. Now to each one the manifestation of the Spirit is given for the common good"* (1 Cor. 12:4, 7 NIV). Then Paul goes on to list a bunch of gifts—preaching, teaching, leadership, helps, wisdom, tongues, etc. The list is not exhaustive, but the key is that no one gets them all, but every Christ-follower gets some. It's far better than Christmas when we might get a huge awesome gift under the tree and iTunes gift cards in our stockings. Following the surrender of our life and receiving assurance of eternal life through Jesus Christ, the Holy Spirit comes to dwell in our hearts. He activates spiritual gifts, given so we can serve Christ and his church with purpose between now and when we meet him in heaven. Question, do you know your spiritual gifts?

Discovering your spiritual gifts is the key to finding great purpose in life and to serving in the church with joy. In fact, in addition to your learning what your spiritual gifts are, also identify your personal passion areas to serve in and your temperament. All of the following are given by God through the Holy Spirit to serve his purposes. It's imperative you discover how God wired you to serve him and others in this world.

a) Spiritual Gifts—Take a Spiritual Gifts Assessment. There are many online and elsewhere that are good. We've used the Network Spiritual Gifts books out of Willow Creek for years and have been pleased with what it offers. It's worth the investment. In addition to spiritual gifts, we help people identify their:

b) Passion Areas—This is simply a document that helps you identify people and issues that you have a passion for. People groups can be kids, elderly, teens, young adults, marrieds, singles, disabled, etc.; specific people with whom you might really resonate. For example, I love kids, but they are not my passion area. My passion area is adults and families. It's critical to understand what your passion area is. A few passion issues are addictions, marriage, prisons, and homelessness to name a few. A key question to ask yourself is this: If I could do anything in the world by helping a specific people group, what would I do and who would that be?

c) Temperament—A great temperament tool is DISC. Using a short version of DISC is exceeding helpful. Here you find out if you are fast-paced or slow-paced, if you are a more task-oriented person or a more people/relationship-oriented person. Again, this is vital to getting people serving on teams in a way that energizes them while serving.

Once we gather all that information we put it all together and encourage people to serve in their gifted areas. Here's a few examples:

Natalie has a strong gift of administration, is passionate about families and is good with people, but is great with tasks and she's a little faster paced. This makes her a great administration person in the church, especially for me, because I'm administratively challenged and really fast-paced.

Jayson has a strong gift of leadership and encouragement and has teaching gifts. His passion area is teens. He's very relational. This makes him a great youth pastor.

Jen has a strong gift of creative communication. She's a little slower-paced. Her passion is women and she is slightly more task-oriented than relationship-oriented. She loves to do crafts and make table center pieces and decorations for women's events.

Charles has the gift of helps and loves to work outside doing gardening. He's does a great job of manicuring the church grounds, keeping bushes pruned and beds weeded. It's the perfect place for him to serve.

**It takes a body:** One thing most church attenders and church leaders don't understand is it takes a body of believers to lead people to Christ and to disciple them. It's not one singular person's efforts. Who designs your website? Gifted high-tech people. That's the first access point for many unchurched people. Who keeps your church campus or grounds clean and landscaped? As I stated above, we have gifted servants doing that. Who makes the coffee and provides hospitality for Sunday morning? Who's that welcoming smiling greeter and usher? Who are the great musicians on stage? Who's doing the tech? Who's in the children's ministry? Who cleans the church and bathrooms? Early on in our church plant and even still to some degree, apart from a few part-time paid staff, most of the work done at our church is by gifted servant-volunteers. They are amazing! And get this, when we do worship services, all of them do their part before anyone who comes hears from me, the pastor/teacher. They set me up for success. Business guru, Patrick Lencione, in his book *The Five Dysfunctions of a Team*, shares the most important part of a movie is the first ten minutes. That first ten minutes are the lenses we view the movie through. That's why it needs to be really good to hook us. I believe the same is true for a church worship service. When a person is coming to your church for the first time, the pastor is not the first person they see. No! They see directional signs, greeters and ushers and coffee! Coffee! Every Sunday morning we have incredible servants who come one hour before our first church service to make coffee and set-up our hospitality carts. They station them front and center, outside on our front porch of the church with a sign above that says "Coffee", but also communicates "Come, relax, and smell and drink the coffee." Imagine, being new and walking up to the church with a bit of anxiety and the first big point of engagement for you is a coffee station. Once you get that cup of coffee in your hand, it's like "Ahh, I'm okay now."

Think about that. Before anyone hears from the pastor or his message, new people and all the regulars have many touch points from many gifted servants in the body of Christ. Here are just a few examples of mid-week and weekend servants who affect the first 10 minutes and beyond on Sundays:

- Building & Grounds nice landscaping and entryway: Jeff and Charles
- Greeters smiling and pleasant: Andy, Angela, Deb, Vickie, and Bob
- Hospitality coffee and donuts: Karen, Kim, Jill and Missy
- Program data entry and inserts: Lisa and Diana
- Church Cleaning Team: Amy, Pat, Marcella, and Jen
- Usher Program handed out and seating: Scott, Tae, Dustin and Erik
- AV Tech booth: Steve, Alan, Randy, Fred, Dylan and Noleen
- Children's Ministry check-in: Cathy, Laila, Marie and Becky
- Children's Ministry Teachers: Bob, Kym, Rovi, Mary, and Steve
- Worship Team: Jayson, Heidi, Dylan, Tom, Brie, Kelly, Miguel, Nathan, Jadyn
- Prayer Team: George and Eileen
- Video Crew: David and Aaron
- Pastor/Teacher: Stan, Roger, Jerry, and Brad

That's about the order of how the gifted servants are played out and encountered on Sunday morning at our church and most churches. And there are many more for each category. Sure, you can add or subtract categories. Most of those gifted servant-volunteers don't get a dime. The crazy thing is they actually pay the church in tithes and offerings and they love it.

That's another insane paradox of the kingdom: pay to serve! Are you kidding me? No! And most love it more than their jobs when they are serving in their passion areas, leaving their serving time more energized than when they arrived. That's why we are excited about administering gifts and passion and temperament assessments. We have gifted people, such as Ann, Natalie, and Lisa to help administer those gifts and create a Personal Profile Sheet for each precious volunteer-servant to see the amazing gifts God has given them to serve his purposes in this world.

Rick Warren calls it helping people find their S.H.A.P.E.

S = Spiritual Gifts
H = Heart or Passions
A = Aptitude or Talents
P = Personality or Temperament
E = Experiences

I love that. It's the job of the leaders of your church to help you find your SHAPE and to help get you into your Holy Spirit-gifted place to serve as a vital part of the body of Christ.

**Leadership Tip:** If you are a pastor or church leader, get a book like *Network* or *What You Do Best in The Body of Christ* by Bruce Bugbee. *Fusion* by Nelson Searcy is great too.

Read them and make it a top priority to apply them to help every person in your local church to discover their spiritual gifts. We offer Milestone 1 classes that include a Discovering Your Gifts segment and that teach everything in this chapter.

Here's something to ponder. I have seen it time and again. People who discover their gifts and passions and temperament and serve in an area that fits them spiritually and emotionally are so energized that they are eager to serve in the church and, more often than not, walk away from their serving opportunity filled up and grateful. As a leader, I believe to deny our church body that joy almost borders on pastoral malpractice. Speaking to the church leaders at Ephesus, the Apostle Paul writes, *"Their responsibility is to equip God's people to do his work and build up the church, the body of Christ... So that we will be mature in the Lord, measuring up to the full and complete standard of Christ"* (Eph. 4:12-13 NLT) A leader's God-given responsibility is not to do all the work themselves, but to get every member of our local churches to be ministers!

**Avoid the tragedy at all costs:** John Ortberg told a true story about his grandmother's china when I did my internship at Willow Creek I'll never forget. I will paraphrase: When his grandmother died, a box containing a full set of priceless exquisite bone china was found in the attic. All the family members were at a loss as to where it came from. One of John's elder relatives spoke up, saying it evidently was given to her as a series of gifts piece-by-piece for birthdays, confirmation, graduation, etc. They wondered together, why in all the years and dinners at grandma's house, they hadn't seen it or eaten off of it. An elder relative conveyed she simply felt there was never an occasion that was special enough for it to be used. So, it sat dormant in the attic—never used, never enjoyed for the purpose which it was made. What a tragedy!

Imagine if Babe Ruth never swung a baseball bat or Michael Jordan never shot a basketball. If Einstein were not allowed to play with numbers or study science. If Steve Jobs or Bill Gates never played with a computer. If Michelangelo never picked up a paint brush or a chisel. It would be a tremendous tragedy. That's what happens when many people who come to church and are part of a church family, simply let their God-given spiritual gifts lay dormant. To do so is a great tragedy. I'm convinced Jesus would agree, that you cannot grow spiritually unless you become a servant.

One of the great joys of life is learning to serve in your gifted areas. Don't be guilted into serving. If you keep on reading in 1 Corinthians chapter 13, the basis for serving at all is love. If we don't serve out of love, our serving means nothing. Remember the prime hermeneutic? Love God, Love Others? That's the primary reason to serve, to love God and love others and to grow in both. Find your gifts and lean into your church's mission with all your heart as you serve. You have amazing divine abilities God has given you to serve his purposes. Have you discovered them? Are you using them to serve the world and God's purposes in the church? Read the following statement and score yourself accordingly:

### 1.3–Serve at Church

I regularly serve in the church. I have discovered my spiritual gifts and am using them to serve the Lord in my local church. I believe doing my part and serving in the church is an essential first step to help me grow in serving the needs of others in this world.

| WEAK | 1 | 2 | 3 | 4 | 5 | STRONG |
|------|---|---|---|---|---|--------|

**Memory verse: 1 Corinthians 12:27 (NIV)** *"Now you are the body Christ, and each one of you is a part of it."*

### Questions for Further Reflection and Discussion

1.  Have you taken a gifts discovery class? Share what your gifts and passions are.

2. Read the above memory verse. How much do you feel you are a part of your local church? How would discovering your gifts and serving help you feel more connected?

3. Have you found a ministry in the church where you serve? If so, write or share where and how you like it.

4. If you could to one thing to change the world or the church, what would it be and why?

5. Discuss the paradox of serving and giving yourself away to be fulfilled versus seeking to get all you want and feeling miserable.

## 1.4 Give Regularly

Over the course of my life, I've met some really generous people. Perhaps the most generous was my dad. We didn't have much growing up in a family consisting of six boys and one girl, but one thing my dad made sure of is that we had a roof over our heads, a shirt on our backs, and plenty of food in the cellar. (We really did have a cellar next to the dirt part of our basement.) One night, right next door to us, a natural gas pipe burst and shot flames up to what must have been a hundred feet into the sky. Firefighters came from far and wide, and there were my mom and dad making coffee and sandwiches all night long for the entire army of firefighters—everything paid for out of his hard-earned wages selling used cars. Another time, one of our nearby friends had a fire in their home and had no place to stay. My dad had an old long travel trailer that we never vacationed in, but used to sleep in during warm summer nights. He basically gave it to these folks free of charge for about a year. He was always giving something away—a meal, a car, whatever.

Perhaps that's why I have such a strong view of the amazing generosity of my Heavenly Father.

God is an incredibly generous God. He longs for his children to be generous too! I believe just about everyone wants to be generous. The problem is, often, people don't think they can afford it. Ann and I decided early on in our spiritual journey, just when we thought we couldn't afford to tithe, we realized we couldn't afford *not* to! Oops, I'm getting ahead of myself. I've strategically located tithing—giving 10 percent of your income—in Milestone 2. So, I'll elaborate more on that then. If you have the faith to do it now, don't wait. You'll see why in Milestone 2.4. For now though, begin to give regularly. During that (often awkward) time called the offering in a church service at your church, do your best to get something out of your purse or wallet and begin to learn how to give a portion of your income away. It could be a dollar, it could be five or ten dollars, anything! Just learn to give something regularly. Deep within us all, God has placed giving muscles. Like the six-pack abs that reside deep within my gut, they are there, but those muscles will not grow unless they are exercised regularly.

I've heard it before, "All the church wants is my money!" It's an interesting statement and attitude. Jesus got a similar attitude from the religious leaders who thought that's all the Roman government wanted! So, they asked Jesus, *"Tell us then, what is your opinion? Is it right to pay the imperial tax to Caesar or not?" Jesus said, "Show me a coin used for paying the tax." They brought a denarius, and he asked them, "Whose image is this? And whose inscription?" "Caesar's," they replied. Then he said to them, "Give back to Caesar what is Caesar's, and to God what is God's"* (Matt. 22:17, 19-21 NIV). Jesus *amazed them* it says in the next verse. Why? Jesus, knew they were trying to trap him but was in essence saying, 'Listen, if there is a percentage of taxes you're required to pay the government, pay it!" But when He said, "Give to God, what is God's" Jesus was saying, God want's all of you, not just a percentage. See, everything we have is God's already. Our giving simply acknowledges all we have is his and we are simply giving back a small portion of what God has so generously entrusted to us. The truth is, God could take all we have at any given moment. Sometimes he does. It's called death. And you can't take anything with you. Between now and then, he wants us to grow in the area of generosity. It's like God wants to use you and me to flow his resources to people he knows need it.

If you believe the money you have is actually *your* money and "that's all the church wants is my money," you're just not ready to give. But, do a little self-reflection. If you believe Jesus died for your sins, realize God gave everything for you. "For God so loved the world, he gave . . ." He gave the most, his Son! We can never pay him back for that. It's done. The price has been paid. Only he could pay it. Realize God certainly doesn't need your money. He just wants his children to reflect their Father's generosity because there is joy in giving. Greed leads to grief. Giving leads to great joy. It's really another paradox. But it's true. Really, we tell people, when you give to the church, you're not giving individually to a pastor or the church per se, you're giving to God.

Know this, most churches are pretty diligent when it comes to finances. Our church does a yearly audit to make sure we are financially above reproach. We give locally to hurting single parents and other people who are down on their luck. We give to the poor globally. Without people like you giving regularly, the church couldn't operate and we certainly couldn't help people in need financially.

All I ask of you right now is to pray about it and know God says this about giving, *You must each decide in your heart how much to give. And don't give reluctantly or in response to pressure. "For God loves a person who gives cheerfully."* (2 Cor. 9:7 NLT). Decide in your heart. Don't give reluctantly. God actually takes the pressure off here. If you're not ready to give, it's okay, don't give anyway and be upset about it. A few years ago I attended a session of a youth conference where a young, immature pastor told the crowd of about 1000 young middle and high school students, "Give until it hurts!" I wondered, where did he learn that? Where is that found in the Bible? That's a ton of pressure on young impressionable hearts, no less. That sort of unbiblical teaching can leave a real poor taste in someone's mouth. I would even say, the way he proclaimed it was sinful and wrong. He had no business or authority to say it, because that sort of proclamation does a lot of damage to the church and furthers people's perception that "All the church wants is your money."

Perhaps you've been hurt in a relationship because of money. Maybe a boss or a friend who was a professed Christian stole from you or didn't pay you as you deserved. Maybe a church bilked you out of some money at some point in your life and you swore you'd never give again. Maybe you heard similar statements like the one I heard at that conference and it just turned you off. Those scenarios are painful, and it's understandable that you may not want to give to the church. If you've been hurt financially by a church or religious organization or in an area that causes some bitterness and makes you somewhat reluctant to give to the church, on behalf of the church at large, I want to ask you for forgiveness. I am so sorry you were hurt. Please forgive us! I hope you can. Please go to God with your pain of reluctance and simply ask him to heal you of it and help you to be generous, specifically to his church.

Here's a reason why: The Christian Church does more good for more needy people worldwide than all the other non-profits on the planet combined. For every bad example of a church's financial missteps, there are one hundred good ones. Don't miss out on becoming more generous. It's so good for your soul. The alternative to being generous is being greedy. It's extremely self-centered and self-focused and helps no one; ironically, it does not even help the greedy person.

Early on in my Christian journey, I was a partner in a business. We struggled at first and then, suddenly, it's like God opened the floodgates. In Seattle, there was an intercity non-profit that was doing great work developing jobs and opportunities—primarily for the black community. As I believed God led me, I went to speak to my partner about a giving opportunity I saw. I said, "Hey, God has really blessed us and I think we could bless others by giving five percent of our net earnings to non-profits." I barely got it out and he blasted back at me, "God, what do you mean, God? We've worked d*** hard to get where we're at." I just about fell over. See, I had just read Deuteronomy chapter 8, which says, *"When you have eaten and are satisfied, praise the Lord your God for the good land he has given you. Be careful that you do not forget the Lord your God... Otherwise, when you eat and are satisfied, where you build fine houses and settle down, and when your herds and flocks grow large and your silver and gold increase and all you have is multiplied, then your heart will become proud and you will forget the Lord your God... You may say to yourself, 'My power and the strength of my hands have produced this wealth for me.' But remember the Lord your God, for it is he who gives you the ability to produce wealth... If you ever forget the Lord your God and follow other gods and worship and bow down to them, I testify against you today, that you will be destroyed"* (Deut. 8:10–19 NIV).

My partner totally violated God's word. From his perspective, God had nothing to do with our success. It's was all us, our hard work, our diligence, our savvy! No recognition that, at the very least, God gave us air! As a result, he held on to "his" money in a very tight-fisted fashion. Think about it. God could pull the plug on air at any moment. It's crazy to believe what we do and what we make financially is all us, but that's what we often do. The truth is, my partner had a god, but it wasn't the one true God. It was money. He worshipped it. He adored it. It was his identity. To him, how people perceived him was all about how much money he had or made. Money meant everything to him and it consumed him to the point where he allowed it to destroy many of his friendships and relationships. Greed got the best of him.

Because of his response to my request to give (which never did happen, by the way) and his greed in other areas, as well as my observations regarding how often money issues torch many partnerships, marriages, and friendships, I have decided not let money be a barrier or a destroyer of any relationships in my life. I am determined to take the hit financially, if need be, and not look back. After all, Jesus took an enormous hit to pay for my sins. I can never ever pay him back for that.

Jesus said, *"No one can serve two masters. Either you will hate the one and love the other, or you will be devoted to one and despise the other. You cannot serve both God and money"* (Matt. 6:24 NIV). Money is so messy. No matter how much or how little one has, we either master it, or it masters us. The only way to clean up our money issues is to learn to be generous and begin to learn to joyfully give it away. I have much more to say about this in Milestones 2.4 and 3.4.

How's your generosity quotient? Where are you in relationship to being a regular giver? Read the following statement and score where you land:

**1.4–Give Regularly**
I regularly give to God through the church. I believe that giving helps me become a more generous person and giving to the church really means giving back to God a portion of what he has so generously given me.

| WEAK | 1 | 2 | 3 | 4 | 5 | STRONG |
|------|---|---|---|---|---|--------|

**Memory verse: 2 Corinthians 9:7 (NLT)** *"You must each decide in your heart how much to give. And don't give reluctantly or in response to pressure. "For God loves a person who gives cheerfully."*

71

## Questions for Further Reflection and Discussion

1. How generous were your parents growing up?

2. God spent a huge price to rescue you by giving his Son to die for you on the cross. How do you truly feel about that?

3. What are your feelings regarding giving to the church? Why?

4. How's your generosity quotient? Your greed quotient?

5. What's your perception of the poor? Do you see them equally valuable in God's eyes?

6. Considering everything is God's and he even gave you the ability to make a paycheck, how does that change your perspective on giving?

# 1.5 Support Your Leaders

Authority and submission. In our culture, those words can feel pretty ugly. So many leaders have abused their authority. Submission? Sounds like something you're beaten into. Who'd want to do that? Authority and submission are biblical words that, unfortunately, have a ton of our cultural baggage attached to them.

Hebrews 13:17 (NIV) says, *"Have confidence in your leaders and submit to their authority, because they keep watch over you as those who must give an account. Do this so that their work will be a joy, not a burden, for that would be of no benefit to you."*

Rock star Bob Dylan wrote, "You may serve the Devil or you may serve the Lord, but you're gonna have to serve somebody." You may say, "I'll submit to God, but never to a pastor or leader or any other human being." Here's the truth; if a person will not submit to another human being, especially God's anointed spiritual leaders, they will not and are not submitting to God. Our ability to submit to our pastor goes hand in hand with our ability to submit to God. You cannot have one without the other.

We live in very rebellious times. Rebellion a big part of our culture and we think it's okay, but it's not. David, the second king of Israel, was relentlessly attacked and hunted down by King Saul, who made numerous attempts to assassinate him, but when David finally had Saul dead to rights in a cave, David let him go while Saul was relieving himself. He didn't lay a finger on him other than to sneak up and cut off a piece of Saul's robe. His men couldn't believe David didn't kill Saul. David had every right. He was totally justified to take Saul out once and for all. When they asked him "Why, David, why? Why did you let him go?" David replied to his men: *"The Lord forbid that I should do this to my lord the king. I shouldn't attack the Lord's anointed one, for the Lord himself has chosen him"* (1 Sam. 24:6 NLT). Listen, I know of no pastors who are even remotely as callous and hard-hearted as King Saul. Here's the deal, to come against your spiritual leaders is to come against God. You may have every justification in your heart and mind to do it. Don't! Pray for him or her. Pray for God to intervene. If you see something way out of whack, talk to your pastor about it, but don't gossip. Things often aren't what they seem. Coming against them will not benefit you or the church. Fact is, most often when factions are formed they cause great damage to the church and to people's lives, especially those who are young in their faith walk.

You may not know it, but your pastor is carrying a tremendous burden. People often believe he should be just like Jesus. I'm sure he is trying to grow to be more like Jesus, just like you and me. But, just like you and me, he's not there yet. So, cut him some slack. Rather than figuring out how he's supposed to serve you, perhaps ask him how you can serve him and others in the church. Believe me, that would bring great joy to most pastors.

One of the things I take very seriously as a pastor is that Bible verse which says, "because they keep watch over you as the one who must give an account." Get this, most people will only have to stand before God at judgment and give an account for themselves. Pastors and church leaders will have to stand before God and give an account for all those people in their church, under their care. I have played this out in my mind, God says, "Brad, how did you do with John and Julie and Sam and Sara and Susie and Paul and Jake and so on?" Every individual life that God allowed to come under my spiritual care—I, as a pastor, will need to give an account for. I'm telling you, if that doesn't put the fear of God in you, not much else will. I then imagine myself standing there, in fear and trembling, squeaking out to God in a mouse-like tone, "Well, Lord, I don't know, but you know. you know all things Lord." All I want to hear at that point is these words, "Well done, good and faithful servant." I think most pastors who really understand this have these kinds of thoughts and desires for the flock God has placed under their care.

So, don't be a burden. Find things right about your church, not what's wrong. If you see some areas that could use improvement, be the solution, not the problem.

Never, ever come against your pastor. People who come against their pastors are risking severe punishment from God himself. In Numbers 16, a group of people led by a priest named Korah, came against Moses and Aaron. Read that chapter. It's not pretty. God was so upset with Korah for coming against Moses and Aaron that he opened up the earth and it swallowed him and his con-conspirators and his whole family up. None were spared. Please read that chapter now and don't ever come against your pastor or leaders.

A number of years ago, a married couple got very upset with the fact that our worship pastor wanted the husband to just play keys and to step down from singing, because other, more gifted vocalists had joined our worship team. That couple was deeply offended. So, they began to find many things wrong with the church. They called me to ask for a meeting. At the meeting, they produced a ten-page document with all the things wrong with me, with our worship pastor, and with the church as a whole. Honestly, there were some truths sprinkled into it, but most were petty. At the end of their document, was a small statement, "We know it could be us, but we don't think so." One of the issues that was brought up was that they apparently had given me a book to read, which I had not returned to them. "That," they said, "proves your lack of integrity." Wow! I sat there in disbelief and hurt. So many people come to me and say, "Pastor, read this book. Watch this movie. Here's something you'd like." I accept them in the moment, but rarely read them or watch them. I just don't have the time. And I can hardly remember where they came from if they do make it off my bookshelf. I'm a flawed human being. I admit it. But no pastor deserves that. They shared their grievances, we thanked them and they left the church. Sadly, a few years later they were divorced. A wise man once told me, "The problem is never the problem." No matter where you go, there you are. It's all about our growth, our acceptance, our willingness to submit to the people God has placed in authority over us.

I could tell you a number of similar stories, like one woman who was so angry at me for saying too much about God at a funeral. The irony is that it was for a graduated high school student whose parents were so appreciative of how their child's funeral went and that their child's unwavering faith encouraged non-church going attenders to pursue Christ. However, the angry woman left our church in a rage. The parents of the deceased child stayed. The enraged woman then went out and told all sorts of people what a terrible pastor I was, for years. Five years later, I was still hearing how poison was still spewing from her lips. Her husband supported her in her offense. Some came to me, said, "Pastor Brad, she is so toxic." I'd just say, "Yeah, I know. Pray for her." We did. Again, just a few years later, I hear she's divorced.

I'm no psychologist, but I know often, when a person has major issues with their pastor or spiritual leader, it's more a reflection of their relationship with their very own father. Hurt people, hurt people! They don't realize it, but more times than not, an old wound from their childhood is triggered by an unmet expectation or old fear. That's too deep to get into in this book, but it's real. Believe me. If I could have a conversation with the people who came against me, these days I'd likely start with one question that may help, "You seem to be hurting, how can I help?" People have such high expectations of pastors, sometimes like they've finally found the perfect father, man or leader. Well, get this, Jesus was the perfect man, fully God and perfect human being, the greatest spiritual leader to ever breath air. Look what they did to him—part of the crowd that initially supported him, turned on him and put him to death on the cross. Even he couldn't meet everyone's perceived needs. If Jesus couldn't, certainly no pastor can!

I don't pretend to know all things spiritual. But I'm convinced, when a person comes against their pastors and spiritual leaders, they are bringing the curses of God on themselves and their families. Don't go there! Read Numbers 16. It's a scary scenario. Did I say that already? PLEASE READ IT! If you need more, read Numbers 12 too. It's about Miriam and Aaron, who bogusly criticized Moses. READ IT! The problem in both of the above chapters was the lack of a healthy fear of the Lord. *"Fear of the Lord is the beginning of knowledge, but fools despise wisdom and discipline"* (Prov. 1:7 NIV). Note: "Fear of the Lord" is a healthy high respect or reverence for God. I'm convinced that almost any time a person goes rogue and comes against their pastor or leader, they have old, unhealed wounds and they just don't have a healthy fear or reverence for the Lord, which will truncate and even prevent their growth in just about every area of life. It's interesting that after the first wave of persecution in the early church was over, *"The church then had peace throughout Judea, Galilee, and Samaria, and it became stronger as the believers lived in the fear of the Lord"* (Acts 9:31a NLT). Did you catch that? The church, which is the people of the church, actually became stronger as they lived in fear or the Lord. "And" it says, *"With the encouragement of the Holy Spirit, it also grew in numbers"* (Acts 9:31a NLT). Maybe many churches don't grow mature disciples because we have lost a fear of the Lord. Maybe that lack of fear of the Lord is most evident when they are unsupportive of their pastor. Something to ponder.

That said, know that when a person comes against their pastor, it hurts the pastor deeply. They really still care and love that person. Did you know pastors have feelings too? I know I do. And, sometimes after pastors have taken their unfair share of emotional assaults, they simply quit. They just can't take it anymore. I totally understand. Do you know why? One primary reason: the inability to handle adversity. And often there is a mountain of adversity in the church that few people can handle, without support. We have to be careful with statistics, but I've heard, and it seems reasonable, that in every church across America on average, approximately nine percent of attenders in any given church are disgruntled with their senior pastor at any given time. Don't be one.

I am so glad that we have had many people in our congregation over the years that totally get supporting their pastor and leaders. When I have taken a big hit, I've often gone to see a wise Christian counselor, paid for by the church. Our church body supports that. I really want to know what I need to work on. How I could have prevented it? What growth steps do I need to take to handle the situation better next time? A few times over the years both Ann and I have gone to extended "retreats" where we are one-on-one with a Christian counselor or in a group. It is so healing. We really do work on our stuff for the good of our marriage, our kids, and our church family and friends.

Here's the deal: if you have a problem with your pastor, or anyone in the church, the Bible directs us to go to them, and seek to resolve the issue one-one-one. It's all in Matthew 18—read it and practice it.

The devil wants to destroy the church. If he can take out the leader, he knows he can cripple the church. If he gets your help and the help of a number of others, especially for petty reasons, know he's laughing all the way to the bank of hell!

Lastly, parents, show your kids how to support leaders, first by supporting their teachers and principals. Parents are notorious for getting upset over small issues regarding classrooms and teachers. And parents, if you have an issue with your church or church leaders, don't badmouth them at home with your spouse in front of your children. That's modeling such negative, toxic behavior to them. Remember, the fruit doesn't fall far from the tree. Again, if you have a concern with someone, respectfully and prayerfully go directly to the person you have an issue with. As I mentioned earlier, Jesus teaches us this in Matthew chapter 18. Again, please read and practice it. Don't just leave your church if you have an issue. Go to your pastor or leader and work it out. Remember, it's your kids' church too. I have seen parents rip their families out of their church with no regard to their kids. I've seen my own kids lose good friends because of other parents' toxic actions. It's painful to watch. Seek always to restore a relationship and reconcile. I share more on this and how to reconcile in Milestone 3.8.

## 1.5–Support Leaders

I wholeheartedly support and obey the church leadership. I am learning to resolve any issues I have with my leaders or others directly with the person involved in an emotionally healthy fashion.

| WEAK | 1 | 2 | 3 | 4 | 5 | STRONG |

**Memory verse: Hebrews 13:17 (NIV)** *"Have confidence in your leaders and submit to their authority, because they keep watch over you as those who must give an account. Do this so that their work will be a joy, not a burden, for that would be of no benefit to you."*

**Questions for Further Reflection and Discussion**

1. How do you feel about your pastor and spiritual leaders?

2. What are your expectations of them?

3. Read Numbers 16 and Proverbs 1:7 and discuss the idea of how fearing the Lord and supporting your pastors and leaders go hand in hand.

4. What do you do to support them? How can you support them better?

5. What was your relationship with your own father and/or mother like growing up?

6. How do you respond to people in a role of authority?

7. What can you say to someone who is complaining about the pastor/leaders or the church?

# 1.6 Be Real

When I first became a Christian, I knew right away I didn't want to be a phony one. I had seen late night televange-lists preach on the wretchedness of sexual immorality one night, then read about them getting caught sleeping with an assistant the next. I knew very quickly that I was capable of doing some really stupid stuff like that, and the only way to prevent it was with God's help. I just didn't want to be a poser. Jesus spoke to this tendency among the Israelites and spiritual leaders at various times, but one time he made it clear as day was in the gospel of Matthew chapter 23:3 and 5, he said, *"So practice and obey whatever they tell you, but don't follow their example. For they don't practice what they teach. Everything they do is for show. On their arms they wear extra wide prayer boxes with Scripture verses inside, and they wear robes with extra-long tassels"* (Matt. 23:3, 5 NLT). They talked the talk, they just didn't walk the walk. They wore all the religious garb, pretended to be so spiritual. And if you read the rest of the chapter, Jesus calls these religious leaders "hypocrites." He uses the word five times to point out many of their hypocritical behaviors. Hypocrite: It was a term used for actors in Jesus' day. A person who has a mask on. They do everything for show, Jesus said. Know any? Before you answer that question—go look in the mirror. Ask God, and ask yourself if you are posing, pretending to be someone you're not in any area of your life. And know this, God loathes spiritual posers. It's so vain. I'm convinced being a spiritual poser is perhaps the greatest violation of the third commandment, worse than saying God d*** it!" (Not giving permission to say that, though. Don't!) The third of God's top ten says, *"You shall not take the name of the Lord your God in vain"* (Exod. 20:7 ESV). Think about it, those Pharisees, all that garb and flowery prayers and judgment they were passing on everyone in the name of God— total vanity! Carly Simon sung, "You're so vain, you probably think this song is about you." For some, even when they pose to be about God, it's all about them. Let's not have it be about you or me. Okay? Be Real. Sometimes it's harder than you think.

Years ago, when I was in seminary, I was taking a preaching class. Entering that class, I knew I wanted to be the best preacher ever. I sat under the teachings of one of the best in the world at my church in Chicago, Bill Hybels. He was so good, still is! I wanted to be just like him. Why not? So, I prepared my sermon I was to give in class. I went 40 minutes instead of the allotted 25. Didn't matter, I knew it was great! I was so proud of myself. Then came my meeting with my seminary professor to critique my sermon. First words out his mouth were, "Brad, what was that? Or should I say, WHO was that?" My professor's brutally honest critique rocked my boat so much I went to see a Christian therapist. Yeah! Really! In two sessions, I concluded that I was trying to be Bill Hybels, not myself! It was the best 180 bucks I ever spent. I came to realize I needed to be the best Brad Brucker I can possibly be. That's all God wants of me. I now know for certain, no one can be a better Brad Brucker than me! I'm the best at it. Hear this: Be the best you God made you to be. No one can be a better you than you! If you do that, you will be truly real! And stop being what others want you to be, or what you think others want you to be. Even if it's your mom or dad. Just tell them "Sorry, I'm going to be who God made me to be, not what you want me to be."

There are some practices that can help you with being real like being appropriately transparent and vulnerable. Don't just share all that is going well with you all the time. At times share where you struggle. That's being transparent. Be honest. When I first went to AA for my alcoholism 30 years ago, they started every AA meeting with a reading from Chapter 5 "How it Works" in the book *Alcoholics Anonymous*:

> *Rarely have we seen a person fail who has thoroughly followed our path. Those who do not recover are people who cannot or will not completely give themselves to this simple program, usually men and women who are constitutionally incapable of being honest with themselves.... They are naturally incapable of grasping and developing a manner of living that demands rigorous honesty* (pg. 58, 1976 edition).

When I first heard those words—"rigorous honesty"—it sounded like work to me. Hard work! I knew to be rigorously honest it was going take a lot of work for a liar like me. I knew I couldn't fudge the truth anymore. I couldn't embellish a story. I couldn't tell a white lie anymore. Being real is being totally honest. The deception of a lie is that really good lies always have a bit of truth sprinkled in, to make them believable. That's why the devil used scripture, albeit twisted scripture, to tempt Jesus in the wilderness (see Luke chapter 4). Boldface lies just aren't very believable. If we decide we are going to be mostly honest, it's still a lie. Fake is fake, even if it looks real. Counterfeiters don't try to pass monopoly money at grocery stores. No, they do their best to copy real ten and twenty dollar bills so they can sneak them by a cashier.

Ever heard the saying, "He is as honest as the day is long?" All my favorite superheroes are incredibly honest. Captain America—totally honest. Superman—100 percent honest, except when Lex Luther poisoned him with kryptonite.

When someone is honest, we say, she's really solid. That's a huge compliment. There is something about honesty that wreaks of integrity and humility, in a good way. *God opposes the proud but gives grace to the humble* (James 4:6 ESV). A humble person is generally an honesty person. Honesty coupled with humility is incredibly attractive. Hypocrisy, on the other hand, repels people. If you are honest with your shortcomings as well as your victories, people will want what you have. They will likely even follow you as you lead them to a deeper relationship with Jesus. That's really the key to Jesus' success. He was the most real and honest person who ever walked the face of this planet, even though he never sinned. More people have wanted what he had and has for the past two millennia than anyone who ever lived.

Recently I attended an all staff meeting where all of our campuses came together. My oldest son was attending his first ever all staff meeting as one of our interns. After the meeting, I asked him what he thought. He said, "Wow dad, it was awesome! I just felt so honored and privileged to be able to be there." Honestly, I was taken aback when he said that. I had just become so used to church meetings, that can sometimes feel monotonous, rather than feel privileged to attend. That's honest. That said, my son's freshness retaught me something very important; to be able to see being part of God's people is a huge honor and privilege, which I never want to lose. Also, it reminded me, no matter how long I'm in the game, I can always be taught by someone new, someone younger. In this case especially, my son.

Being honest means when you go to church, don't pretend you know everything. Being honest means not pretending to be more spiritual than you are. Sometimes Christ-followers like to share a bunch of Bible information, just to impress someone. I've learned over the years, I have no need to impress anyone. My goal is to be more like Jesus. Then I'll increasingly become the best Brad Brucker God created me to be.

CS Lewis' book *The Great Divorce* heavily influenced my early Christian journey. To paraphrase, the story goes a group of ghost people board a bus in hell that takes them to the outskirts of heaven. As they get off the bus, everything there is more solid, the water, the grass, even the people—they are the solid people. At one point, some heavenly people come down out of the mountains, and they are really solid. The point is, the closer we get to Jesus and living the kingdom of heaven here on earth, the more solid we become. I so want to be a solid person. Being solid is synonymous with integrity! A big part of our journey with Jesus is becoming more real and being less hypocritical. The world wants to mold us into hypocrites, where everyone is pretty much the same. The irony is God gave every person on the planet a different and unique set of fingerprints. Yeah, it helps police detectives track down the bad guys, but I'm sure that's not why God created our prints uniquely. I believe it goes way deeper.

They say, "You are who you hang with." If we hang with Jesus and walk with him on this spiritual journey, we will become more real and more like him, all the while becoming more like ourselves—the very original and unique masterpiece our Creator made us to be. It's really pretty cool. No one can do a better you! You are so great! As the old saying goes, "God made you an original, don't die a copy!"

So, are you getting more real? Do you want to become who God made you to be? No one can do you better than you! Score yourself and be real!

### 1.6–Be Real

I know I am a sinner saved by grace alone. Therefore, I am transparent, authentic and honest and not a spiritual poser. I keep a short list of my sins and confess any sin issues I have. With the help of God, I'm becoming the real me.

( WEAK    **1**    **2**    **3**    **4**    **5**    STRONG )

**Memory verse: Matthew 23: 5 (NLT)** *"Everything they do is for show. On their arms they wear extra wide prayer boxes with Scripture verses inside, and they wear robes with extra-long tassels."*

### Questions for Further Reflection and Discussion

1. Who, if anyone, growing up was someone you wanted to be like and why?

2. What do you think of people who seem to always have it together?

3. What's your greatest fear about people getting to know who you really are on the inside?

4. Discuss what being honest and transparent means to you. How can you grow in being more authentic and real?

5. Do you believe Jesus knows all about you and at the same time completely loves all of you? What does that mean to you?

## 1.7 Reach Out

E ver have someone invite you to a party? Ever been asked to play on a team? Ever had a call from someone special who wanted to have coffee or lunch with you? How did that feel? Pretty good, huh! Now, how about being left out? Not being invited? Not being asked? Never getting that phone call? Depressing and painful, huh? One of the most amazing things about being a Christ-follower is the Christian faith is incredibly inclusive. Honestly, we'll take anyone. No matter how challenging they are. Yeah! That even means you and me!

The problem is, it's pretty common knowledge among church leaders that within five years of becoming a Christian, a new Christ-follower does not have many or any non-Christian friends. That means two things: First we need to be intentional about reaching out to those who don't know God. Second, if you are just beginning your spiritual journey and you're at Milestone 1, chances are you still have a number of friends who don't know Jesus yet. That gives you a distinct advantage over many long-term more "mature" Christians. I want to encourage

87

you to use your location on The Spiritual Journey map strategically to advance the kingdom of God and win friends, neighbors, classmates and co-workers to Christ. How do you do that? The Apostle Peter, one of Jesus inner three disciples, gives us a clue: He wrote:

> *"Always be prepared to give an answer to everyone who asks you to give the reason for the hope that you have. But do this with gentleness and respect"* (1 Pet. 3:15) NIV.

"Always" is the key word. Be ready in every situation. You may think, "No way! I'm not ready! In fact, I'm scared! People just won't understand." I get it. Remember the Spiritual Curiosity part of your own journey, "Why am I here? What is my purpose in life?" Just about everyone asks those questions. You did, right? So, share it with a friend. Ask, "You ever wondered if there is more to life than this? You ever wonder what your true purpose is in life?" Remember Spiritual Curiosity? Just go back there and gently and respectfully go through it with the person God has put in your path.

***Share Your Story*** of becoming a Christ-follower. A great process to follow for formulating your testimony is BC + Cross + AD. What was your life like Before Christ? How did you receive God's grace and believe in Christ's death on the Cross for all your sins? What was your first real Easter like when you realized Jesus actually did rise from the dead? And how's your life been since? That's the After Decision piece. Keep it to five minutes or less and it will be really effective. But be careful not to be too pushy thinking you need to save everyone you meet. As Peter says in the above verse. Share your story "with gentleness and respect."

***Keep your testimony pure, live*** with integrity. Be Real! What's amazing is, most non-Christians have an idea how a Christ-follower is supposed to conduct their lives from a moral perspective. Personally, over the years I have engaged in many conversations with unchurched men who drop f-bombs at will. They curse up a storm not having a clue what I do for a living. At some point in the conversation I ask them what they do for a living. Most of the time, they easily share their vocational calling with me. After all, it's a great way to connect and show you are interested in them. Then the table is turned to me, and they ask me what I do. "Oh, I'm a pastor," I nonchalantly say. Suddenly, they do a quick rewind in their mind of all the swear words they littered all over our previous conversation and it's almost like they have a fishing rod and quickly try to reel every bad word back in. "Oh, uh, I didn't mean to swear there!" They say sheepishly. I don't expect anything different from them, because until they receive the Holy Spirit, people will remain worldly in speech and actions. Here's the deal, if you are swearing and getting drunk, and if your life, apart from Sunday morning, pretty much looks the same as it did before you put your faith in Christ, your testimony will be ineffective. Be different on purpose. Ask God to help you and never forget what he did for you. *Christ bought you with a price, therefore honor God with your bodies* (1 Cor. 6:20 NIV). People notice. If you're living a joy-filled life, even when life gets tough, people will want what you have. And what you have is Jesus. There is nothing or no one better! Trust me, at some point they will be interested in what you have. Be careful, though, to first be interested in them.

***Be Interested!*** When I moved from Chicago back to Oregon, we had a house built in a new sub-division. Chris was the contractor's guy that cleaned up all the houses and got them ready to hand over to the new owner. After a few months of interacting with Chris, I knew he was lost and I knew I was the one God sent to bring him the gospel to get him saved. After all, we moved there to plant a new church and I wanted to make sure that new church was filled with seekers and new believers. One day, I strategically asked Chris if I could buy him lunch. "Sure," he said. Loaded for bear with my gospel tracts, pen and Post-It note pad, I was ready to usher Chris into the kingdom. We sat down, ordered lunch, exchanged pleasantries. Finally, the task at hand had arrived. I whipped out my "Steps to Peace with God," which has worked so well for us over the years in sharing the gospel. I walked him through it. I'm sure he gets it. After all, Romans 1:16 says, *"The Gospel is the power of God for all who believe!"* I've got this! God's got this! I draw a few more illustrations out on a Post-It note just for good measure. I'm ready to take the salvation order, and say, "So, Chris, is there any reason you wouldn't want to put your faith in Christ right now?" I'll never forget it. He looks up at me and says, "Gee, Brad, it's pretty hard for me to concentrate right now. See, today is the day my divorce is final." My jaw just about drops to the table. I cannot believe how insensitive I was. I was so interested in my agenda, I never once asked him how he was doing. I weep even as I write this, years later. I heard it so many times, and I thought I got it, but it was then that I learned to be genuinely interested in lost people before I slapped a Bible verse on them. They matter to God.

***Pray for and with lost people.*** Everyone goes through challenges and difficulties in life. When I learn people are struggling, I pray for and with them. That includes my unchurched friends. Remember Jim, my Star Trek theology plumber? Fast forward about eight years. He's at my house, working on my sink. He gets a call. His live-in girlfriend calls him. Jim is visibly shaken. I ask what's wrong. "It's Bethany (not her real name). She just had a seizure!" "Wow, Jim," I gently say, "Can I pray for her?" "Uh, sure," he awkwardly responds. I put my hand on his shoulder and pray for her by name. He tells me, in his 50 years of life, no one has ever done that. One week later he calls me up and leaves a voice mail, "Brad, my friend from way back in grade school, Bob in Florida, just had a stroke. Can, you do what you do, send a few words up for Bob?" I call him back and ask him if I can share his voicemail on my cellphone with the congregation and we'll all pray for Bob." He says "Sure!" So, I do that next Sunday as I'm teaching on outreach. I just put my cellphone up to my mic and play the voicemail from Jim to the whole congregation. Everyone prays for Bob. Two weeks later, I see him at the local supermarket, "Jim, how's Bob?" He looks at me with his head shaking and says, "Brad, I know when I first met you I was all about Star Trek theology. But you know what Brad, Bob is doing a lot better and I'm really starting to believe this s***." A year later he's doing another plumbing project for me. I'm working with him to keep the cost down. We drive to the hardware store together and out of the blue he asks me, "So, Brad, what's Easter all about?" I just about fell out of the car! I thought, "Are you even kidding me?" That's like the best question a pagan could ever ask a Christ-follower! So, I tell him about the death and resurrection of Jesus. He says, "Nah, he really didn't come back from the dead, did he?" "Yep, he really did. If he didn't we would never have the possibility of going to a better place when we die," I energetically reply. "Oh," he says. End of conversation. Over the course of ten years, Jim has become a good friend. About year ten of our friendship he calls me up in crisis, business crisis, relational crisis—total drama! "Jim," I finally say, "I can't help you, but I know who can. Jim it's time!" "Time for what?" he retorts. "Time to say a prayer you need to say!" I boldly proclaim. "Prayer? Me? For what?" he asks. "To put your faith in Christ, Jim! It's time!" "Okay, I'll do it later today." Jim replies. "Jim, you need to do it now." "What do I say?" he asks. So, I give him some words and say, "Just say it out loud from your heart in your own words." "Alright, let me pull over!" He does. And just like that, ten years later, he's saved. How? Relationship, patience and the power of the Holy Spirit. But prayer. Prayer. All people need prayer. It's one of the greatest outreach tools we can use. Pray for your lost friends' and neighbors' salvation and pray with them in times of pain and sickness and need. And lead them in a prayer of salvation at the right Holy Spirit-led time.

*"Live wisely among those who are not believers, and make the most of every opportunity. Let your conversation be gracious and attractive so that you will have the right response for everyone"* (Col. 4:5, 6 NLT). Here, the Apostle Paul was simply teaching that he was hoping he could share the message of Christ with those who didn't know him. How do we do that? Develop relationships with lost people. Have them over for dinner. Develop business relationships. Shine for Christ as a business owner. Honestly, as I alluded to above, I'm pretty strategic about developing business relationships with lost people. It's a risk for sure. We intentionally hired a non-Christian architect to design our church building. He'd come to church for Christmas and Easter and that's about it. Eventually, he came one too many times. We do connection card responses to the message and for prayer requests. He wrote on the card, "Brad, I did it today!" I call him up, "Larry, am I reading this right? You put your faith in Christ on Sunday?" "Yes, I did!" "Wow, so awesome!" The crazy thing is, I didn't get him there. His step-daughter, Deb, did. She invited him. Yeah, we became friends during our building design, but he'd have never come without Deb inviting him. And that's a great way to share your faith.

***Invite them to church.*** I just read somewhere that 96 percent of your friends will come to church if you invite them. Other research says one out of four people asked will come if you invite them. Our church has touch cards the size of a business cards to use as invites. We use them for special outreaches. Often, for Christmas and Easter, people are more prone to come if invited. But first pray for them. And don't be pushy. Just pray for them and invite every now and then, but love them regardless. Then watch and see what God does.

So, how are you doing with reaching out to those who don't know Christ? Read the following statements and the memory verse and then score yourself appropriately.

**1.7–Reach Out**
I am beginning to understand the church's mission of reaching out to people who don't know Jesus yet. I am excited to tell others about my church and about Jesus, even though they might think I'm crazy and, at times, say hurtful things about my faith. I pray for people in my life who don't yet have a relationship with God (1 Pet. 3:15-16).

**Memory verse: 1 Peter 3:15 (NIV)** *"But in your hearts revere Christ as Lord. Always be prepared to give an answer to everyone who asks you to give the reason for the hope that you have. But do this with gentleness and respect."*

| WEAK | 1 | 2 | 3 | 4 | 5 | STRONG |
|------|---|---|---|---|---|--------|

**Questions for Further Reflection and Discussion**

1. Who are five people in your life who don't know Christ? Make a list of their names.

2. If you're in a group study, confidentially share a few of the above names with your group.

3.  Study the beginning of The Spiritual Journey map at the front end of GROW. Try to write it out and memorize it—practice helps us to always be ready. If you're in a group, practice it with a friend.

4.  Write down or share a time when you tried to share your faith and it didn't go so well.

5.  What might you do different next time?

6.  Challenge: In the next few weeks, pray for and invite an unchurched friend to church with you. Discuss your apprehensions.

## 1.8 Forgive

Have you ever been hurt? Live long enough—like five or six years—and eventually people will hurt you. We all get hurt, often by people we love. It's just part of living in this fallen world. How we deal with the hurts is the ball game. That's what forgiveness is all about.

As you move along on your spiritual journey, know forgiveness is often a journey as well. What this milestone point is all about is beginning to develop the same mind Jesus had when he offered us forgiveness on the cross. Peter, one of Jesus' closest disciples, was a great example of a person who grew as he leaned into Jesus. One time, I imagine after Peter had some problems with James and John, his fishing buddies and his fellow disciples of Jesus, he came to Jesus and asked him how many times should a person be willing to forgive. I can almost hear Peter say, "James stole my catch, Jesus!" And, "John ripped my fishing nets, on purpose! Again!" "I'm so tired of it! And they don't really seem to care. It hurts, Jesus, it hurts! God, I wish you'd just smite them, oh, Mighty Smiter!" Ever felt that way? We all have at one time or another. So, what's the answer? "Forgive" Jesus says. "How many times, seven times?" Peter asked Jesus. "Nope!" Jesus replies, "Seven times seventy!" (Matt. 18:21-22). Question: Does that mean 490 times and I'm finally done forgiving that jerk? Nope! I believe Jesus was saying this:

***Pre-forgive.*** Have an attitude that even prior to someone sinning against you and hurting you, you have already pre-decided in your heart and mind that you will forgive them. Why would we? Well, Jesus forgave you! Grace and love, remember? So, when someone does hurt you, what do you do? Forgive. Holding on to unforgiveness leads to bitterness and resentment, which are spiritual and emotional toxins to the soul. It's been said that bitterness and resentment are simply anger with mold on it. So, in my mind and heart, I just prepare for the hurt to come. I call that pre-forgiveness.

Pre-forgiveness is really psychological forgiveness. The word psychology is derived from the New Testament Greek word *psuche*—its means soul, we get psyche or psychology from that word. True psychology is the study of the soul—perhaps the care of the soul. The soul is the seat of our emotions and inner life. In the Old Testament, the Hebrew word for heart is *LEB*—it has a similar meaning as soul in the New Testament. Proverbs 4:23 says, *"Above all else guard your heart [or soul], for it is the wellspring of life."* I love the word wellspring. I picture an ice cold pure spring bubbling out of the rocks in the mountains. It's totally clear and unpolluted. This proverb captures the heart of God toward how we are to care for our own hearts and souls. God says to us, "Guard your hearts. Don't let any toxins or pollutants in." When we allow unforgiveness to fester, our wellspring becomes toxic. The only way to clean it is to forgive. The way to keep it clear is pre-forgiveness. Think of pre-forgiveness as a spiritual and emotional filter that keeps your heart and soul fresh and pure no matter what someone throws at you—no matter how anyone tries to hurt you.

During this past baseball season, I had just finished watching my son Nathan's game. It was a great win against a tough team. I was a happy guy. Winning is way more fun than losing! It's a guy thing, I think. As I giddily strolled out to my car, I observed a gash across both doors. "Ouch, what the... ?" Someone had hit my car and left. No note, no nothing. A bit of anger and dismay struck me. "Must have been some jerk from that other team," came to mind. What to do? Get angry? Get really ticked-off? Go ballistic over something I can't do anything about? If I'm honest, I've gone down that path before. But it's a dead-end. And I'm growing. So, nope! I pre-forgave!

In addition, one of my life verses I had really been taking to heart prior to that scrape is Ephesians 4:2, *"Always be humble and gentle. Be patient with each other, making allowance for each other's faults because of your love"* (NLT). As true Christ-followers, we need to deeply understand the heart of this verse. Jesus made a huge allowance for our faults. He gave his life for you and me because of his love for us. As he was taking a big hit, being spit on, flogged with a lead-tipped whip that was ripping deep gashes into his back and then nails were driven into his hands and feet to pin him to that cross. As he hung there in agony, what does Jesus say? *"Father, forgive them for they do not know what they are doing"* (Luke 23:34 NIV). I'm convinced, Jesus was guarding his heart the whole time, not allowing the devil to deposit any toxic hate, or bitterness or resentment into his soul.

So, we need to make an allowance for other people's faults. Why? Because of our love. Love! It always seems to get in the way, doesn't it? Aren't you glad? Yes, I had to make an allowance for the time it took me to take my car in to get it repaired. I had to make an allowance—to actually write a check for the $500 deductible I had to pay. And just get over it quickly and not allow toxins to enter into my heart. Why? For love's sake!

After Jesus imparted his 7 X 70 pre-forgiveness wisdom to Peter, he told Peter the parable of the unforgiving servant to drive home his point:

> *"A king wanted to settle accounts with his servants. A man who owed the king ten thousand bags of gold, was brought to him [twenty years of wages]. Since he was not able to pay, the king ordered that he and his wife and his children and all he had be sold to repay the debt. The servant fell on his knees and begged the king, 'be patient with me and I'll pay it all back.' So, the king took pity on the servant and canceled his debt and let him go."* (Matt. 18:23-27 NIV).

Twenty years' wages might as well have been the national debt in America of twenty trillion. He had no way to repay. This is a picture of what God does with us. He sees us exactly how we are. We have hurt him every time we sin and owe him a sin debt that we could never repay. But he paid it for us and forgives us—100 percent! So, here's the deal. Because God forgives we need to forgive.

*Forgive*: It means to cancel the debt. Every time someone forgives us, they pay what we owe and cancel the debt. Every time we forgive someone else, we pay what they owe and cancel their debt. If it's canceled, it's done, over. One of my mentors and pastors, Matt Hannan, taught me years ago, "True forgiveness is giving up the right to bring it up again." If you have forgiven someone and still bring it up and still hold it over them, you really haven't forgiven them.

Who hurt you? Who owes you? Have you forgiven them even though they didn't ask for it? Even though they didn't deserve forgiveness? Even though you know they are going to do it again? Even though they did it again and again? Are you angry still? Have you said, "To hell with them?" Hard, isn't it? Pause right now and ask yourself, "Would I want God to have that attitude toward me?"

In the movie *The Mission*, Rodrigo Mendoza, played by Robert De Niro, was a mercenary in the jungles of South America in the 18th century. Armed with guns and swords, Rodrigo hunted down and enslaved the Guarani natives high above the falls. He was a mercenary who was merciless. One day, he returns home to find his very own brother sleeping with his wife. In a moment of rage, he killed his brother he deeply loved. He's now lost everything, his brother, his wife, everything worth living for. He slumps into a deep depression. Father Gabriel, a Jesuit priest who established a mission to the very natives Rodrigo was hunting down and killing, comes to Rodrigo to offer hope. He asks Rodrigo to pack up all his weapons and armor to drag them from the lower basin up the falls to face the natives who hated him for all the death and carnage Rodrigo brought to their lives. Rodrigo agrees. With a thick net full of weapons and armor tethered to his back by a long rope, Rodrigo makes the arduous journey through cascading waterfalls and up sheer rock walls, until he finally arrives, on his knees, exhausted. The natives see him and warn all the others. They know him well. In a moment of high tension one of the Guarani warriors runs up to Rodrigo with knife in hand and on Rodrigo's throat. As the native is waiting for instructions of what to do next, it appears Rodrigo will finally get the fate he deserves. However, with one order from the chief, the warrior shows mercy and cuts the rope from Rodrigo's back and dumps the weapon-laden net off a cliff and into the river. Rodrigo, overwhelmed by grace and sensing enormous relief and joy, begins to weep uncontrollably finally understanding he's forgiven. The Guarani gave him total grace. As many of the natives run up to him, Rodrigo is trembling, while smiles and joy break out everywhere. Amazing grace how sweet the sound that saved a wretch like Rodrigo, like me! What was once lost is now found and forgiven! Rodrigo is forgiven, I'm forgiven, you're forgiven. But make no mistake, the Guarani paid deeply. God paid deeply!

The king in Jesus' parable paid deeply for his servant's forgiven debt—ten thousand bags of gold! So, you'd think, the servant would get it. He didn't. Once he's set free it says, *"But when that servant went out, he found one of his fellow servants who owed him a hundred silver coins. He grabbed him and began to choke him. 'Pay back what you owe me!' he demanded"* (Matt. 18:28, 29 NIV). And this fellow servant too begged for patience. But the forgiven servant had the man thrown into prison for pocket change in comparison. No mercy!

Can you believe this guy? Ever done that? You accept God's forgiveness for all your sins, but you could not or cannot forgive someone who hurt you? Perhaps even someone you love? I decided a long time ago that no matter what someone does to me, steals from me, abuses me—I'm going to forgive them. Because if I don't, there are huge emotional and eternal consequences.

In Jesus' parable, the king finds out the servant he forgave ten thousand bags of silver, would not forgive one of his old buddies 100 silver coins. The King (God here) is really ticked off (that's called wrath in the Bible). So, he calls in the servant and says, *"You wicked servant, I canceled all that debt of yours because you begged me to. Shouldn't you have had mercy on your fellow servant just as I had on you?" In his anger his master handed him over to the jailer to be tortured, until he should pay back all he owed"* (Matt. 18:32-34 NIV). Obviously, that servant could never pay his own debt to the king and neither can we.

Jesus punctuates the parable with *"This is how my Heavenly Father will treat each of you unless you forgive a brother or sister from your heart"* (Matt. 18:35 NIV)

In this life, the torture is not so much from God as from our own hearts and minds. Our unforgiveness most often hurts us so much more than the person we have not forgiven. We self-sentence ourselves to a toxic, harsh reality when we choose not to forgive. And that toxicity ends up leaking all over other people we love. In the next life, this verse gives us a glimpse of hell. It's not pretty. So, we need to pre-forgive, forgive, and let me give you one last forgiveness step:

***Re-forgive***: This is emotional forgiveness. It's truly from our hearts. Have you ever been hurt by someone and you've forgiven them, but when you see them on the street or at the grocery store that old pain comes back a little or a lot? What to do? Re-forgive them. Say to yourself and to God, "I forgave them, I really did." My old psychologist friend Dixon Murrah, taught me, we have an emotional memory from that hurtful event we need to wear out. That takes time. Just because we feel the pain again and again, doesn't mean we haven't forgiven them, it just means there is still some lingering emotional pain from the event that needs to be exorcised. Every time you see that person, hear about that person, think about that person or the event that hurt you, re-forgive. Say the words, "I forgave them. It's over!" Don't rehash the event. Just say the words and re-forgive. Little by little, you will wear out that old emotion until one day you might feel love and positive emotions toward them again. And then thank God for them and for his forgiveness of you once again.

Some "experts" say, "Forgiving isn't forgetting!" Honestly, that may be true, but I sure try to. Certainly, the deeper the hurt, the greater the pain and the longer it takes to forgive and be free of the hurt. God says, *"For I will forgive their wickedness and will remember their sins no more"* (Heb. 8:12 NIV). That sure sounds a lot like forgetting to me. However, God didn't totally forget the debt of the unforgiving servant when he wouldn't forgive the man who owed him. Nope! When we get it, and forgive others like God forgave us, God does treat us like it never happened. He wipes out all debt in our sin account. We get a fresh start with him. That's what I try to do. Really, I do just forget it ever happened. I like to live like that. For us humans, I'm convinced "forgetting" takes practicing a lot of re-forgiveness and practicing not talking about the old hurts and giving them life again. I know I can forgive and I may be a bit of a numb skull, but I choose not to remember the hurts I've forgiven. When I do, I just tell myself, "Brad, you forgave that, remember! Let it go." So, maybe forgive and forget is to choose not to remember, when something jogs our memory about a certain hurt.

A number of years back a man in our church came to me after seeing a psychologist about all the pain his step-father caused him in his childhood. The psychologist told him, "Joe (not his real name), there are some things in this life that are just unforgivable." I was shocked a licensed psychologist told him that. I said, "Joe, that's psychological malpractice." And I believe it's totally contrary to what the Bible teaches us about the importance of forgiveness. Sure, sometimes we're not ever going to be best friends with people who hurt us deeply and likely will do it again. That, however, does not exempt us from forgiving them and allowing God to remove all the toxic bitterness and resentments from our souls. Not forgiving kept Joe in the dungeon of unforgiveness. Forgiveness allows us to be free.

There's an old story of a woman who was raped in the South. They caught the perpetrator and her day in court came. The rapist was tried, convicted, and sentenced. After the sentencing hearing, on the courthouse steps outside, a reporter seeking to get a statement from the woman asked, "So, your rapist was convicted and sentenced, how do you feel about it all now?" The woman replied, "I forgive him!" "What!" the offended reporter exclaimed, "How can you forgive him?" The woman calmly replied, "He had me for a day, I'm not going to give him the rest of my life." She got it. We need to too. 7 X 70! Pre-forgive, Forgive, Re-forgive!

***Practical tips on forgiveness:*** Don't ever go tell someone you forgive them unless they ask you for forgiveness. You could cause deeper hurt. When someone asks you for forgiveness, say, "Yes, I forgive you." Not just, "Oh, no problem. Don't worry about it." It's a big deal when someone humbles themselves to ask for forgiveness. Use the words of forgiveness. When you need to go ask someone for forgiveness say, "Please forgive me for (insert specific offense) I'm so sorry I hurt you."

So how are you doing on forgiving people? This chapter was bigger that most so far for a reason! It's really the ball game! Read the following paragraph and score yourself. Then work on the questions. More questions on this one too!

## 1.8–Forgive

I am willing to forgive those who hurt me, even when it's hard. I understand that unforgiveness is unhealthy and toxic. Mostly, I believe that God has forgiven me and paid the ultimate price by sending his Son to die on the cross for all my sins. Therefore, I must forgive others and not hold resentments against them.

| WEAK | 1 | 2 | 3 | 4 | 5 | STRONG |
|------|---|---|---|---|---|--------|

**Memory verses: Matthew 18:21, 22 (NIV)** *"Then Peter came to Jesus and asked, 'Lord, how many times shall I forgive someone who sins against me? Up to seven times?' Jesus answered, 'I tell you, not seven times, but seventy times seven.'"*

Take a little test: Answer these questions yes or no: (Dixon Murrah 1989):

1. Have I been hurt?

2. Do I often think about the hurt?

3. When I remember the hurt, do I have strong feelings of anger?

4. Do I avoid the person or not communicate with them, when it would be pretty easy to communicate?

5. Do I have physical symptoms of tension (tightness, stomach disorder, insomnia, or a desire to sleep a lot)?

6. Am I irritable and angry over little things?

7. Do I indirectly attack the person who hurt me (mild putdowns, hostile humor, fail to cooperate, neglect being supportive)?

8. Am I highly critical of myself (discontented, self-demanding, self-condemning, dissatisfied with self)?

9. Do I remember a lot of details about the hurt (where it happened, the clothes they wore, the day of the week, the time of day, my own clothing, the events leading up to it)?

If you answer yes to any of the above questions you probably need to forgive.

### Questions for Further Reflection and Discussion

1. Write down or discuss a situation where you have been hurt and if you have forgiven that person.

2. Write down your thoughts or discuss the method of pre-forgiveness—making a prior decision to forgive no matter what someone does to you.

3. When was a time where you may have hurt someone, but never resolved it by going and asking for forgiveness?

4. Discuss how ready you are to pay the price to forgive someone else and never bring it up again.

5. Discuss how Jesus forgave you for every one of your sins: past, present, and future. Go to him in prayer and thank him for what he paid to make that happen.

6. Do you ever see someone in the store or in public you avoid because you hurt them or they hurt you? What can you do about that? Remember re-forgiveness!

## 1.9 Rest—Reflect—Record

After reading through Milestone sections 1.1 to 1.8 now is the time to pause and reflect on what you've learned and perhaps even implemented in your life since reading it for the first time. Don't be surprised if you've grown in certain areas.

So, again, read the following statements and evaluate yourself accordingly:

### 1.1–Attend Church

I attend weekly church services. Attending a church service and joining in worship is an essential first step to help me grow in loving God.

WEAK    1    2    3    4    5    STRONG

**Memory verse: Hebrews 10:25 (NLT)** *"And let us not neglect our meeting together, as some are in the habit of doing, but encourage one another—and all the more as you see the Day approaching"*

## 1.2–Attend a Small Group

I regularly attend a small group or Bible study. Attending a small group is an essential first step to help me grow in loving people.

WEAK    1    2    3    4    5    STRONG

**Memory verse: Acts 2:42 (NIV)** "*They devoted themselves to the apostles' teaching and to fellowship, to the breaking of bread and to prayer.*"

## 1.3–Serve at Church

I regularly serve in the church. I have discovered my spiritual gifts and am using them to serve the Lord in my local church. I believe doing my part and serving in the church is an essential first step to help me grow in serving the needs of others in this world.

WEAK    1    2    3    4    5    STRONG

**Memory verse: 1 Corinthians 12:27 (NIV)** "*Now you are the body Christ, and each one of you is a part of it.*"

## 1.4–Give Regularly

I regularly give to God through the church. I believe that giving helps me become a more generous person and giving to the church really means giving back to God a portion of what he has so generously given me.

WEAK    1    2    3    4    5    STRONG

**Memory verse: 2 Corinthians 9:7 (NLT)** *"You must each decide in your heart how much to give. And don't give reluctantly or in response to pressure. "For God loves a person who gives cheerfully."*

## 1.5–Support Leaders
I wholeheartedly support and obey the church leadership. I am learning to resolve any issues I have with my leaders or others directly with the person involved in an emotionally healthy fashion.

| WEAK | 1 | 2 | 3 | 4 | 5 | STRONG |

**Memory verse: Hebrews 13:17 (NIV)** *"Have confidence in your leaders and submit to their authority, because they keep watch over you as those who must give an account. Do this so that their work will be a joy, not a burden, for that would be of no benefit to you."*

## 1.6–Be Real
I know I am a sinner saved by grace alone. Therefore, I am transparent, authentic and honest and not a spiritual poser. I keep a short list of my sins and confess any sin issues I have. With the help of God, I'm becoming the real me.

| WEAK | 1 | 2 | 3 | 4 | 5 | STRONG |

**Memory verse: Matthew 23: 5 (NLT)** *"Everything they do is for show. On their arms they wear extra wide prayer boxes with Scripture verses inside, and they wear robes with extra-long tassels."*

## 1.7–Reach Out
I am beginning to understand the church's mission of reaching out to people who don't know Jesus yet. I am excited to tell others about my church and about Jesus, even though they

might think I'm crazy and, at times, say hurtful things about my faith. I pray for people in my life who don't yet have a relationship with God (1 Pet. 3:15-16).

**Memory verse: 1 Peter 3:15 (NIV)** *"But in your hearts revere Christ as Lord. Always be prepared to give an answer to everyone who asks you to give the reason for the hope that you have. But do this with gentleness and respect."*

WEAK　1　2　3　4　5　STRONG

### 1.8–Forgive
I am willing to forgive those who hurt me, even when it's hard. I understand that unforgiveness is unhealthy and toxic. Mostly, I believe that God has forgiven me and paid the ultimate price by sending his Son to die on the cross for all my sins. Therefore, I must forgive others and not hold resentments against them.

WEAK　1　2　3　4　5　STRONG

**Memory verses: Matthew 18:21, 22** *"Then Peter came to Jesus and asked, 'Lord, how many times shall I forgive someone who sins against me? Up to seven times?' Jesus answered, 'I tell you, not seven times, but seventy times seven.'"*

*Milestone 2 Goal—God is Using You to Transform Other People's Lives*

*At Milestone 2, the way we love God is to practice a daily devotion. The way we love people is to lead or support a small group that meets weekly. The way we serve the world is to go on a mission trip outside your church, across your city or somewhere else in the country or the world. In addition, there are five other significant stops that will enable you to grow in Milestone 2. At milestone 2.9 make sure you pull over for to the Rest Area and reflect on where you're at and record your journey.*

MILESTONE

2

## 2.1 Practice Daily Devotion

A few years back my daughter, Sarah, went off to Australia to spend two years at the Hillsong Leadership College. I was excited for her, but even more excited for myself—at long last I had the opportunity to go to Australia to check off my #1 Bucket List item—Dive the Great Barrier Reef. So, after a year of her schooling, my wife sent me off for a two-week vacation to visit her. I made all the plans, secured a hotel in Sydney, found a Dive Shop in Cairns to get our diving certification and off I went. We spent a few days in Sydney together and then flew to Cairns. I was so excited, finally, my dream would come true, to explore the expanse and wonder of the Great Barrier Reef. It didn't take me long to realize the extra bonus God had afforded me—to do it with Sarah. What a joy! We had so much fun. After we enjoyed three days and two nights on a live-aboard boat diving the reef, we spent our last night in Cairns, having a ball. It was during that last night it dawned on me, after 20 years of being Sarah's father, my goal of parenting had been realized—Sarah and I had become best friends. Something happened down under to me and Sarah that was more important than my #1 Bucket List item. And when the day came to head back to Oregon, I met Sarah at my hotel a few blocks away from the Hillsong campus, I walked her to the corner and we said goodbye—it hit me like never before—tears welled up in my eyes, I already missed her. Just the thought of leaving her on that rock called Australia with a Pacific Ocean and the equator separating us, made me long for her. And within days, once again, my heart ached to see her, to be with her again. Why? Love, deep relationship.

Over the years, I've come to realize a similar phenomenon with God. To date, I've been reading my Bible and journaling/meditating on scripture daily for almost 20 years. Oh yeah, there are days I've skipped my Bible reading and journaling, but when that happens, I've come to miss him. Why? Love. It's been said that God has no favorites, just intimates. Jesus was the model for us of being the Father's intimate, and I believe God desires each of us to be one too. Honestly, I think I am one now. But anyone can become one. The Lord longs for intimacy and deep friendship with all his children. God is ready. We have role to play.

Again, our model for intimacy with God is Jesus. *"Before daybreak the next morning, Jesus got up and went out to an isolated place to pray"* (Mark 10:35 NLT). Time and again, Jesus placed a huge value on spending quiet time with the Father. I'm convinced Jesus loved to spend time with his Father and knew it was essential to his purpose and mission on this earth. We need to ask ourselves, "If Jesus needed to spend regular quiet time with the Father, how much more do we need to?

## FEED or BE FED?

Picture a calendar with a plate of food on it for every day of the week as depicted above. Let's say Sunday there is a huge platter—a feast scheduled. That's the weekend church service! Your pastor works hard in his spiritual kitchen every week to cook an amazing feast to serve you and all who come to church on Sunday morning. Question: After you "eat" his feast, when will you be hungry again? When will you miss being fed? Monday? Tuesday? I can tell you with certainty, if you wait to eat 'til the next Sunday, you will starve to death! Yet that's what many Christ-followers do.

We all need to be fed spiritually. The best and most nourishing way to be fed is to feed ourselves, by praying, reading scripture and journaling *daily*. Here's something to consider. Either we take responsibility for our own spiritual growth and read scripture daily or we will be fed by something else—in most cases—the devil. See, once again, we are spiritual beings and we need spiritual input. We cannot remain status quo. Either we're moving toward God intentionally, or moving away. There is no middle ground. We'll end up consuming much of the spiritual trash that comes out in some movies, on the internet and even these days in many sitcoms.

God says, we are in a spiritual battle and calls us to armor up (Ephesians 6). Picture a real live battlefield. Can you imagine army troops walking out in the line of fire naked—no training, no clothes, no gun, no helmet, no nothing and being surprised that they took a round from the enemy in the leg or arm or chest. Guess what? There is a spiritual war raging all around us and yet many Christ-followers do exactly that every day. We wake up, smart phone in hand, checking out social media, perhaps posting something on Instagram or Snapchat, perusing other posts or pages sometimes for fifteen minutes or sometimes for an hour or more prior to heading out on the battlefield of life, with no thought of putting on our spiritual armor. And that is incredibly dangerous. Spending time with God, reading scripture, praying and journaling is a key time-tested method to armor up for your day in the spiritual realm, which, by the way, is everywhere.

We are most protected and most satisfied when we spend time with God in his word and reflect on and apply his word to our lives on a daily basis. It's *the* key spiritual discipline for growing. But the other side of that is, if we don't feed ourselves spiritually, the devil and his cronies will whisper seeds of discord and dissatisfaction into our lives. That's what the devil does: sows seeds of division, dissension, discouragement, dissatisfaction, bitterness, and unforgiveness into our lives. He literally "disses us" in every conceivable way and place. He does it in marriages, families, parenting, businesses, churches, relationships, and individual lives.

If you're dissatisfied with your church, I can confidently predict that you're not reading scripture daily and "cooking your own meals." Or you're drawing comparisons to some other church that you might think is better than yours. You're likely looking for someone else to feed you and satisfy all your spiritual needs. Ultimately, that's pretty self-centered. In addition, it's spiritually and emotionally immature. In America, studies have been done that show only about 10 percent of Bible-believing Christians read their Bible regularly. God spoke to this through the prophet Amos:

*"The time is surely coming," says the Sovereign Lord, "When I will send a famine on the land— not a famine of bread or water, but of hearing the words of the Lord." Amos 8:11 (NLT)*

God Himself sends this famine on the land. A spiritual famine from not consuming the word of the Lord. Ironically, in the next verse God says:

*"People will stagger from sea to sea and wander from border to border searching for the word of the Lord, but they will not find it."* Amos 8:12 (NLT)

That is a picture of people who are spiritually famished. As I read this, my first thought to God is, "Why, Lord, would you not allow people to find your word? God, isn't that what you want? Surely it is!" I've concluded that most people are looking in all the wrong places. We're looking for others to feed us. The right pastor, the amazing radio preacher, the new Christian song, the great rock star pastor blogger. Hey, nothing wrong with these if they're in addition to your own quiet time with God. Just don't make it your primary means to being fed. That stuff simply becomes spiritual fast food! No one can eat for you and daily spiritual bread can't be saved up. But, we go days without eating. The result is that we're starving while our most nourishing meals are waiting to be cooked—as our Bibles sit untouched in our bookshelves and nightstands. Think about it: amazing spiritual meals, just sitting there waiting as we starve and exclaim our dissatisfaction to our church leaders.

What's the answer to the famine? We need to learn to cook our own spiritual meals, friends. They are incredibly encouraging to our souls. When we feed ourselves on God's word daily, an amazing thing happens—the spiritual feasts we are served on Sunday taste so much better. If you've been a Christ-follower for five, ten, twenty years or more and ever say, "I'm not really being fed by my pastor," that's more likely a commentary on your own spiritual maturity than the ineptness of his messages. Feed yourself during the week, and I promise you it will provide sumptuous seasoning for his or her messages. This is the single most important thing we can do, not only spiritually, but in our lives. It will impact our marriages, our friendships, our parenting—*everything*. Jesus promises it will bear amazing fruit in every area of our lives:

> *"Cling to the vine and you will bear much fruit... fruit that lasts."* (John 15).

And the best way to cling to the vine is to have daily intake of God's word in our lives. You get this one right and it will enormously impact every other milestone point! You will grow like wildfire! Great books have been written on this that have helped me get into the Bible over the years. Here are a few: *Too Busy Not to Pray* by Bill Hybels. *The Divine Mentor* by Wayne Cordiero is perhaps the best book I've ever read on the subject. Wayne's Bible reading plan and SOAP method is what I recommend for our entire church body. You can find the SOAP method and a daily Bible reading plan that will work for you in the appendix in the back of this book.

Get this, I'm for praying on the fly: while I'm driving, while I'm waiting in line at the store—anywhere really. But I believe the God of the universe deserves and desires a daily segment of time where I give him my undivided attention. I mean, if the President of the United States knocked on your door and wanted to spend 30 minutes just with you, would you be texting your friends or busy doing something else while he was there with you? Sure, a selfie would be fine! But I'm pretty sure you'd give him your undivided attention, no matter what you think of him. How much more should we carve out a daily quiet time with our almighty God to give him his rightful honor and respect?

My typical daily quiet time consists of first making a pot of coffee early in the morning—gotta have coffee! Then I find my "dad" chair in the living room, get on my knees, and pray, thanking God for another day and praying for my loved ones and any other issues people in my life may have. I also often ask God to show me my sins! I don't like praying that, because he just about always does. I then ask him for forgiveness. Then I look at my Bible reading plan app and see what I'm scheduled to read that particular day. I read through the Bible every year cover to cover and the New Testament twice. I often ask God to show me a verse he wants me to apply to my life. As stated in the above paragraph then I SOAP on that verse and end it with some specific prayer, most often including blessings for every family member by name, Ann, Sarah, Elliot, Willie, and Nathan, so far. I also ask Jesus my King, Savior, and Lord to lead me that day. I ask the Holy Spirit to fill me and provide counsel for me that day and I ask my Abba/Father/Daddy to use me to advance his kingdom that day. The cool thing is, I have about 40 journals from the past 20 years filled with Bible verses, thoughts, meditations and prayers. It's truly radically changed my life.

**Hint for leaders:** If you're a preacher, teacher or youth pastor or leader, I highly recommend every now and then, at certain points in the middle of your message, to pause and grab your journal and share a pertinent journal entry—your SOAP. It reminds your flock of the importance of a daily quiet time. It's great modeling and it leaks all over in a very good way!

Parents, get up a little earlier to spend time with God and let your kids "catch" you doing it. My oldest son, Willie, and my daughter, Sarah, and her husband, Elliot, all young adults now, do this on a daily basis. Most parents would agree that we want our children to be successful in life. It's my strong conviction that success is spelled J-E-S-U-S! They don't need to go to the best college or have the awesome white collar job. They can be enormously successful and have a hugely fruitful, fulfilling life if they are a butcher, baker or candlestick maker, as long as they cling to Jesus. That's not my idea, it's Jesus' promise!

So, where are you? Read the following paragraph and score yourself. If you already do a regular quiet time, be generous in your assessment. If there are some things you might embrace that you've learned here, just make a note of it. If you think you're apt to employ this key spiritual discipline and haven't before, it's okay to give yourself a 1 now. As I stated above, if you diligently begin to do this one, it will impact every other milestone point. I promise! Remember, you can score yourself again in a few months to see all the progress you've made. So, go for it.

**2.1–Personal Devotional Time**
I practice a daily quiet time. Giving God my undivided attention though prayer, Bible reading, and journaling is one of the most important steps to loving God and growing closer to him every day.

| WEAK | 1 | 2 | 3 | 4 | 5 | STRONG |

**Memory verse: John 15:5 (NIV)** *"I am the vine; you are the branches. If you remain in me and I in you, you will bear much fruit; apart from me you can do nothing."*

**Questions for Further Reflection and Discussion**

1. What's was most impactful for you about this chapter?

2. What one thing from this chapter are you going to start doing and why?

3. Consider and reflect on the above memory verse spoken by Jesus. What are implications for your life?

4. How does the idea that clinging to Jesus ultimately will be the primary factor for success in life strike you?

5. What do you think of the title of Bill Hybels' book, *Too Busy Not Pray*? Do you get it?

6. Are you prone to be distracted when you pray or have a quiet time? How can you discipline yourself to give God your undivided attention for a period of time each day?

## 2.2 Lead or Support a Small Group

M any times I've seen small groups stay together for many years—same leader, same house, same people. I know, it's awesome how close those people got over the years. It's an amazing thing. However, if we believe what we really say we believe, we are going to have all eternity together. In this life, is not the time to create a long-term holy huddle. Now is the time to make ourselves available to be used by God to help lost people find Jesus and new believers grow. It's called "making disciples!" Jesus specifically said, "Go do it!" He didn't say, "Stay and huddle up!"

So, go for it! Lead, co-lead, or simply support small groups. By support I mean bring some cookies, help with childcare, get there early to help set-up. You get the idea. Don't leave it all on the leader. Small groups are one of the best vehicles to make disciples. Leading can be scary at first, sure! But get this: Being a small group leader or support person is not the same as being a teacher. Most churches have different approved small group curriculum, study guides or they are studies based on Sunday's sermon. A leader's job is simply that of a facilitator. It's actually

pretty easy if you get some guidelines. See the small group interaction tips below. We provide small group training for leaders
and coaches/mentors to guide the leaders at times should certain issues come up. A support person can host a group at their
home, provide hospitality or even make sure things are organized for the leader. The Apostle Paul wrote, *"He makes the
whole body fit together perfectly. As each part does its own special
work, it helps other parts grow, so that the whole body is healthy and
growing full of love"* (Ephesians 4:16 NLT). There those words
are again; grow and love! That's what it's all about. Everyone
has a role to play to make it happen, especially in small groups.

Maybe you don't feel you're ready to lead. Do you have
a clean home that could host a group there? That's awesome!
Leading or supporting small groups is a great way to move forward on your spiritual journey while helping others to grow too.
This is a key milestone in your spiritual journey!

The following are some tips to hand out to your small group
right from the start. If they get these and abide by them, you'll
do great.

**Small Group Interaction Tips**

- Come! It is vitally important that you attend your small
  group. Your attendance is imperative to your spiritual
  growth and the growth of other small group members.
  Make this a top priority! You won't regret it.
- Be interested in your fellow group members. It has been
  said that you must first be an interested person to be an
  interesting person.
- Being in a small group is more about how God is going
  to change you rather than how you're going to change
  others. It's not about giving advice to people in your
  small group or giving the "right" answer. Don't try to
  "fix" people.

- A small group is a safe environment that facilitates authenticity and spiritual growth. Confidentiality is an enormous value for a healthy small group. What you hear in your group should stay there.
- Be appropriately vulnerable. Everyone has life issues and a small group is a great place to get some answers. However, don't dump all your baggage at once, but do dump a little at a time. Dumping a "truckload" at once can be too overwhelming for some in your group. It takes time to develop deep relationships.
- Be careful not to comment on everything that your fellow small group members say. Often, we just need someone to listen.
- Pray regularly for your fellow group members. Regarding prayer request time: It is important not to try to fix people here. This is often the most vulnerable time in your group. Simply be empathetic—saying something like, "That must be difficult for you," is a great way to show you care. Use "You must feel . . ." statements rather than "I think you should . . ." statements. Keep prayer requests close to home—not some obscure situation that is distant to you.
- Ask your leader how you can serve the group. By getting involved and serving you are implementing the high Biblical principle of servanthood.
- Inevitably, you're going to have one or two people in your group that will really bug you. That's God's way of humoring us. The point is, it's probably more about God changing you than you changing them. Talk to your leader if you have a problem with a person that you are uncomfortable addressing yourself.
- Remember you're not in this alone. God is with you and so are your leaders and pastors. If you have any questions, contact your leaders and/or pastors. They are there to support you and serve you in any way they can.

- Your group can be an amazing place for deep, heartfelt community. What you put into it is what you'll get out of it. Also, get together with your group members outside of your regular group time.

- Serve together at church or somewhere in the community as part of your group experience once or twice a year. It's amazing how serving together can deepen small group life together.

Again, leading or supporting a small group is a great opportunity to grow. That said, sometimes crazy things happen in the context of the small group. For example, early on in our church plant, we were looking for leaders in any way, shape or form. We did not have this GROW book. One day I found out that one of our small group leader couples, after the group had ended that night, invited some of the group downstairs in their basement for bong-hits! Can you even believe that? So, I met with them, and remember, we are in Oregon (at the time, recreational use of marijuana was not legal, it was illegal). I had to confront them—first saying, "Listen, no matter what, if it's illegal we don't do it!" And I had to ask them to step down because they just weren't as spiritually and emotionally mature enough to lead as I thought they were (see, 2.5). The new laws are making it even more challenging. Now I often say, "Just because it's legal, doesn't make it right."

Grow, move forward, and lead, co-lead, support, or host a small group in your home, the local coffee shop, or a place of business. It's the best!

Are you leading or helping to support a small group? Do you understand that new people need a place to grow and therefore your church needs you to lead, co-lead, or host a group? Score yourself based on the following statement:

### 2.2–Lead or Support a Small Group

I regularly lead, co-lead, or support a small group. I understand that it's great to be a small group participant, but now I also feel responsible to help others grow by leading, co-leading, hosting, or supporting a small group.

( WEAK    **1**    **2**    **3**    **4**    **5**    STRONG )

**Memory verse: Ephesians 4:16 (NLT)** *"He makes the whole body fit together perfectly. As each part does its own special work, it helps other parts grow, so that the whole body is healthy and growing full of love."*

**Questions for Further Reflection and Discussion**

1. Have you ever been a leader in a small group? How was your experience?

2. Look over the above small group interaction tips. Which one(s) do you find most helpful and why?

3. Read and discuss the above memory verse related to leading and supporting small groups.

4. If you're not currently involved in leading or supporting a small group, how and when can you do that?

5. Discuss with your group leaders and participants how your one group could become two groups soon and perhaps meet in different places and times.

## 2.3 Go on a Mission

Mission—I love the word! It's filled with adventure. I hear the theme song from the movie *Mission Impossible* right now: *dunt, dunt, dunt, dunt, dunt dunt. Da da da... da da da.* Do you hear it?

Missions in the church can be as exciting as any Tom Cruz *Mission Impossible* movie, but way more impactful.

When I first became a Christ-follower, it wasn't long before my church in Seattle offered an opportunity to go on a VWAP—Vacation With A Purpose mission trip—to the jungle of Costa Rica. This was right up my alley! I had no idea at first what I was in for. When we arrived in Costa Rica and took a long dugout canoe up the Rio Toro, I was thrilled to see alligators and large iguanas lining the river bank. Our mission was simple: help a war-torn people survive by digging latrines and clearing brush to set-up fields to plant cash crops. I slept in a mosquito-netted jungle hammock next to a pig pen. As a young Christ-follower, I was amazed that God had brought me to such a place—if even for week.

Over the course of my spiritual journey, I have now gone on and led many mission trips, both locally and globally. Every time, it's more about God growing me to be more like Jesus than what I'm going to bring to the people we serve in the mission field. That said, Jesus told us to *"Go, make disciples of all nations"* (Matt. 28:19a NIV)—that word *nations* in the original Greek language is *ethnon*—we get the world ethnicity from that word. I believe that's significant. There is something about spending time with people of different ethnicities, especially for your average American. It's such a rich, life changing experience. Mission trips have radically altered my life for good, and I've seen many other people's lives totally transformed by the mission experience.

It works a lot like this: when I was a junior in high school, all my buddies skied. The Pacific Northwest is a great place to ski—lots of mountains and lots of snow most winters. I wanted to learn how. I tried it once a weekend for four weeks and still wasn't getting it. Well, my expert friends decided to take a trip up to Crystal Mountain, Washington for spring break. They invited me. I was all in! We got there, and I went to the rental shop. They strapped on these heavy steel skis with bad bindings. At the time, I had no idea they were really bad, because they were better than what I had, which was nothing. Up the chair lift I went with my bros. I got to the unload zone and slipped off and fell. They said, "Follow us, Brad!" The path looked very tame, flat; *so far, so good*, I thought. Then we came to the monster run—double black diamond. It was called Exterminator for a reason. Moguls were over my head. Off my friends went, hopping down the mountain with relative ease. I'm adventurous, so I pushed off and got lost under a mogul—I face-planted and my skis fell off. I got up and tried it again. Same result. On I went a few more times. I looked more like a messy yard-sale than a skier. The yard-sale called Brad seemed to have parts all over the mountain.

Halfway down, I finally collected myself, took my skis off, and walked down the mountain. I went into the rental shop and asked them to give me some demo skis. They gave me K2 Holiday fiberglass skis with much better bindings. So much better! I avoided all the black diamond runs for most of the week. I skied on round-circle-green runs with the little kids at first. Then I graduated to gentle square-blue runs with beginners like me about mid-week. As the week progressed, I felt more sure of myself. With a few lessons from my friends, I was actually learning how to ski. The last day, my buddies challenged me to try Exterminator again. Being sixteen and a guy, I had an ego to stroke, so I went for it. I made it all the way down on my skis—without falling. Now, it wasn't pretty by any means, but that's where I became a skier, one who would go on to ski any run on any mountain fairly well. What made the difference? Going skiing every day for six days straight. Putting those days back to back enabled me to learn at an exponential rate; it was far better than skiing once a weekend for an entire season.

I'm convinced the same is true with going to church once a week and going on a mission trip, where you are immersed in the things of Christ from sun up to sun down for a week or two. I've seen it in myself and, as I've led mission trips, I've seen exponential growth in many people who've been on my mission team.

When my daughter, Sarah, was a senior in high school she went on a 17 day mission trip to Africa. I figured this would be a great trip for her, but I had no idea what God would do in her. She came back and was asked to speak at her school and share about her trip. As a dad, I couldn't wait to hear her share, so I showed up at the assembly. She got up, shared some of cool things that she did and saw, then she said, "My faith to this point in my life has always been my parents' faith." I gasped, sadly thinking, "Really?" But then she said, "On this trip, God became so real to me and my faith became my own and I now know I need God's word in my life every day." She's never been the same since. These days, she's pure joy in Jesus! As a dad, what could be better?

As a leader in the church, I believe we need to do everything we can to get our youth, our students out on short term mission trips. Like the best way to learn Spanish or French or another foreign language is to go to a country and immerse yourself in the language and the culture, mission trips are the best way to immerse yourself in the ways of Jesus. And, like the best time to learn another language is when you're young so it has more sticking power and becomes part of your DNA, young people going on missions does the same for their faith.

One church I know of in the upper-Midwest actually raises hundreds of thousands of dollars annually to fund short-term youth mission trips. I can't wait to hear stories of students who went on those trips and see how many still have a vibrant relationship with Jesus ten years from now. Every opportunity Ann and I get, we try to send our kids out on missions. We believe that it will pay off in spades, not only for our kids, but also for our future grandkids (God willing).

Jesus sent his disciples on short-term missions. He sent 72 out one time two by two for what appears to be a week or two to local towns and villages. He gave them some instructions, part of which were, *"Do not take a purse or a bag or sandals"* (Luke 10:10 NIV). These seem to be odd instructions, but I believe Jesus was telling them, "I don't want you to rely on or trust in anything or anyone but God." In essence, Jesus was shoving them off a cliff to experience the goodness of God as they relied solely on him. That's what many mission trips do for immature believers. It thrusts them out of their comfort zone, so they have no choice but to trust God. It stretches their faith in such a way that they can never return to the place they once were. *"Trust in the Lord with all your heart, lean not on your own understanding, in all your ways submit to him and he will make your paths straight"* (Proverbs 3:5, 6 NIV).

*"The seventy-two returned with joy and said, Lord, even the demons submit to us in your name"* (Luke 10:17 NIV). They were amazed. They had never experienced anything like that in the local synagogue. No, they had to get out on mission to truly experience the power of God. Just to temper their excitement and reign them in a bit, Jesus affirmed the power he gave them, but he replied to them, *"Do not rejoice that the spirits submit to you, but rejoice that your names are written in heaven"* (Luke 10:20 NIV). I love Jesus' brilliance. These guys came back feeling like rock stars, so Jesus reigns in their egos with the awe that ordinary people like them have been given an extraordinary gift from God that they never deserved—their names are written in heaven. Wow!

A number of years ago, I was prompted to go on a mission trip to Africa, a trip I really didn't want to go on. It was the same trip my daughter was going on. It was with Jose Zayas, an evangelist from another church in the area, and my wife sensed a prompting of the Holy Spirit that I should go along too. I told her, I met the leaders from the other church and I'm not going to protect Sarah, who was just entering her senior year in high school. Ann, said, "No, I think God wants you to go too." I was unconvinced. A week or so later a servant in our children's ministry, Susan told me, "Brad, God told me you need to go to Africa with Sarah." Now, know when God tells someone else that I need to do something for him, it really messes with my theology. Why doesn't he just tell me, I think. Susan was a great woman that I led to Jesus years earlier, really my spiritual daughter, so I said, "Susan, thanks, but I don't have any time to go to Africa." The next Sunday there is Susan again, "Brad, so you're going to Africa, right?" "No Susan, I have no time to head off to Africa." She gently responds, "Will you at least pray about it?" So, I do. That was my first big mistake! I prayed and sensed maybe this is something God does want me to do. The following week I shared all this with my elder board, saying, "I think God may want me to go to Africa but I have no idea why."

And I ask them to make the decision for me. They all prayed and came back and told me, "We all think you need to go to Africa, Brad." Okay! Now it's just a matter of obedience, because I still have no idea why I'm going to Africa. I go! The first day the team took a boat ride across Lake Victoria in Uganda to an orphanage called Bethany Village. Sarah and I met an orphan named Nkenga Joshua, who lost his parents through the ravages of a war-lord up by the Sudan. One look into Nkenga's eyes and all we saw was sadness and hopelessness. It was in that moment, God took a wrecking ball to my heart. It's like he told me, "I want you to reach these people, Brad. This is where I'm working! Come, join me!" The next day we went and presented the gospel at schools. At one school, Jose tells me, "Brad, you're up!" Up? "Yeah, go present the gospel to these kids." Okay, I can do that. But even though I've done it many times in the USA, this was a first time doing it like this. There were about 120 students present and by the end of my presentation of the gospel about 60 put their faith in Christ for the first time. I was in awe. During that week, that was the norm. At times, I felt like I had time travelled back into the book of Acts. It was amazing. And I've been back many times.

Now I lead mission teams to Africa to plant churches. In our sessions prior to going we do cultural awareness training, safety sessions, etc. But I tell them at some point I'm going to push them off a cliff, as they will have to go to schools, go house to house, business to business and share the gospel message. Be ready. Always be ready! We also put a schedule together where every team member leads the team devotion at least one morning on the trip. They all are involved in making it happen, everyone on our team shares the gospel and they are amazed people come to Jesus. Often in droves. Finally, we can say with conviction, *"I am not ashamed of the gospel, because it is the power of God for salvation to everyone who believes!"* (Rom. 1:16 NIV). It really is! When mission team members see it and experience it happening, yes it has a rock star feeling to it, but we always bring them back to a humble spot to know it's God working through an ordinary, willing person doing extraordinary things. The amazing thing is, they are never the same again. Not even close. A few weeks of that wrecks a person in a good way, forever. Often, people ask, "Why do you go to Africa when there is such a need here in America?" My friend, Jose says, "We take people there so we can reach people here." I love that. Jayson, our campus youth pastor, has come with me to Africa a number of times. Up to the time he went there, he had never personally led anyone to Christ in America. Well, he did there. He actually took my youngest son, Nathan out one day door to door where God gave them plenty of practice and lots of results. It was great mentoring for my son to do that with his youth pastor. Now, back here in America, it's common place for Jayson to lead youth to Jesus.

Locally, I have a pastor partner named Armando who leads our Hispanic campus called Esperanza. Before he started Esperanza I took him to Africa with me. Armando is not your typical Mexican. See, he was a gang leader in Los Angeles prior to coming to Christ. And he's one big hombre! I kinda feel like he's my body guard. One day in Africa, we were going to the Rukungiri Police station and Armando was up to share the gospel. He came to me early that morning, "Pastor, where is the passage on submitting to government authorities?" "Romans 13," I say. We got to the police station. The officers were wearing uniforms that looked more like military garb and had AK 47 assault rifles strapped to their sides. I'm thinking, "Everyone, be really good!" The whole police department assembled outside, behind the station—chief, captain, 20 plus officers and administrative staff. We did a few worship songs, a gospel skit, then Armando's up. Out of his mouth comes, "I'm the type of guy out on the street that you don't like!" "Oh, no!" I lament. "You know," he says, "The guy who gives you no respect, who doesn't acknowledge your authority. The guy who says, there is no way I'm going to submit to your authority, I got drunk and

I did drugs and I didn't care who you are." I'm totally freaked out by now! "What the heck, Armando?" I'm beginning to seriously wonder if I will ever see my wife and kids again. I look at the faces of the Ugandan police staff. They don't seem to be entertained in the least. Then he says, "Yes, I got drunk, and I did drugs, but that was not my problem. You know what my problem was? My problem was submission." Then Armando brilliantly took the police staff and us through the Romans 13 passage and shared how all their authority is from God. Then he tells them that him not wanting to submit to their authority was telling God, he wouldn't submit to his. Smiles begin to surface across the Ugandan crowd. Then came the clincher, "If you want God's blessing and authority, first you have to submit to the greatest Authority in the universe." And he asks, "Do you salute here?" All the police say "Yes." Armando commands, "Then if you want to accept Jesus Christ as your commander and chief, please stand up and salute him right now, while I say this prayer." And every single person, chief, captain, administrative staff people and officers stood up and saluted and gave their lives to Christ, right there. It was amazing! That town will never be the same. Where and when do you get to do that? Only on a mission trip.

Armando loves to reach out to lost people. What I love is we encourage people at our campus to go serve on a mission for a half-day with Armando at Esperanza during their shoe and toy giveaway at Christmas time. It's a great way to get your feet wet in the mission field and his Spanish speaking campus is only five miles away from ours.

Jesus said, as he sent those 72 out, "*The harvest is plentiful, but the workers are few. Ask the Lord of the harvest, therefore, to send out workers into his harvest field. Go! I am sending you out*" (Luke 10:2, 3a NIV). Go Jesus says, don't stay. Go. We need people willing to go on missions. Will you? Ask your pastor if your church has mission trip opportunities. If not, there are a number of great mission organizations who offer trips. Find one and go! Jesus' orders, not mine! Our EPIC website periodically lists opportunities for life-changing trips available for your teams—<u>epicglobalmissions.com</u>. So, do you want to go on a mission trip and have your life radically changed?

Read the following statement and score this section two ways, first your experience on a mission, but also your desire to go. I mean, if you've never been, score a 1. But if you really want to go, score yourself a 5 and average both as your final score.

**2.3–Go on a Mission**
I love serving in a mission opportunity, across town or out of the country. I have a passion to serve outside the borders of this church and be involved in expanding God's Kingdom both locally and globally.

| WEAK | 1 | 2 | 3 | 4 | 5 | STRONG |
|------|---|---|---|---|---|--------|

**Memory verse: Luke 10:2 (NIV)** *"He told them, the harvest is plentiful, but the workers are few. Ask the Lord of the harvest, therefore, to send out workers into his harvest field."*

**Questions for Further Reflection and Discussion**

1. What do you think about going on a mission trip?

2. Do you have any fears about going? If so, what are they?

3. Have you ever personally led someone to faith in Christ? Do you know any people you long to tell about Jesus, but don't?

4. Read Luke 10:2 above. What strikes you? How can you live out that verse?

# 2.4 Tithe

People are generous. I believe that. And most people know it's a good thing to give to the church, especially if it's not money. So, often, they look to give something to the church in one form or another. In the early days of our church plant, we got a few calls from well-intentioned people wanting to donate their old copiers. Their place of employment just bought a new one, so, they'd ask if our new little church needed one. I was so excited. "Absolutely!" And the first one was dropped off. "Wow," I thought. "So generous!" Then it died within a week. "Bummer!" A few weeks later, I got another call, "Our business just bought a new copier, but our old one really works good. Do you still need one?" "Yes! Praise God! He knows all our needs!" So, we go to downtown Portland and up into the office building, I lay my eyes on this amazing copier. It collates, staples, prints on both sides—slices, dices and makes curly fries! It's incredible! Thank you, Lord! Now, it's a beast, and it took quite an effort to get that baby out of the building into our old church pickup and back to our in-home office. So exciting... until it started acting up later that week. Then for the next two weeks it began to cough and sputter and chew up reams of paper, limping along at best. Within three weeks, I knew that copier's only positive contribution to the planet would be an anchor for a barge in the bottom of the Willamette river. Fool me once, shame on you. Fool me twice, shame on me!

About 2400 years ago, God spoke about giving broken down copiers to the church through the Prophet Malachi. Did you know that? Yeah! God let the people know what they were offering on the altar was defiled. The people couldn't believe God thought that so they asked God, *"How have we defiled you?"* *"When you offer blind animals for sacrifice, is that not wrong? When you sacrifice lame or diseased animals, is that not wrong? Try offering them to your governor! Would he be pleased with you? Would he accept you?" says the Lord Almighty"* (Mal. 1:7b–8 NIV). Back in Malachi's day, people were bringing in broken down, diseased animals to satisfy their tithe requirement. It made them look generous, but they were simply pretenders. Posers. And God was not about to bless them.

Now, I believe the people who donated the copiers were well intended. But I had to ask myself, "Did God bless their good intentions?" Perhaps. But then I thought, "What if? What if a company got a brand-new copier, looked at their old copier and said, "Gee, this old one still works. Let's give the new one to the church." Somehow, I think God would really bless that company, if that were the attitude and spirit of generosity they held. God does not need or want our leftovers, or our hand-me-downs. He wants our best. Proverbs 3:8 says *"Honor the Lord with your wealth, with the first-fruits of all your crops."* The first-fruits means the best! Let's say, Tom Hanks, Chris Pratt, Jennifer Lawrence, Brad Pitt or your favorite movie star was coming to your house for dinner. Would you pull some old cold, half-eaten pizza out of the fridge and throw it into the microwave and slap it on a paper plate and announce, "Dinner is served?" Can you imagine? No! But that's often what we do with God with our offerings until we learn the spiritual exercise of tithing.

Tithing—what's that? It simply means ten percent. And it means the very first ten percent of everything that passes through your hands should go to God as an offering and act of worship to him, out of love and appreciation for him and gratitude for all he's given.

Many people say, "I can't afford to tithe!" I get it. But, it's really not about affording to or not. It's about faith. Trusting in the Lord to provide all you need. It's really proving your trust in the Lord, even and especially with your finances. Ann and I have been tithing faithfully for over 27 years. God has always provided all we need. Sometimes things get pretty tight, but we still tithe and God provides. The fact is, as some people say, "I can't afford to tithe", we say, "We can't afford not to." God speaks through Malachi very clearly why: *"Bring the whole tithe into the storehouse, that there may be food in my house. Test me in this,"* says the Lord Almighty, *"and see if I will not throw open the floodgates of heaven and pour out so much blessing that there will not be room enough to store it"* (Mal. 3:10 NIV). The first reason we tithe is, God promises to bless us. Know this, I'm not into "Health and Wealth" teaching or "Give to Get." No! What Ann and I do trust God for though is to always take care of our family and provide for all our needs. To date, we've never lacked a meal, a bed or a roof over our heads for even one day. God has always provided. I never have to be afraid that he won't. He blesses us is so many other ways—with great friends, great kids who believe in Jesus, and a great church family.

God tells us the second reason why we should tithe through Malachi, *"I will prevent pests from devouring your crops, and vines in your fields will not drop their fruit before it's ripe,"* says the Lord Almighty (Mal. 3:11 NIV). Picture holding an umbrella over you and your entire family in a torrential downpour. It's a big strong umbrella that's protecting your whole family from getting sopped. Now, take away that umbrella, what happens? See, when we tithe, it's like God holds an umbrella of protection over us. The economy can tank. The stock market can plummet. Many people can lose their jobs and be filled with fear for the future. But, in general, faithful tithers seem to be okay. 2008 was a bad year. The housing bubble burst. The construction industry tanked. The job market blew up. It was really, really bad. However, my own personal survey among faithful tithers in our congregation was they seemed to be okay. Most kept their jobs. Some had to take a cut in pay, but they made out fine. I believe God protected them with his umbrella of protection. He sure did us! And get this, in all my years of being a pastor, I've never, ever heard of anyone who tithed regret it. Most are grateful to God for all he's provided them and the opportunity to give back a little bit of what he has entrusted them with.

See, that attitude says, "It's all God's. Who am I to not give him back in worship what rightfully belongs to him?" Fact is, God says, *"Will a mere mortal rob God? Yet you rob me. But you ask, 'How are we robbing you?' "In tithes and offering. You are under a curse—your whole nation—because you are robbing me"* (Mal. 3:8–9 NIV). That's pretty serious business. If we call ourselves Christ-followers and don't tithe, we are robbing God himself.

Over the many years, I've seen people come to church for every reason under the sun, messed up marriage, messed up kids, sickness, you name it. But perhaps more than any reason, what's motivated people to come to church and seek God is messed up finances. I cannot give a home finance course in these pages, but if you begin to faithfully tithe, which is an act of faith to give control of your finances over to God, I believe God will bless you. Tithing is like getting the top button of your shirt buttoned right. If that happens, all the rest seem to line up pretty well, and God provides for us and protects us.

Sometimes he even throws open the floodgates of heaven. Jayson and Jen got into an adjustable rate mortgage that adjusted way upward and put them into financial peril. It got to the point where they tried to modify their loan seven times with their bank. All seven times they were rejected. During that period, they decided to continue to tithe no matter what. They prayed and prayed for God to help them, especially when foreclosure seemed imminent. Jayson told me he came to the point of realizing they needed about $100,000 to save their home. They prayed for that amount and prayed around their home and continued to tithe. At what seemed the last moment, a letter appeared from their bank that totally remodified their loan forgiving $108,000 and giving them a two percent fixed rate for the duration of their loan. Call it what you want. I call it God making good on his promise to test him. He's amazing!

God says bring the whole tithe into the storehouse. I believe the storehouse is your local church, your primary place of worship. Tithe to your church. We personally don't count in our tithe sponsoring children abroad or contributing to other vital ministries or non-profits, which we do. That's above and beyond. Know that your church is trying to do all they can to minister to people and it simply takes money to do that. Somehow the bills need to be paid; the lights need to be turned on. Normally, in most churches that comes out of peoples tithes and offerings. The problem is in the average church in America only something like 15 to 20 percent of regular attenders actually tithe—give a full ten percent faithfully. Imagine what your church could do to minister to many needy people locally and globally if 50 percent or 75 percent of the church body actually tithed. It would be amazing! If you don't already tithe I want to encourage you to help your church increase the percentage of tithers, by adding you.

If you're afraid that, somehow, you're not going to have enough, choose faith over fear. More on that in Milestone 3.4.

Now, some theological thoughts on tithing. I have heard people, even pastors say, Tithing is an Old Testament Law that doesn't apply to New Testament believers anymore. Interesting.

My response is, how do you explain the principle of tithing being present in the Old Testament as *"Abel brought an offering— fat portions from some of the firstborn of his flock. The Lord looked with favor on Abel and his offering"* (Gen. 4:4 NIV). We don't see the word tithe here, but strongly implied was Abel's best. It certainly wasn't old, dried up Papa Murphy's pizza from the fridge. Then we see Abram tithe when Melchizedek, the priest and king of Salem, shows up. *"Then Abram gave him a tenth of everything"* (Gen. 14:11 NIV). Many theologians believe Melchizedek was Christ's representative way back then! The night after Jacob saw the "Jacob's ladder" vision to heaven he said, *"And this memorial pillar I have set up will become a place for worshipping God, and I will present to God a tenth of everything he gives me"* (Gen. 28:22 NLT). That's effectively Jacob's promise to God; to tithe on everything that comes his way as an act of worship.

All of these accounts were present even before there was an Old Testament Law of any sort. Further, Jesus affirmed tithing in the New Testament when he was "challenging" the Pharisees, he said, *"You should tithe, yes"* (Matt. 23:23 NLT). Jesus' concern with the Pharisees was that they made everything a religious rule devoid of love and compassion which just put a huge weight on the commoners. Never make tithing a strict rule that isn't given out of love and faith. And know, you cannot tithe your way into heaven. Jesus paid the full price for your ticket to heaven when he died on the cross and we can never pay him back for it. All that said, some Bible-believing Christians seem to do a ton of theological gymnastics to somehow biblically justify not tithing. It's sad and misguided because it misleads others and prevents God from blessing and protecting them.

One of the most gratifying things for me is to watch our adult children tithe. I remember a few years ago when I breezed through our admin office while our offering counting team was counting the offering from the previous Sunday. I normally don't look at what people tithe, but just happened to look down at the table as I passed and saw a check from my son, Willie. It was for exactly ten percent of what he got paid from his job at the time. My spirit soared! I thought, "Wow! And I didn't even tell him or prompt him to tithe, he did it all on his own." Then I thought about God. I wondered and thought, in a few weeks say he's out of money and needs a $20 for gas and he comes to me and asks me like he's done a thousand time before, "Hey dad, I'm out of gas in my car, can I borrow (he really means *have*) twenty bucks?" Seeing Willie tithe, I'm much more apt to say, "Sure!" I think that's what God's like. Honestly, I'm not bad with money, but I'm also not the best guy when it comes to finances. My wife is way better than me. She keeps us on track. Sometimes I spend too much. But we always tithe and somehow God seems to fill in the gaps, especially when we need it.

This is a huge step because it's the biggest faith step next to and in response to God's gift of salvation and eternal life to us. When this top button of your shirt gets fastened, the Holy Spirit is unleashed to move us right through the remaining milestones. You will look back in a year and be amazed where he took you without your even realizing it when you retake your assessment. Remember, it's not the overall amount, but the percentage. One wife I know wanted to tithe, but her husband didn't allow her to. I suggested that when she received spending money and other cash gifts she tithe on those. She was set free, because God the Creator of the universe can take a $10 bill and multiply it just like the loaves and fishes. He created the fish in the first place. Springs of water from a rock! He wants us to invest seeds in his work and in his servants, in caring for the poor and orphans. Want to see modern day miracles? I suggest try tithing for three months or six months. Every month you have enough try another one. God says, "Test me in this!" I say, if you don't like it or you're upset you did, I'll give you your money back. To date, no one has taken me up on refunding their tithe. Faithful tithers are never disappointed they tithe. Remember, it's a tenth off the top—that's before you pay your rent or mortgage, food bill, etc. It's not giving God a tip or giving what's left over. It's the faith step like no other. Begin and get ready for a front seat to God's miracles. Even through hardships he will be faithful—and you will have a new set of eyes to see his provision all around you.

Jesus said, *"Where your treasure is, there your heart is also"* (Matt. 6:21 NIV). It's been said, show me your checkbook or credit card statement and I'll show you where your heart really is. Believers often talk a great faith game, but this is a place where way too many people just refuse to trust God and grow in. There is no time like the present.

What do your finances look like? Are you a tither? Are you ready to take the leap of faith and trust God with your finances? Read the following and score yourself. If you don't tithe yet, in six months when you retake this survey, know you can be a 5 and be so blessed and protected. Deal?

## 2.4–Tithe
I faithfully tithe to my home church. Faithfully giving ten percent of my income is an act of worship that helps me grow my faith in God, who always provides all I need.

WEAK   1   2   3   4   5   STRONG

**Memory Verse: Malachi 3:10 (NIV)** *"Bring the whole tithe into the storehouse, that there may be food in my house. Test me in this,"* says the Lord Almighty, *"and see if I will not throw open the floodgates of heaven and pour out so much blessing that there will not be room enough to store it."*

**Questions for Further Reflection and Discussion**

1. What is your take on this chapter and tithing?

2. What scares you about tithing?

3. Read the above verse; discuss how you can act on it.

4. How have you experienced God's blessing and protection as a result of tithing?

5. If you don't tithe, would you be willing to spend some time in prayer and ask God to help you grow in your faith, and make it a goal to tithe in the next few months?

## 2.5 Grow Up—Emotionally

Grow Up! Ever have anyone say that to you? Have you ever said it to someone else? Every time, the intended communication is *grow up emotionally* isn't it?

Years ago, when we were selling our first house in Oregon, an ice-storm hit the Portland area and a tree from our neighbor's yard fell onto the front corner side of our house. The tree was about six inches in diameter and 20 feet tall. Not huge by any means, but big enough that it needed to be dealt with. I went over to my neighbor to inform him his tree was on my house and it would be great if he could get it off, as we were expecting home buyer traffic and the tree would not be viewed as an upgrade. He mentioned he really didn't care for the tree and planned to get rid of it. A few weeks went by and he didn't touch it. My emotional stress level in selling our house began to rise. Then I had a friend, Tim, stop by to help us with some repairs at our house and he happened to have a saw with him. So, I asked him to cut that tree down and throw it on my neighbor's front lawn. Tim did. Big mistake! That night my neighbor pounded

145

on my door when he got home. He was deeply offended and he told me his wife had decided she wanted to save the tree. I reminded him he told me he was going to get rid of the tree. I was doing him a favor (in my eyes). Now, to be sure, I was a bit ticked-off that my neighbor didn't deal with the tree sooner by propping it back up off our house if they intended to salvage it. After all, it had been a few weeks for crying out loud! That said, honestly, I did have my buddy drop the tree on my neighbor's front yard, just to make a small statement. Know what I mean? I was actually offended that he was offended! Ever been there? After the initial emotional storm passed, I went over to his house, asked him for forgiveness and gave him a check for $150 so he could buy a replacement tree. That seemed to make a proper amends and restore neighborly relations. I was glad.

Since then, I've grown up quite a bit. I think more than twice before I react to someone. I never send a potentially emotionally charged email anymore. I've just learned that's stupid and I have been "stupid is what stupid does" too many times to count over the years.

Why would I do that? Why would I get offended with him in the first place? One reason: emotional immaturity. And then, why would I spend my hard earned money for something that was ultimately, really his fault and negligence? Answer: I'm growing up to be more emotionally mature.

Human beings hadn't been on the planet long when emotional immaturity got the best of Adam and Eve. God told Adam and Eve, "Don't eat that fruit." The devil appealed to Eve's emotions, and then it says, "*The woman was convinced. She saw that the tree was beautiful and its fruit looked delicious, and she wanted the wisdom it would give her*" (Genesis 3:6 NLT). And, Adam, afraid of the serpent, afraid of offending Eve, just watched it all happen while humanity was being taken to the cleaners. Adam, emotionally enabled Eve. We do that too. Then they have kids. This first family was also the original dysfunctional family. Adam and Eve have Cain and Abel. Cain is emotionally toxic! He gets offended just because God tells him to bring the best crop offering to him, not just anything. Effectively, Cain's offering isn't as good as Abel's. It wasn't that Abel brought meat and Cain brought veggies. No, Abel brought the best of what God had given him. Cain just brought "some" it says, not the best (Genesis 4). So God says, "Go to make it right." So, what does Cain do? He literally "Raises Cain!" He disobeys and instead goes and kills his brother, Abel. Then when God confronts him, Cain cops an attitude— *"Am I my brother's keeper?"* (Genesis 4:9b). Most wars and disputes that have not been easily and quickly settled are due to emotional immaturity.

There will always be disagreements and at times we are all at fault to some degree. How we handle these faults and disagreements emotionally, is vital. *"Always be humble and gentle, be patient with each other, making allowance for each other's faults because of your love* (Ephesians 4:2 NLT). I stated these in Milestone 1.4 in relationship to money, but perhaps a bigger area of challenge is when it comes to emotionally charged situations. I've been challenged by God to memorize that verse and live it out, emotionally. Over the years I've learned that I have to "make an allowance" for other people's faults and emotional issues, just like I'd like them to make an allowance for mine. And mine are many!

I think of it like this: I have an emotional bank, in which God has made some significant deposits. I try to keep my emotional bank full.

"Do unto others as you would have them do unto you!" Jesus said it. Why? Because of your love. God's instructions to us always comes back to that. Love! Love God, Love Others! I'm convinced, more than in just about any other area, church people need to get this and grow up in emotional maturity. Certainly, the secular world is learning this—it's called emotional intelligence. Many business gurus make a living teaching Emotional Intelligence. They often say, to be successful, your EQ is more important than your IQ. I totally agree!

Over the years, I've observed that most relational, business and financial human train wrecks in life can be traced to very immature, emotionally-based choices and responses. Think about it. The media thrives on people being offended. It sells news. Many reality TV shows are all about the other person or party being offended. Politics—everyone seems offended!

I love John Bevere's book, *The Bait of Satan*. He states that being offended is the primary bait the devil uses to destroy relationships—in families, friendships, marriages, businesses—in life. Look around you. Look in your relational wake of life. See any bodies? It's been said,

> *"The most spiritually mature person in the room is the person least likely to be offended, when they have every right to be."*

Jesus was rarely, if ever, offended. On the other hand, the religious leaders in Jesus' day were constantly offended and jealous of Jesus.

I'm learning we are offended and angered too easily. The devil loves it, because it destroys relationships. After a blow up in our church a few years back, some dear friends exited the church and our lives and it left a scar on my heart that still stings from time to time. That summer, my wife and I went on a personal retreat for 10 days of healing in the high Sierras at The Mountain Learning Center. Guided by Russ Veenker, a Certified Pastoral Care Counselor, we were led into a fresh realm of learning about how anxiety drives many relationships. There was a moment when I was explaining what happened in "the blow up" when I realized my part in adding to the high anxiety in that relationship that had long been present and building over a number of years. And, in a confrontational interaction, my own angst and anxiety pushed the relationship to the tipping point. As I was sharing the blow-up experience with the counselor, God spoke to me from his word in 1 Peter 5:7 and 8, which I already had memorized; *"Cast all your anxiety upon him because he cares for you"* (1 Pet. 5:7 NIV). I have tried to practice this verse for years. Love it. What I've never done is put the two verses together. Verse 8 is key, *"Be alert and of sober mind. Your enemy the devil prowls around like a roaring lion looking for someone to devour"* (1 Pet. 5:8 NIV). Wow! If I don't cast my anxiety upon Jesus, I just increase my anxiety and the anxiety of others in relational interactions, sometimes to the point of a painful explosion or break up. That's what happened. And to date, while that relationship has not been fully reconciled as I'd hoped, I have been working on seriously growing up!

When God asked Cain to "Make it right," he also told Cain, *"Sin is crouching at the door; it desires to have you, but you must rule over it"* (Gen. 4:7 NIV). Think about it, sin is crouching at the door and desires to have you. Your adversary, the devil, prowls around like a roaring lion looking for someone to devour. Sin and the devil seem to be one and the same here. The devil is just longing to pounce on us and devour our relationships. I tend to believe, most, if not all of our sins can be attributed to emotional immaturity. The devil just preys on our emotions. I've come to believe that *anger* follows right after *anxiety* in the emotional alphabet. And if it's not arrested, relational carnage ensues and the devil wins. I'm learning I need to grow up emotionally and become more and more aware of anxious situations with others. I'm learning to walk away and just chill out when my kids push back too hard. I'm learning to bite my tongue in some business meetings. I'm learning my emotionally immature, high anxiety responses to my wife and others I love can cause a lot of pain that doesn't need to be.

It is a deeply spiritual issue. Peter Scazarro, in his amazing book, *The Emotionally Heathy Church*, writes, "You cannot be spiritually mature and emotionally immature at the same time." Wow! There's something that's a mind blow truth. A few years ago, I read Peter's book. That year, I read completely through the Bible again, but this time I paid particular attention to emotions. I noted so many occasions where supposedly spiritually mature people acted incredibly emotionally immature; I think of Adam, Eve, Cain, Abraham at times, Lot, Joseph's brothers, King Saul, and King David. One amazing example is King Solomon. He was the wisest man to ever live to that point, yet his failure to master his emotions got him in so much trouble. The New Living Translation's version of the last part Genesis 4:7 is, *"Sin is crouching at the door, eager to control you, but you must subdue it and be its master."*

### Master Your Emotions

Too often, the devil has his way with us. I've determined the best way I can combat him is to seek the Holy Spirit's help to master my emotions—my anger, especially. That's my growth edge. I'm not saying don't feel your emotions. Heavens no! To feel joy and love and passion is what makes us human. My primary goal is to be able to be calm and not let an emotionally volatile situation get the best of me and destroy a relationship. Paul wrote, *"As far as it depends on you be at peace with all everyone"* (Rom. 12:18 NIV).

As a pastor, I have to deal with a lot of marriage and family breakups and breakdowns. It's painful to watch. A surprising truth came to me from my friend, Dixon Murrah. He states the number one reason for divorce: **No Fun Anymore!** Sounds so unspiritual. But it's deeply spiritual. Think about it. When a couple meets, why do they want to be together—it's so much fun! He's fun, she fun. Life has so much meaning now, so much joy. Then, years later, it becomes toxic emotionally and that's never fun. No fun anymore is also the reason some young adults don't really want to come home much or at all when they move away. They are just sick of the toxic emotional atmosphere they lived in at home for so many years. It's no fun! Why go there?

With the devil prowling around attacking our marriages, it can get real painful and difficult for all of us who are married.

That's why we need to lean in more to maturing in Christ and seeking to grow up emotionally. You may be reading this and you're on the other side of having been divorced. No one approaches marriage with a plan to end up divorced 15 years later. You need to know God's grace and healing is available to you; lean into your faith and commit to grow emotionally for yourself, your kids and those around you.

### Parents, listen up!

As I think about all the young men, sometimes teens, who walk into schools or theaters or shopping malls all over America and begin to let bullets fly on complete strangers, I'm convinced those acts are utter wickedness. And, psychologists would rightly say they have deep emotional issues. But it's more than that. It's a deeply spiritual issue. Sure, they've been wounded, probably by their parents somehow, most all of us have to some degree. When that happens I can't help but think of Cain—Raising Cain. Sin and the devil are crouching at their door; they subdued and mastered the young men who in turn became the devil's slaves. And we know *"the thief comes only to steal, kill and destroy"* (John 10:10a NIV).

What's the answer? Parents, please, please get your children and teens to a youth group that is not just fun and games. Get them to a youth group that trains them to read the Bible, and SOAP and serve and go on missions. One that helps them learn to feed themselves so they grow both emotionally and spiritually. As I stated back in Milestone 1.1, getting them to church regularly is so much more important than soccer, football, baseball—any sport. Only 1 in 1000 at best go on to play college sports and even then, getting your kids spiritual training will serve them, you, God, their communities and future families better than any team they've ever been on. I promise! Jesus promises! Read the book *Sticky Faith* by Dr. Kara Powell and Dr. Chap

Clark. Get them into a church that embraces the ideals set forth in that book. Okay?

**Can you handle being told "No"?** A great self-test on your emotional growth is how you handle a "no." Are you okay with a "no, you cannot do that?" Or do you get upset and even lash out when someone tells you no?

My youngest son Nathan just got his driver's license and, unfortunately, his girlfriend moved about 50 miles away down I-5. It's both a good thing and a bad thing. Good, that at this age they aren't enmeshed with each other every waking hour. Bad, it's a logistical problem with the use of our car. The time it takes for him to go to see her or her coming up here is a two hour turn around. So, Ann and I have imposed some healthy boundaries. One of which is he can drive down twice a month, during the day. One week, Nate told us his girlfriend bought some tickets to a concert that he was going to go to with her in Portland. "Okay," I say, "Who's the band?" Now, Nate is not into illicit music, he plays keys on our worship team and generally is a great young man. But, I look up the band online and find a song they play. First song, they drop a few f-bombs. That's seals the deal. NO WAY! So, I tell him, "Can't go Nate, forget it!" He pushes back. "Dad, come on, most of their songs don't have any swear words in them." "NO! Not happening!" "Dad?" "NOPE! End it." Well, a day later he's scheduled to drive down to his girlfriend's and very windy raining weather hits the area. I looked at the weather report. He's a new driver. I talk it over with his mom. I'm feeling it, but we conclude, he's going to have to postpone his visit until another day. I tell him. He's not happy. "Dad, come on!" I just say, "Nate, too much can go wrong that doesn't even depend on you. There are lots of semi-trucks on I-5 and sometimes they get sideways and cause bad accidents. Sorry, no!" A little later I get a text from Nathan. "Dad, two times this week I really wanted to do things that I thought I was going to do and you told me I couldn't, that's really hard." I text back. "That's fair, come and talk to me rather than text." So,

Nate comes up and we talk. I explain again the difficulty of both decisions and ask him to be okay with it. "We only make these decisions because we love you so much—trust us." "Okay," he says. About twenty minutes later, he comes up, perfectly calm and begins to wash the dishes. No fit, no tantrum. No angst. I say, "Nate, come here, let's talk for a minute." I say, "How are you doing with all of that?" "I'm good, dad," he says. I smile, "Nate, I'm so proud of you for being so emotionally mature. Many adults my age don't have the kind emotional maturity you have displayed." And I gave him a big hug! Being able to handle some difficult nos is such a tell-tale sign of a person's emotional intelligence and growth!

How do you handle "nos?" Do you need to have your own way? It's interesting that God gave his children a bunch of nos in the Ten Commandments. How do you handle them emotionally? Think about it. Do you gladly embrace them? Are you okay with a "no" from your boss or teacher or parent or pastor or even God?

Considering this chapter, where are you in growing up emotionally? Read the following statement and score your emotional maturity accurately.

## 2.5–Grow up—emotionally

I am not offended by others. I am learning to love people who hurt me, to give others the benefit of the doubt when I don't understand their actions, and to not pass judgment on them. I don't need to have my way.

| WEAK | 1 | 2 | 3 | 4 | 5 | STRONG |
|------|---|---|---|---|---|--------|

**Memory verse: Ephesians 4:2 (NLT)** *"Always be humble and gentle, be patient with each other, making allowance for each other's faults because of your love."*

**Questions for Further Reflection and Discussion**

1. Discuss a time when you were really offended and a relationship was destroyed.

2. Consider Ephesians 4:2. How could you have made an allowance for the other person's faults?

3. Discuss the statement and apply it to your own growth: "You cannot be spiritually mature and emotionally immature at the same time."

4. Are you okay with a "no" from your boss, teacher, parent, pastor, ministry leader, or even God?

5. How's your anger factor?

6. What is your growth edge to master your emotions?

## 2.6 Be Mentored Spiritually

Guess what? Not to brag, but I graduated second in my class in high school. Yeah, second from the bottom with a 1.2 GPA. Can you believe it? And you've read this far! Ha!

I couldn't have graduated nor done anything without some key people pouring into my life. Take a moment and reflect back on your life. Who, if anyone, really invested in you and made a positive impact? I remember when I was in high school and my parents had just divorced—I was more than a rebel, working 40 hours a week at a grocery store. I just didn't see the value of school. I mean, I was making five bucks an hour, which was pretty good cake back in 1975. I'd get in trouble skipping classes. I was smoking dope and drinking, just seemed like school was no fun. Then I found out, with my absences and grades so poor, I was very close to not graduating. That's when Mr. Wendt stepped in. He went to bat for me. He tutored me and brought me in as a teacher's assistant so I could pass my classes and get some much needed credits for being a TA. I'll never forget graduation night. Mr. Wendt walked up to me and handed me an envelope with a card in it. I opened it up, it had a check for $20 in it and he had taped a piece of thread on the card. He wrote, "Congratulations Brad, here is the thread your diploma has been hanging on the past four years. Now it belongs to you." He has no idea what his mentoring and tutoring really did for me. I doubt I'd ever made it to college or seminary without a high school diploma.

I love the fact that we see many mentoring programs in schools, especially for kids who are struggling. I love the inner-city mentoring programs that happen. It's an awesome thing. Churches need to get more involved there. However, one of the areas I see a huge need and an easy fit, but rarely happens is spiritual mentoring within the church. I'm for church services. I'm for small groups. But I'm also for one-on-one or one-on-two spiritual mentoring. It happened back in Jesus' day. We see it in the Bible. We just don't see it much in churches, but it's vital for spiritual growth.

If we could talk with the Apostles Peter and John, I imagine they would share how special it was to have Jesus as their mentor. Think about it, Jesus was a small group leader, but he had a special mentoring relationship with Peter, James and John. We kind of know, all three of those guys needed some special attention. They were likely foul-mouthed fisherman when Jesus first met them and chose them to be his disciples. We know by a number of accounts that Peter was incredibly emotionally immature and impulsive. James and John wanted to destroy a village and Jesus had to rein them in. John seemed to have some self-esteem issues and when he finally overcame them, he was totally enamored with the fact that Jesus would actually choose him and referred to himself as *"The disciple Jesus loved"* (John 21:20b NLT). Amazingly, as Jesus mentored these three, you would have never known the impact they would have after Jesus was gone. In the gospel of Luke, Jesus takes his inner three mentees up with him on the Mount of Transfiguration and Luke records, *"And as he was praying, the appearance of his face was transformed, and his clothes became dazzling white. Suddenly, two men, Moses and Elijah, appeared and began talking with Jesus. They were glorious to see."* (Luke 17:29-31a NLT) It's hard to understand at first, why Jesus would take these numbskulls up there. They all fall asleep. Peter suddenly wakes up and sees what's happening, and true to form it says, "Peter, not even knowing what he was saying, blurted out, *"Master, it's wonderful for us to be here! Let's make three shelters as memorials,—one for you, one for Moses and one for Elijah"* (Luke 17:33b NLT). Then Peter, James and John witnessed one of the most important things in all of scripture, which is what I call the other Prime Hermeneutic of the Bible, "Then a voice from a cloud said, *"This is my Son, my Chosen One. Listen to him"* (Luke 17:35 NLT). Amazing! What happened here that's so important—that Peter, James and John had the amazing privilege to witness? Well, the two most important, most decorated Hebrew prophets of the Old Testament show up with Jesus and the Father says in effect, "As important as Moses and Elijah were, know this; my Son is now most important—it was always about Jesus. So, listen to him to avoid any confusion." Jesus trumps everyone. This was a mentoring moment that they'd never forget. In fact, some 38 years later, Peter wrote about this amazing experience, *"We ourselves heard that voice from heaven when we were with him on the holy mountain"* (2 Pet. 1:18). Peter's name was Simon before Jesus changed it to Petros, which means rock. And if you read 2nd Peter chapter 1, you realize Peter had become ''The Rock' Jesus saw in him way back in Matthew 16! In fact, we know, Peter went on to become a key leader in the church—a Rock. Many towns and cities and churches all over the world are named after him to this day. Why? He was mentored.

When I first became a Christ-follower God put some men in my life that mentored me. Rich, a singles pastor at a Presbyterian church I attended in Seattle, took me under his wing for a few years. He introduced me to Father Francis, a Catholic monk, who mentored me once a week for over a year. He was so wise. I was so amazed by how he seemed to emulate Jesus. After a year of knowing him, I went to him and said, "Father Francis, I think I want to become a Catholic." He smiled and laughed, "Ha, Brad, I think you should just seek to be a good Presbyterian." He knew I had a great loving community at my church and what's more important? He had my best interests in the Lord at heart. There's a great attribute of a mentor!

When I first got sober from alcohol and drugs I spent a number of years in Alcoholics Anonymous. AA strongly encourages all newcomers to get a sponsor to mentor them. Recovering alcoholics have a much greater likelihood to of staying sober when they regularly engage with their sponsor. I had some great sponsors who had what I wanted; long-term sobriety. When people get saved in the church they are really recovering sinners, we all are! And, when we get a mentor, our chances of staying mostly free of sin and not slipping back into our old worldly life is greatly enhanced. I often think AA could teach the church a number of things that make it work so well. This is certainly one of them.

Over the years, I've sought out men to mentor me who were obviously far beyond my spiritual maturity. I would never be where I'm at without them. If you want a mentor and you see someone that has a special glow of the Lord that you want for your own, ask them if they would mentor you. They may say no for good reason. Don't take it personally. Just take it to the Lord in prayer. It does take some boldness and some humility to ask someone to mentor you. Oh, and never seek a mentor of the opposite sex. Men mentor men and women mentor women for adults as well as youth.

The key to being mentored is, you need to want it more than your mentor wants it. You need to be F.A.T. Faithful, Available, and Teachable. All three are vital. Apart from Judas, I'm sure all of Jesus' other disciples were faithful and teachable, but maybe Peter, James and John were simply the most available. Availability is really key. Humility and teachability are synonymous in my book and they are part and parcel to being a disciple. There's a great word: Disciple; the ancient Greek word is *Mathetes*. It means *learner / pupil/ apprentice.* As a disciple of Jesus, we are learners first and foremost and learners lean into Jesus always. Part of what that means is when you mess up, and we all do, you need to be honest and wiling to confess any slip ups or sinful behaviors you've engaged in. You need to be willing to spend daily time on your own in God's word. You really need to be willing to take every aspect of this book seriously so you can, like Peter, grow and become all God has created you to be. Peter writes, *"The more you grow like this, the more productive and useful you will be in your knowledge of our Lord Jesus Christ"* (2 Pet. 1:8 NLT).

There is something special that happens when one man meets with another man or one woman meets with another woman who is further along in their spiritual journey and intentionally wants to grow in their faith. *"As iron sharpens iron, so one person sharpens another"* (Prov. 27:17 NIV).

Are you ready to be mentored? Score yourself in both your desire to be mentored and whether or not you're currently being mentored. Then average the two scores below. If you aren't being mentored and want to be, make sure you let a pastor or leader at your church know.

## 2.6–Be Mentored Spiritually

I regularly meet with a special mentor and/or an accountability partner who is further along on The Spiritual Journey than I am. I want to be held accountable and embody what it means to be faithful, available, and teachable.

| WEAK | 1 | 2 | 3 | 4 | 5 | STRONG |

**Memory verse: Proverbs 27:17 (NIV)** *"As Iron sharpens Iron, so one man sharpens another."*

**Questions for Further Reflection and Discussion**

1. Share about a person who had a very positive impact on you. Who and why?

2. Talk about how Jesus chose some foul-mouthed fisherman who would be so key to carry the message to future generations.

3. Do you love Jesus deeply, yet are unsure of yourself like John was? If so, that means you're ripe for mentoring. Discuss John and Peter's issues, and how, by being mentored and with the help of the Holy Spirit, they totally overcame them. What does that mean for you?

°5. Understanding that *Disciple* means learner/pupil. What does that mean for you?

## 2.7 Persevere

We are a baseball family! I'm one of those dads who brings a baseball glove to the hospital for the birth of his son. So, my boys played baseball. One year, after the regular summer league was over, my oldest, Willie was twelve years old, and he played up with thirteen to fifteen year olds. At the time, he was a very good catcher, even though he was left handed. One late summer afternoon his team was playing a team with a fifteen-year-old kid who must have weighed in at 225 pounds—about 100 more than Willie. This big kid, let's call him Jed, was very athletic and had a big ego and an attitude to go with his size. Jed's up to bat and spanks a single to left. Steals second and third, all the while taunting the pitcher and mouthing off to whoever would listen. The pitcher has the ball, but Jed decides to steal home. The pitcher throws the ball to Willie. Willie steps up about five feet toward third. Jed pauses about halfway home, then digs in and comes barreling home. Willie braces for impact, tags Jed and is completely bowled over, flattened on his back. Now, as a baseball dad, yes I'm concerned about my son, but first things first—"Did Willie hold on to the ball? Did he drop it?" Those were my first thoughts! Don't tell my wife, his mom! Well, to my delight, he did hang on! The umpire calls Jed out. Not only out, but out of the game and out of the park for his flagrant bullyish play. I march over to the opposing dugout, luckily, the cyclone fence is between me and Jed, otherwise I may be writing this book from my prison ministry. Honestly, I could have killed him! I shout "Dude, that was my son! What were you thinking?" He blares back, "You want to go at it?" Raises his hands motioning me toward him, and yells, "Come on!"

Wow! I shake my head, collect myself, and calmly walk away. Later that day, I'm driving with Willie and I asked him, "Willie, when that guy was coming at you and you knew you were going to get flattened what were you thinking?" I'll never forget his response. "Dad, one thing. I knew I had to hang on to the ball, because I didn't want to waste the pain." Those words, "I didn't want to waste the pain," were prophetic in more ways than one.

That told me more about Willie and the future God had for him than just about anything. I was so proud of him. In the midst of suffering—even knowing he was going to take a serious hit, in a flash, he played it all out in his mind to persevere through it.

Don't waste the pain! When Jesus was talking about the end-times he said,

During that time, it's going to be really difficult, *"But whoever stands firm [perseveres] to the end will be saved"* (Matt. 24:13 NIV). A quick important theological caveat here, Jesus was talking about the end-times tribulation, not about how a person is saved. The important idea here is there will be suffering. It will be hard. What we can take from that is life is hard. It's painful at times, sometimes continually. Persevere! Be willing to take the hit. And when you do, don't cave! Don't quit! Don't waste the pain!

My grade school PE teacher, Mr. Mathews, used to say, "Winners never quit and quitters never win." That stuck with me all my life.

I look around at the relational landscape and I see bodies, so many relationships terminated, littered across the decades of people's lives. We hit the eject button on relationships so easily. So many relationships and marriages end because of a lack of perseverance. The sad thing is just five years after the divorce a large percentage of people who were for ending their marriage wished they never had.

Here's a question: At the end of your life, what do you want to be known for? I want to be known as a person who persevered to the end; in my marriage, in my parenthood, in my friendships, in my job. In my relationship with God. I want people to know, they can count on me, with God's help and grace. A favorite stretch of scripture is in Romans where Paul writes, *"We know that suffering produces perseverance; perseverance, character; and character, hope. And hope does not put us to shame, because God's love has been poured out into our hearts through the Holy Spirit, who has been given to us"* (Rom. 5:3b-5 NIV).

Suffering produces perseverance; perseverance, character. They all work together. Character comes out not so much when things are going great in our lives. That's easy! Character shows most when life is hard, when we suffer.

Southwest of Portland, Oregon, in the Willamette valley, on a rare clear day, you can look east and see the snowcapped Mt. Hood. It's amazing! We are known for our amazing fir trees in the Pacific Northwest, and looking up at the mountain, you can see the tree line. What is obvious from afar is that nothing grows on the mountaintop. The same is true in our lives. When things are going great—when we are at the top of the mountain of life—it's exhilarating! Great view. Very encouraging. Take it all in while you can. But we don't grow up there. It's only in the valleys of life where we really grow. That's why when life gets hard, we don't quit, we grow!

Paul, writing his second letter to the church at Corinth, said, *"That's why we never give up. Though our bodies are dying, our spirits are being renewed every day. For our present troubles are small and won't last very long. Yet they produce for us a glory that vastly outweighs them and will last forever"* (2 Cor. 4:16-17 NLT).

Our troubles produce a glory! I believe the glory is the increased character. We are all going to have amazing character in our glorified state in heaven. But, while we are on this earth, our character is being developed through suffering and perseverance.

Quitters never win and winners never quit. Christians are winners because of Christ, which means there's no quitting for the Christ-follower. We are called to persevere! Aren't you glad our Lord, Savior and Leader, Jesus, persevered to the end? Aren't you glad he didn't quit when he was getting mocked, flogged and spit on by the Roman soldiers? Aren't you glad his perseverance produced for us a glory that will never fade away?

When Willie was 17, he went through an extended period of darkness in his life. As a dad and a parent it was so difficult. One morning I was on my knees, talking to God about it all. A thought came, "Let go and let God." That's was so spiritual! Had to be from God I thought. So, I prayed, "Lord, I'm letting go of my son and giving him to you. I'm done. I can't take it anymore." God got in my face in that moment, "No you don't!" And he gave me one word, "Tenacious! Like never before, you tenaciously go after your son!" Wow! A few weeks later, I was scheduled to take Willie out to dinner just to talk and connect. It was November and getting cold at night in the Pacific NW. I texted him after school. "When can I pick you up?" "Later dad, I just need a little space right now." "Okay." A few hours go by. I text again, "Willie, let me pick you up and we'll go eat." "Not yet." Two hours later, "Willie, what's up." Text: "Dad, I'm not worthy to be called your son." Whoa, tears! My text back: "What? Where's all this coming from?" And he goes dark. Off the grid! No response. I'm scared. Ann's scared. Our youngest son, Nathan is very concerned and begins to pray. We pray and pray and pray, all the while calling friends and trying to text him. Nothing. We spoke with Sarah in Australia and she gets a prayer chain going with her college friends at Hillsong. About midnight, I fall asleep till about 2 am. Still no Willie. I lay in my bed and start praying again. "Get up! Go look for him," is all I hear. (We learned later this was the exact time our daughter was lifting her brother up in worship and prayer Down Under.). So, I start driving out of our little town toward the town his school is in, about 8 miles. I cry out to God, "Lord, my son is lost, I'm lost and I have no idea where to look. But Holy Spirit, you know, you know exactly where he is!" The night was dark and cold as I drove along, looking in storefronts hoping I might see him. Nothing. "Turn right," I hear in my spirit. I'm now driving toward the school. "Turn left," I hear. "Turn right." And I come up on an elementary school. I drive toward the back and shine the lights of my car into a covered play area. Nothing there. I begin to back out and I hear in my spirit, "Get out!" I get out, turn my iPhone flashlight on and go around the corner and there, on the ground curled up in a sleeping bag, is my Willie. Tears! Joy! Relief! Awe! I tear up every time I tell that story, because it is such a God story! God never gives up. He always perseveres. He just wants us to hang in there a little longer, keep going, don't give up. Persevere! I never want to quit on my kids or my wife or you. Why? God doesn't. The father of the prodigal son never gave up—he ran out to his son who was lost when he saw him heading home from a long way off. (Luke 15).

Tradition has it that James, the younger half-brother of Jesus, and pillar of the early church in Jerusalem was severely persecuted for his faith in his Big Bro. The irony is James didn't even believe in Jesus until after Jesus rose from the dead, but Jesus' resurrection totally convinced him. Some called James, "James the Just". He loved the poor and always fought for their rights. Seems he couldn't stand phony religious people. It's said that James spent so much time in prayer that his knees were calloused. Evidently, James was called upon by the Jewish leaders to denounce Jesus and was taken up to a wall to proclaim his change of heart to all of Jerusalem. Well, instead of caving on Jesus, James used the occasion to proclaim the gospel message and encourage everyone present to put their faith in Christ. The Jewish leaders finally had enough of James and threw him off the wall to his death. I can't help but wonder how many people James influenced by his perseverance in his faith all the way to his death? James wrote, *"Consider it pure joy, my brothers and sisters whenever you face trials of many kinds, because you know that the testing of your faith produces perseverance. Let perseverance finish its work so that you may be mature and complete, not lacking anything"* (James 1:2-4 NIV). Mature and complete. He also wrote that we should not be merely hearers of the word, but doers also. Faith without works is dead. James lived it and died for it. Count it pure joy. I imagine James having a smile on his face sharing the gospel of his big brother Jesus, knowing full well, he would see Jesus again in the blink of an eye. James was the real deal, mature! That's what I want and I know that's what God wants for you and me.

Don't waste the pain! Persevere! So much pain is wasted by quitting. Our Lord redeems everything. It's his nature. All your painful experiences can and will be used by God to bring others to him, to encourage others who are currently going through similar difficulties that you've already navigated. But if you cave... it's lost and wasted. Don't waste the pain. It's too costly! Let God use it and you for his glory and yours. Persevere! Why? Love! It's always about love, remember?

> *"It [love] always protects, always trusts, always hopes, always perseveres. Love never fails"* (1 Cor. 13:7, 8a NIV)

My good friend and pastor Stan Russell says, "The best thing I've ever done is not quit" I totally agree. I never want to quit on my marriage, on my kids, on people around me, even on my church. As a result of persevering, I've seen so much fruit in people's lives. It saddens me to have known people who quit, who never got to experience the fruit of lives transformed, being used by God to change a life. Nothing is better, but it takes perseverance.

How about you? What's your perseverance quotient? Read the following statement and score yourself:

### 2.7–Persevere

I am not a quitter. I am so glad Jesus did not quit on me and persevered all the way to the cross. I know suffering is part of life and although I don't like it, I know often that's where I grow most. Therefore, I'm committed to persevere to the end.

| WEAK | 1 | 2 | 3 | 4 | 5 | STRONG |
|------|---|---|---|---|---|--------|

**Memory verse: Romans 5:3b-5 (NIV)** *"We know that suffering produces perseverance; perseverance, character; and character, hope. And hope does not put us to shame, because God's love has been poured out into our hearts through the Holy Spirit, who has been given to us."*

## Questions for Further Reflection and Discussion

1.  What struck you most about this chapter and why?

2.  Have you ever quit on something or someone and wish you hadn't? Share the story.

3.  Have ever you felt like quitting on something or someone but didn't? What or who was it and why did you persevere?

4.  Spend some time talking about Jesus and how glad you are that he persevered all the way to the end.

5.  What do you think about counting suffering as pure joy?

6.  How does perseverance hone our character?

7.  Is there something you need to persevere in right now?

# 2.8 Obedience

Telling someone to obey feels like kindergarten. We live in a world that says, "Do your own thing!" or "Whatever works for you!" God says obey me and things will go well with you. Disobey me and it won't. It's quite a contrast.

On my trip to Australia to see my daughter, Sarah—we needed to get certified before we went out on the live-aboard boat to dive the Great Barrier Reef. Part of the Diver Certification process was classroom time and pool time in Cairns. One thing they taught us is, "Never hold your breath when you dive. Always keep breathing." "Fish never hold their breath," the instructor emphatically stated. Why? Why not hold your breath? To kill our fun? To make it so we use up the tanks quicker so we can't enjoy the dive as long? No, that's not it. As you descend, pressure increases and it actually takes more oxygen to fill your lungs. The deeper you go, the more oxygen you use. As you ascend, the air expands. So, imagine if I'm diving at 60 feet. I take a deep breath and I hold it all the way up. What happens? Well, the air that filled my lungs nicely at 60 feet expands greatly on the way up and my lungs burst and I die! It's that simple. Question: Do I obey the instructors' wisdom on this or literally blow it off? I obey! It's a matter of life and death.

The same is true with God. Let's take a few of the 10 commandments. Number 7—You shall not commit adultery. Should we blow that one off? Is God trying to kill our fun? So much pain and even death has happened over the centuries and millennia because many people have disobeyed this command. It's preventable! Just obey. How about Number 6—Thou shalt not murder? Obey or disobey? Please say obey! Number 8—Do not steal! Number 9—Do not lie! Ever had someone steal from you or lie to you? How did that feel? Hurts, doesn't it?

Like obeying the dive instructor, and having the greatest opportunity to live and thoroughly enjoy the splendor of the Great Barrier Reef, obeying God brings us life and blessing and honestly, fun! Disobeying God brings death, curses and so much pain upon us. It's just that simple. Moses reflects the voice and heart of God he writes, *"Oh that their hearts would be inclined to fear me and keep all my commands always, so that it might go well with them and their children forever!"* (Deut. 5:29 NIV). God says this right after he gives Moses the Ten Commandments. You can hear the voice of a loving Father in this verse—*"Oh that their hearts would be inclined"*. God knows what's best for us. He so wants our lives to go well. Every sane father or mother loves it when their child obeys them. God longs to have us obey him, not for his good, but for ours. When diving the Great Barrier Reef, for my own good and my daughter's own good, our very lives depended on obeying every aspect of our dive instructor's teachings. The instructions regarding the water, the pressure, the tanks, the regulators, time down, depth of our dives, rate of descent and ascent, even the weight belts called for our strict obedience. All those elements and more needed our attention and obedience to have a fun, safe dive. If you were there and you had any sense about you, I'm sure you'd agree wholeheartedly. It's a logical and tangible matter of life and death. In the same way, from God's perspective, all of his commands are a logical and tangible; a matter of life and death, blessings or curses. He made us; he knows what's best for us, even when we think it's no big deal. In fact, it's arrogant for us to think better than our Creator. It would be similar to saying, "I've seen the space shuttle take off on TV, therefore I know better than the men and women who designed it." How insane would that be? But often that's exactly what we do when we disobey God's Word. What we have to understand God is a God of life. All life emanates from his very being. Every time we obey God, we take a step or two toward him and we experience life. On the other hand, every time we disobey God, we take a step or ten away from God and experience death. Sometimes slow and painful. God said, *"See, I am setting before you today a blessing and a curse—the blessing if you obey the commands of the Lord your God that I am giving you today; the curse if you disobey the commands of the Lord your God . . ."* (Deut. 11:26-28 NIV). God makes it pretty clear. Obedience or disobedience? Blessings or curses? It's our choice.

It's really all about God's will. God's will is for us to obey him. It's always the best choice. It's the choice of life! You may ask, "How do you know it's God's will?" Great question. If it's clear in the Bible, we know it's God's will. No reason for debate. What if it's not in the Bible? Every possibility of every choice for good and evil is not in the Bible. Sure! Here's something I learned from a Catholic monk named Father Gregory while on a retreat at a monastery years ago in the high mountain desert of Southern California. He said, "Generally speaking, if it's easy to do up front, and we can project that we might regret that choice, often it's not God's will. However, if it's hard to do on the front end and you can see it's likely to be of benefit in the long run, it's more likely to be God's will." Easy—the devil's will. Hard—God's will! Not always, but generally. I've mentioned that I'm a recovered alcoholic and drug addict who's been sober for 30 years. So, grateful! Saying yes to drugs and alcohol for me was so easy back then. Saying "no" was so hard. What was God will? What's God's will for you in that regard? Will you say "yes" or "no" to drugs? How about being married and getting drunk at a bar on a business trip then getting seduced and sleeping with another person you just met? God's will? Doing that is the stuff of death! Death of a marriage and sometimes the adulterer. What about charging credit cards up and mounting up huge debt? So easy to do that everyone is doing it. God's will? The hard choice is to live within your means. Get it?

Now, the truth is, at times we all mess up. At times, in this life, we are going to disobey. What then, death? No! Repentance! To repent is to change course. Its when we fall into disobeying God, and then suddenly we realize we are walking away from God and make the decision to turn back toward him. To repent literally means to "turn around." Repentance has fallen out of vogue this days, but it's such a gift. It's the doorway to grace! When we do repent and confess our disobedience, God forgives everything and welcomes us back wholeheartedly as a son or daughter. John the Apostle writes, *"If we claim to be without sin, we deceive ourselves and the truth is not in us. If we confess our sins, he is faithful and just and will forgive us our sins and purify us from all unrighteousness"* (1 John 1:8, 9 NIV).

The most amazing thing is it's all about love. Real love demands a choice between right and wrong, good and evil, obedience and disobedience. You cannot have real love without the possibility to choose hate. John wrote, *"We know we have come to know him if we keep his commands. Those who say, "I know him, but do not do what he commands are liars, and the truth is not in them. But if anyone obeys his Word, love for God is truly made complete in them"* (1 John 2:3-5a NIV). A child who obeys their parents shows love and respect for them. When God's children obey him, we show him the honor and respect he deserves.

So, what's your obedience factor? Are you beginning to understand the beauty of life-giving obedience? Do you desire to really obey God, especially now? Read the statement below and make an honest evaluation of yourself and your choices.

## 2.8–Obedience

I have an increasing desire to read, understand and obey the Bible. I believe the Holy Spirit gives me the wisdom and power to understand and obey God's word, and shows me how to apply it to my daily life.

| WEAK | 1 | 2 | 3 | 4 | 5 | STRONG |

**Memory verses: 1 John 2:4, 5a (NIV)** *"Those who say, 'I know him, but do not do what he command are liars, and the truth is not in them. But if anyone obeys his Word, love for God is truly made complete in them.'"*

## Questions for Further Reflection and Discussion

1. When you hear the word obedience, what comes to mind?

2. Read out loud and discuss the memory verse above.

3. Discuss the idea that doing God's will is often the difficult choice and share an example where you made the right choice and, if you're bold enough, the wrong choice. What were the consequences?

4. Discuss the blessings of God when we obey and the curses we bring on ourselves when we disobey. Give some examples of both in your own life.

5. Connect fun to obedience. Is disobeying really more fun? Discuss the gift of repentance.

6. What can you do to learn to obey and do God's will on a more frequent basis?

## 2.9 Rest—Reflect—Record

After reading through Milestone sections 2.1 to 2.8, now is the time to pause and reflect on what you've learned and perhaps even implemented in your life since reading it for the first time. Don't be surprised if you've grown in certain areas. So, again, read the following statements and record yourself accordingly:

### 2.1–Personal Devotional Time
I practice a daily quiet time. Giving God my undivided attention though prayer, Bible reading, and journaling is one of the most important steps to loving God and growing closer to him every day.

| WEAK | 1 | 2 | 3 | 4 | 5 | STRONG |
|------|---|---|---|---|---|--------|

**Memory verse: John 15:5 (NIV)** *"I am the vine; you are the branches. If you remain in me and I in you, you will bear much fruit; apart from me you can do nothing."*

### 2.2–Lead or Support a Small Group

I regularly lead, co-lead, or support a small group. I understand that it's great to be a small group participant, but now I also feel responsible to help others grow by leading, co-leading, hosting, or supporting a small group.

| WEAK | 1 | 2 | 3 | 4 | 5 | STRONG |
|------|---|---|---|---|---|--------|

**Memory verse: Ephesians 4:16 (NLT)** *"He makes the whole body fit together perfectly. As each part does its own special work, it helps other parts grow, so that the whole body is healthy and growing full of love."*

### 2.3–Go on a Mission

I love serving in a mission opportunity, across town or out of the country. I have a passion to serve outside the borders of this church and be involved in expanding God's kingdom both locally and globally.

| WEAK | 1 | 2 | 3 | 4 | 5 | STRONG |
|------|---|---|---|---|---|--------|

**Memory verse: Luke 10:2 (NIV)** *"He told them, the harvest is plentiful, but the workers are few. Ask the Lord of the harvest, therefore, to send out workers into his harvest field."*

### 2.4–Tithe

I faithfully tithe to my home church. Faithfully giving ten percent of my income is an act of worship that helps me grow my faith in God, who always provides all I need.

WEAK    1    2    3    4    5    STRONG

**Memory Verse: Malachi 3:10 (NIV)** *"Bring the whole tithe into the storehouse, that there may be food in my house. Test me in this," says the Lord Almighty, "and see if I will not throw open the floodgates of heaven and pour out so much blessing that there will not be room enough to store it."*

### 2.5–Grow up—Emotionally

I am not offended by others. I am learning to love people who hurt me, to give others the benefit of the doubt when I don't understand their actions, and to not pass judgment on them. I don't need to have my way.

WEAK    1    2    3    4    5    STRONG

**Memory verse: Ephesians 4:2 (NLT)** *"Always be humble and gentle, be patient with each other, making allowance for each other's faults because of your love."*

### 2.6–Be Mentored Spiritually

I regularly meet with a special mentor and/or an accountability partner who is further along The Spiritual Journey than I am. I want to be held accountable and embody what it means to be faithful, available, and teachable.

WEAK    1    2    3    4    5    STRONG

**Memory verse: Proverbs 27:17 (NIV)** *"As Iron sharpens Iron, so one man sharpens another."*

## 2.7–Persevere

I am not a quitter. I am so glad Jesus did not quit on me and persevered all the way to the cross. I know suffering is part of life and although I don't like it, I know often that's where I grow most. Therefore, I'm committed to persevere to the end.

| WEAK | 1 | 2 | 3 | 4 | 5 | STRONG |

**Memory verse: Romans 5:3b-5 (NIV)** *"We know that suffering produces perseverance; perseverance, character; and character, hope. And hope does not put us to shame, because God's love has been poured out into our hearts through the Holy Spirit, who has been given to us."*

## 2.8–Obedience

I have an increasing desire to read, understand and obey the Bible. I believe the Holy Spirit gives me the wisdom and power to understand and obey God's Word, and shows me how to apply it to my daily life.

| WEAK | 1 | 2 | 3 | 4 | 5 | STRONG |

**Memory verses: 1 John 2:4, 5a (NIV)** *"Those who say, 'I know him, but do not do what he command are liars, and the truth is not in them. But if anyone obeys his Word, love for God is truly made complete in them.'"*

*Milestone 3 Goal—God is using you to Multiply Christ-followers locally and globally*

*At Milestone 3 the way we Love God is to 1) Learn to meditate on God's Word and practice Solitude. The way we Love Others is 2) Mentor Others. And the way we Serve the World is to 3) Be On Mission. In addition there are five other milestone points to really help you mature in your relationship with Christ.*

## 3.1 Practice Meditation and Solitude

We live in noisy world, likely the noisiest world since time began. We see and hear messages and news spin cycles that have the potential to suck us in or take us out. Channel surfing or surfing the internet is common place. Grown men often spend hours playing violent shoot'em up video games on a daily basis. I read recently that smart phone addiction is becoming a serious problem. We love being connected, but it's often disconnecting us from God and others at a deep level. All this and much more are sucking us dry.

What's the answer? Meditation and Solitude. Here's a question: Is your daily and weekly routine increasing your love for God? David wrote this about people who long for the goodness of God and love him with their whole hearts: *"They delight in the law of the Lord, meditating on it day and night"* (Ps. 1:2 NLT). Meditating on God's word day and night. Imagine that. Instead of spending so much time with phone in hand, checking out social media and whatever else, we meditate on God's word day and night. Ever tried it? I believe it's a lost art that this world desperately needs to rediscover, starting with you and me.

At Milestone 2.1 you learned the spiritual exercise of having a daily quiet time. It's vital. And 3.1 basically starts there, but here we take it up a notch. When we seek to fill the void in our lives with noise from this world, we think somehow it's going to make us happy, but it simply leaves us empty. Psalm 119 is the Gold Standard for meditation of God's word and an amazing exercise in focused meditation. The psalmist used all twenty-two letters of the Hebrew alphabet as his outline, with 8 verses under each letter for a total of 176 verses, virtually all referring to God's word. Theologian J.A. Motyer, referring to Psalm 119, states, "Our God is a God who speaks and it is the possession of that verbal revelation which marks his people off from all others on the earth" (p. 566 New Bible Commentary). When God speaks to us, we need to listen intently and make it part of who we are. That's what meditation is all about. Here's a sample of some verses in Psalm 119 NIV:

*1 Blessed are those whose ways are blameless, who walk according to the <u>law</u> of the Lord.*

*2 Blessed are those who keep his <u>statutes</u> and seek him with all their heart—3 they do no wrong but follow his <u>ways</u>.*

*9 How can those who are young keep their way pure? By living according to your <u>word</u>.*

*11 I have hidden your <u>word</u> in my heart that I might not sin against thee.*

*20 My soul is consumed with longing for your <u>laws</u> at all times.*

*24 Your <u>statutes</u> are my delight; they are my counselors.*

*30 I have chosen the way of faithfulness; I have set my heart on your <u>laws</u>.*

*33 Teach me, Lord, the way of your <u>decrees</u>, that I might follow it to the end.*

*78 May the arrogant be put to shame for wronging me without cause; but I will meditate on your <u>precepts</u>.*

So, so good. We are instructed to meditate *on* God's word and repeatedly *be in* God's word. But what does that mean? Here's Google's definition for Meditate: "To think deeply or focus one's mind for a period of time." That's pretty good. I'd add, think deeply ON GOD'S WORD and focus your mind and heart on it, so much so, as to to live it out. Years ago, I went on a small retreat to a Benedictine monastery when my mentor, Father Francis lived. There, his Benedictine brother, Father Luke instructed us in the ancient practice of Lectio Divina. That's Latin for Divine Reading. It's a Benedictine practice of reading scripture for the purpose of meditation. Father Luke defined it as "Listening to scripture with the ear of your heart." Lectio Divina dates back to Origen who was one of the Early Church fathers in the 3rd century. The word of God is not simply to hear, it's to penetrate our hearts and direct our lives. Take one of the above verses. Just one. Let's go with verse 11 *"I have hidden your word in my heart that I might not sin against thee."* Read it. Repeat it over and over and over again. Memorize it. Think about it in utter silence. And then do you best to keep it at the forefront of your thoughts all day long in everything you do. As we do this day after day, just one verse at a time, God's word truly is hidden in our hearts and the likelihood of sinning against him becomes less and less over time and our lives are *transformed by the renewal of our minds* (Rom. 12:2). And our actions are sure to follow. It's amazing!

I'm a passionate guy and even though I have amazing people I work with, I can get upset over things not going my way (more on this in Milestone 3.5). I've learned over time, when I disagree with something, to bite my tongue in the moment, most of the time. That said, things can get me going down the road to a confrontation where I'm going to straighten someone out. Some mornings, before I get out of bed, I've already got a plan to strategically call or meet with the person who needs my wisdom on a particular contentious issue. The good news is, before I go out the door, I spend time in prayer and meditation on God's word. Inevitably, God changes me, changes my attitude. I come to understand he's still in control and doesn't really need my help. Meditation on a particular verse gives me a sense of peace and then I'm good to go! It's happened too many times to be coincidence. God works deeply on our souls when we meditate on His word. That doesn't mean I just cave when I disagree about a direction our church or our family is headed and not say anything. No, but by meditating on God's word, God often gives me much more helpful, calm insights to share in order to advance the initiative and ultimately the kingdom of God.

Think about it, as Christ-followers, shouldn't we be seeking the King's Precepts, His Instructions, His Statues, His Decrees, His Commands, His Laws, His word daily in order to do His will, not ours? *"Seek the Kingdom of God above all else, and live righteously, and he will give you everything you need"* (Matt. 6:33 NLT). Meditation is vital to keep our hearts and minds and souls seeking his kingdom first and foremost, not our own. Meditation and prayer at home daily and throughout the day pours vital spiritual nutrients into our souls. I know Jesus did it and so should we.

Jesus also had another spiritual practice that goes hand in hand with meditation called solitude. Time and again Jesus got away from the noise and clamor to spend time with the Father, alone. Before Jesus started his public ministry in earnest, he spent 40 days praying and fasting in the wilderness alone (Luke 4; Mark 1:12-13). The day before he chose the 12 Apostles Luke records, *"Jesus went up on a mountain to pray, and he prayed all night to God"* (Luke 6:12 NLT). Here he had a huge decision to make, which would impact all subsequent human history. What does he do? Gets alone to pray all night and get some input from His Father. Ever done that when you had a big decision? It's a pretty good idea! After a heavy day of ministry he knew the only way to refill is to practice solitude: *"Before daybreak the next morning, Jesus got up and went out to an isolated place to pray"* (Mark 1:35 NLT). After the feeding of the 5000, *"immediately Jesus made the disciples get into the boat and go on ahead of him to Bethsaida, while he dismissed the crowd. After leaving them, he went up on a mountainside to pray"* (Mark 6:45-46 NIV). Again, Luke records, *"Jesus often withdrew to the wilderness for prayer"* (Luke 5:16 NLT). Question: If Jesus, who was God come to earth, needed solitude and carved out alone time with the Father, how much more do we need it?

Jesus not only practiced solitude himself, he encouraged his disciples to practice it too, especially after a hard day's work; *"Come with me by yourselves to a quiet place and get some rest. So they went away by themselves in a boat to a solitary place"* (Mark 6:31b—32 NIV).

Do you ever feel, you just gotta get away? Away from the rat race? Away from the crowds? Away from the kids? Just away? Sometimes I get so tattered, I'm seriously thinking about umbrella drinks in Tahiti! My problem is, until I met Jesus, I wanted to get away, but my escape route was misguided. The bar, a bong hit, parties, anywhere that's fun. Believe me, I still love fun places and fun vacations and warm tropical beaches and I highly recommend them. Just don't leave Jesus behind. Again, Augustine of Hippo said, *"Our hearts our restless, O Lord, until they rest in thee."* We can try to fill the void in our souls with noise and fun and food and booze and sex and everything else under the sun, but our souls need rest and solitude in Jesus. God made us that way. Nothing else works—I know, I tried.

Jesus said, *"My sheep listen my voice, I know them, and they follow me"* (John 10:27 NLT). We need meditation on God's word to recognize God's voice and we need periodic solitude to pause, quiet our souls and really hear Jesus amidst all the noise of our world. The irony is, God could shout, he could stop us in our tracks, but for some reason, he refuses to compete for our time and our space. He just says, *"Come to me, all you who are weary and burdened and I will give your rest"* (Matt. 11:28 NIV).

As I write this chapter, I'm alone up our little shack of a cabin on a little island in the west Puget Sound, have been here for four days now. There is no way I could do any of this with all the noise of home. This is one of my solitary places. Sometimes it's camping. Sometimes it's fishing. Sometimes I go out on our little boat in the middle of the water and put on worship music and just worship God by myself. Often I might fast while practicing solitude. If you're going on a holiday or a vacation, plan some alone time with God. It's so good. It can be scary to get alone with God, but once you do it a few times, God shows up and you can't understand how you ever did life without it.

Meditation on God's word and solitude are spiritual disciplines that enable us to really integrate God's word into our lives more than just about anything else. I love how Wayne Cordeiro puts it:

Just in your head: Information.
Just in your heart: Inspiration.
When it bleeds out of you: Incarnation.
I'll paraphrase Wayne:
Information alone will make you a Pharisee.
Inspiration only will make you a fanatic.
Incarnation will make you an authentic follower of Jesus.
(*The Divine Mentor*, page 120)

Jesus was the word who became flesh. That's called incarnation. He lived out scripture like no one else. As his faithful followers, we too should be living it out—incarnating God's word. Meditation and solitude will enable you to do it like nothing else.

So, where are you at? Interested? Remember, if Jesus did it and felt he needed meditation and solitude, don't we even more? Read the statements below and score yourself.

### 3.1–Practice Meditation and Solitude

I regularly meditate on God's word and periodically get away to a place of solitude to be recharged and filled up by God. I believe these are key spiritual practices that help me to develop and maintain an intimate relationship with the Father, Son, and Holy Spirit.

WEAK   1   2   3   4   5   STRONG

**Memory verse: Mark 6:31b–32 (NIV)** *"Come with me by yourselves to a quiet place and get some rest. So they went away by themselves in a boat to a solitary place."*

## Questions for Further Reflection and Discussion

1.  How does meditating on God's word sound to you? Why?

2.  Explore Lectio Divina, listening to the word of God with the ear of your heart. What are your initial thoughts on it?

3.  Share a place or a time where you just got away alone. Was God there?

4.  Discuss Jesus' practice of solitude.

5.  Do you ever feel, "I just gotta get away?" Why?

6.  How can you practice solitude periodically?

## 3.2 Mentor Others

Ever heard something from someone that rocked your boat so much that you just could never shake it? In a good way? When I was doing my internship at Willow Creek in Chicago and John Maxwell was the guest speaker one weekend, he said something that has haunted me since, "There is no success, unless you have a successor!" Those words are constantly on my mind. They are in part the reason for this book. I believe the primary way we can be sure to have successors is by mentoring others. The ancients got this—Socrates mentored Plato, Plato mentored Aristotle, Aristotle mentored Alexander the Great. And as much damage Alexander the Great did, he helped pave the way for the gospel to be spread all over the Mediterranean. He insisted that Greek be the common language; the language in which the New Testament was originally written.

A ripple effect started with Socrates, of all people, that has even reached you and me. Ever heard of the Ripple Effect? *Merriam Webster* defines it as *"A situation in which one event causes a series of other events to happen."* It's the *idea* that a butterfly flapping its wings in China one year can be the starting point of a hurricane in the Gulf of Mexico the next.

**Stay on the path! Don't step on the butterfly!**

In 1952 Ray Bradbury wrote a sci-fi short story called *A Sound of Thunder*. It became the script for a 30-minute movie in 1989 on the Ray Bradbury Theater. I'll never forget it. The setting was 2055 during a democratic election. A company called Time Safari had developed a time machine where they took hunters back 60 million years to hunt dinosaurs, specifically the T-Rex. One very boastful hunter who had already bagged every conceivable trophy on the planet paid the exorbitant fee to make the trek back in time. Supported by a guide, he and a few other hunters board the time machine and back they go. Once they arrive at their destination and open the time machine a mechanical pathway extends way out from the door. The key directive from the guide is "Stay on the path! Do not step on a plant or a bug that may alter the future via a ripple effect." The T-Rex is baited in and the macho hunter is so scared when he hears the dinosaur he falls off the path. After misfiring and being collected by an angry guide, they board the time machine and head back to 2055. Upon arrival, they are received by angry Nazi's rather than the kind people who existed in the pre-trip democracy. The ego-shaken hunter looks at the bottom of his boot and finds a squished butterfly he had stepped on when he fell off the path. The ripple effect was catastrophic over 60 million years! The corrective in this case would be "Stay on the path, don't step on the butterfly!"

Ripple effects can have both positive and negative consequences. The question is what will the ripple effect of your life be?

In Ancient Israel God gave the Hebrew people the Ten Commandments and then the Great Shema as follows to abide by so every person's life would have a positive ripple effect.

*"Hear, O Israel: The Lord our God, the Lord is
one. 5 Love the Lord your God with all your heart
and with all your soul and with all your strength.
6 These commandments that I give you today are to
be on your hearts. 7 Impress them on your children.
Talk about them when you sit at home and when
you walk along the road, when you lie down and
when you get up"* (Deut. 6:4–7 NIV).

God asked parents to mentor their children and be their
guides, so they would "stay on the path and not step on the
butterfly!" And be blessed, not cursed.

As we are on our spiritual journey, being a mentor is a sure
way to stay on the path... the path that Jesus laid out of us. We
can be wooed by so many things, and "step on the butterfly."
But Jesus shows us the way to make kingdom ripple effects.

Jesus made the greatest ripple effect for good, more than
anyone who ever lived. Intentionally mentoring three of his
disciple was the brilliance in it. While Jesus chose 12 disciples
initially, He mentored three of them—Peter, James and John.
We know James, the brother of John, was martyred soon after
Jesus went to heaven, but Peter and John continued to lead the
church and have had more profound influence for the Christian
faith, apart from Jesus, than anyone who ever lived, except perhaps the Apostle Paul. You have to ask why? I believe, the answer
is Jesus intentionally mentored them. Jesus modeled mentoring
others, but now it seems to be a lost art. Jesus so easily could
have had a mega-church immediately after the feeding of the
5000 or the 4000. But each time he told his disciples to "Go".
Then he'd go away to pray and meet them. Jesus met and mentored Peter on the water. It was a great mentoring moment. He
took Peter, James and John up on the Mount of Transfiguration
with him, where they alone saw Jesus with Moses and Elijah.
He took those three into the house of Jairus where he brought
Jairus' daughter back from the dead. He took only Peter, James

and John into the garden of Gethsemane to be with him one last time prior to his arrest and crucifixion.

Why did Jesus seem so much more interested in mentoring a few than growing a big following? He knew the paradox of doing far more with less. He knew by focusing on three intentionally it would have a far greater long-term impact than ministering to 3000 or 30,000 once a week.

Recently I took my mother to her eye doctor. Accompanying her into the examination room, I was surprised to see my mother's 60ish Optometrist who called in two significantly younger doctors to also examine my mother's blind eye. He said, "Take a look, but keep your diagnosis to yourself and we will discuss it together." After each one had their go at my mom's eye, the younger physicians each gave their assessment. Each one missed what the older doctor saw only by experience. I sat in awe. I knew exactly what was going on. My mom's doctor was mentoring those two younger ones. To make sure, I asked the doctor what was going on there. He stated, that both those men were fully qualified and certified eye doctors who could go out and start their own practices and make a lot of money, but choose to come in to be in a mentoring fellowship under his care for a year, to learn things that could only be taught in that type of an environment. I loved it. Just think how the wisdom of my mother's doctor could be multiplied by mentoring two or three fellows each year, for as long as my mom's doctor could. That's a huge ripple effect! *As Iron sharpens Iron so one person sharpens another* (Proverbs 27:17 NIV).

My big question is why is this not common place in the church? Is it we're just not prioritizing the value of mentoring? Is it the busyness of each day that just overwhelms us? Is it the elixir of large crowds that mesmerizes us and strokes our ego that we just don't go there? Do we think we are just that good that no one can replace us? Are we that emotionally insecure that we believe we alone must be the all-wise dispenser of God's truths? Are we not trusting God and are we so full of fear of letting go of control that we can't pass off leadership to qualified, next generation leaders and pastors?

Over the years I have developed many relationships with pastors in Africa. We can learn much from our African brothers and sisters on this matter. Pastor Peter mentored Elisha and Jonathan, both who went on to plant great churches. Elisha mentored Sam, Ivan and Patrick – all who have planted churches with our EPIC group. Jonathan is mentoring Isaac and Michael, who are involved leaders in the ministry. That's just the tip of the iceberg, or maybe the tip of the rhino horn in this case.

Jesus mentored. It's happening in the secular world, which calls it coaching. The church, more than any other organization on the planet, needs to make mentoring a priority. There is no success unless we have successors! So many men and women have wisdom they need to give away. It's a huge part of how we find fulfillment. The writer of Hebrews said,

> *"You have been believers so long now that you ought to be teaching others. Instead, you need someone to teach you again the basic things about God's word. You are like babies who need milk and cannot eat solid food. For someone who lives on milk is still an infant and doesn't know how to do what is right. Solid food is for those who are mature, who through training have the skill to recognize the difference between right and wrong"* (Heb. 5:12-14 NLT).

This seems to be an admonishment to those who had been believers for a number of years, to grow up and start teaching and training others. But it's obvious they were unable because they were still struggling with the basics after many years of "knowing" Christ. If we are being trained up to grow in Christ in a healthy fashion, after just a few years we should be mentoring others—Peter did, James did, Paul certainly did. They easily knew the difference between right and wrong. And just knowing that helps us to avoid silly mistakes that can have enormous consequences.

One of the strange phenomena of getting older and moving into middle age is a train wreck called midlife crisis. Midlife crisis is best and broadly generalized in the 50 year-old male who has a deep need to be young again and proceeds to get a gold chain for his neck, a fast sports car, divorces his wife of 25 years and finds a younger woman to pursue, all of which he believes will bring meaning and fulfillment to his life, again. It's a lie too many men and now even women buy into. Sure, it may last up to five years, but it's fraught with problems and pain. The person acting out midlife crisis is seeking to go back to relive their youth again. It's the stuff of fools! You can never go back any more than we can board a time machine and go back 60 million years! Talk about stepping on the butterfly!

What's the answer? To intentionally stay on the path and give away all the wisdom you have gained and deposit it into the next generation. At my age, it's one of the single most fulfilling things I do. This next generation so wants to be mentored. They are hungry and looking for people with wisdom to impart so they can negotiate the minefield of an exceedingly volatile and complicated world. Who better to do it that than those of us who rely on the One with all wisdom!

I'm currently intentionally mentor my son-in-law Elliot and my son Willie, just to name a few. There is nothing more gratifying. They are both leaning in and I know they will be so much more effective than me in the long run, because they started so much earlier. Think about that, me spending my time with them, pouring into them, rather than chasing some youth fantasy. I know this, my wife is very pleased! Praise the Lord! Why do I do it? Remember this, the only way to keep it is by giving it away.

### Pastor Brad's Definition of the Mentor/Protégé Relationship:

What is a spiritual mentor? Well, I define it as someone you look up to spiritually. What is the protégé? The person being mentored. For our purposes, a mentor is someone who has Godly attributes that you want for yourself. Someone who is willing to take their time to help you become all God has for you. I mentor a few people and, honestly, it seems God grows me through those relationships as much as them. But I ask them to really, really want what God has for them. Lean in! If I'm going to mentor someone, I say, "It's incumbent upon you to call me, set up mentoring appointments. I will not chase you down." In essence, they have to want it for themselves more than I want it for them.

Back to some thoughts about why Jesus chose Peter, James, and John to mentor, and not the other disciples. As I stated in Milestone 2.6, the basics requirements of mentoring someone are they need to be F.A.T. I want FAT people—Faithful, Available, and Teachable. I'm sure Peter, James, and John all consistently displayed those attributes. I have seen and interacted with many people who are both Faithful and Teachable, however they are not Available. Most often it's a stage of life they are in or the job they hold. It's just part of the deal. I get it. No fault or shame on their part. That said, as I think about Peter, James and John, we know they were fishermen. And fisherman generally fished early in the morning and sometimes all night. That seems to mean they likely were more available during the day. Matthew, one of Jesus' disciples, was likely not quite as available as Peter, James, and John, because he had to man the tax booth all day. Some of the others were shepherds and it would have been more difficult for Jesus to chase them all over the hills. These are not facts, but some thoughts on why I believe Jesus mentored these three fishermen. Availability is key!

A number of years back I connected with a F.A.T. guy named Armando in our congregation and began to mentor him. He was a great protégé. He did everything I asked of him and was always hungry for more. I had seen him grow enormously over the course of just a few years. And then the Lord showed me something amazing. I was at his house for a Thanksgiving gathering. He and his wife, Rosie, invited 30 or so people from our church for dinner. Two-thirds were Hispanic. Everyone sat down to eat. Armando passed out a preprinted Thanksgiving table prayer and began to lead them all in a Thanksgiving devotion. As all eyes were locked on Armando, leaning into every word he uttered. Suddenly, I have a Holy Spirit "a-ha! moment." I think, *Even though I'm all these people's senior pastor, I'm not their pastor, Armando is!* And it wasn't long after that that we sent Armando out to plant a church to reach the Hispanic population. And he's amazing!

A mentor's role is to discern where and in whom the Holy Spirit is working and go there, alongside the Holy Spirit, and help to foster growth in an individual. That's what we did with Armando. If it's just me, plus 100, that's addition. But if it's me and Armando x 100, now it's multiplication. I challenge those I mentor with books to read—specifically scripture, journaling, praying and even marital fidelity and parenting. It's all spiritual, really.

**The Following are some guidelines for the Mentoring relationship:**

- Make the mentoring meeting a TOP PRIORITY IN YOUR LIFE! Set up a standard meeting time. For example, Tuesdays at 7 am at the local coffee shop. Make the mentoring meeting about an hour.
- Make sure it's a good fit—try it for a few weeks to a month and see if it works. The more natural the relationship the better. Mentoring or being mentored by

someone in your small group or serving area may be best. Do NOT be offended or hurt if it doesn't work out.

- Have a plan for when you meet and KEEP IT SIMPLE! Use the GROW survey tool in Appendix A every quarter or so to assess spiritual growth in your protégé. Reading Scripture using the SOAP method in the appendix is a very good plan. Find a Bible-in-a-year plan for your protégé or less imposing is to read through the New Testament in a year and stick with it – see Appendix C.
- Read a prescribed chapter of scripture (prescribed by the reading plan or mentor).
- SOAP journal on a verse of that chapter prior to or even during the mentoring meeting. Note: If you are SOAPing daily you should have plenty to discuss.
- You are not the Guru! Jesus is! If issues come up—seek God's wisdom in his Word to answer those issues— don't be the answer man/woman!
- Mentors should point protégés into scripture to dig for God's answers. While other books can be helpful, it is strongly suggested to avoid other books for this process—use the Bible. This will enable people to learn how to fish and feed themselves. Other books, even GROW, are milk; only the Bible is solid food and provides the best nutrients for spiritual growth.
- As you use the GROW Survey as a guideline for spiritual growth, if you or your protégé are scoring low on a particular statement—go to the Bible verse referenced by that statement. Read the verse(s) and the context that verse is in and SOAP on a verse in your reading that seems to resonate. I believe the Holy Spirit will provide the answers and the power to overcome any roadblocks.
- The mentor relationship should not be a therapy session. Unless you are a licensed and trained counselor, DO NOT say or make reference that you're providing counseling. Although certainly as the Holy Spirit works, your

time with your protégé can be therapeutic, but more than that, it will be transformational—Romans 12:2.

- Mentors should be faithfully tithing and solidly in Milestone 2 and growing in Milestone 3.
- Mentors should be in scripture daily, praying, feeding themselves. You cannot give what you don't have.
- Men mentor men and women mentor women. I once had a male parishioner who brought his female 'protégé' to our first service on Sunday morning and his wife to the second service. It was a train wreck. Never mentor one-on-one a person of the opposite sex, unless it's your spouse, child or very close relative of some sort.
- The protégé should want it more than the mentor wants it for him or her. I never chase protégés down and I make it their responsibility to chase me down. Recently my son, Willie asked me to mentor him—I was shocked. But I said, "Two conditions. First, we set a time every week and you make sure you make it. It's up to you to chase me down, I'm not going to chase you down." He said, "Okay, Dad." "Then," I said, "Second—and this is harder—you do what I say." It's been amazing. I have seen him grow exponentially in the Lord!
- Last but not least—those seeking to mentor, please read *The Divine Mentor* by Wayne Cordiero—it's the best book on mentoring I've ever read and it's simple! Embrace what Wayne offers, you will be richly blessed by it.

How you doing here? Are you a good mentor? Are you ready to mentor someone? Pray and ask God to show you someone or bring someone to you if you aren't yet mentoring someone. Remember, this is the stuff of Jesus! This was and is key to his plan of making disciples. Score yourself now.

## 3.2–Mentor Others

I regularly mentor others. I'm a mature follower of Jesus Christ and want to give away what God has given me to help others to also become committed, mature followers of Christ.

| WEAK | 1 | 2 | 3 | 4 | 5 | STRONG |

**Memory verse: Hebrews 5:12a (NLT)** *"You have been believers so long now that you ought to be teaching others. Instead, you need someone to teach you again the basic things about God's Word."*

### Questions for Further Reflection and Discussion

1. Consider the ripple effect. What do you envision your ripple effect will be?

2. Think about F.A.T. Faithful, Available, Teachable. How available are you to mentor someone else?

3. Read Deuteronomy 6:4-7. This is all about modeling and mentoring. How are you obeying these verses?

4. Look at and reflect on or discuss the guidelines for the mentoring relationship. Discuss them if you are in a group.

## 3.3 Be On Mission

A few years ago, I led a team to Ishaka, Uganda to launch a new church. It was an amazing trip. God provided a new building through some generous donors and our individual team's fundraising efforts prior to going. Hundreds of locals came to participate in the very first church service. Many came to Christ. The indigenous pastor, Sam and his wife, Prossy, were overwhelmed by the presence of God and how he sent Mzungus (white people, typically of European descent) to help them achieve their dreams. As a missions team leader I was so grateful. The mission had been an overwhelming success. Now, feeling a very good sense of tired, it was time to get a good night's sleep and head back to the USA to be reunited with our loved ones and first stop, Five Guys Burgers and Fries for an American cheeseburger. The mission was basically over and I couldn't wait to get home.

The next morning, we were just finishing breakfast, longing for home and wrapping up some loose ends. We still had a few books and Bibles left over, so some team members brought them out to the table where I was having breakfast. Just then a rather large Ugandan man, I came to know as Sheeba, and a younger woman happened into the inn to have breakfast. Somehow, we engaged in conversation and he asked me "What are you doing here in Ishaka and what are all those books?" I briefly shared about the Bibles and the books and why we were here, not thinking too much about it. He asked, "Can I have a book and a Bible?" I smiled, "Absolutely!" Then he asked, "Why do you do this?" I told him I used to be a party animal and a business man and how Christ changed my life, in some detail. With that he proclaims, "That's what I am too, a business man and a party animal!" We engaged in an amazing conversation about how tiring partying is and how it gets so old. How there just has to be more to life. Then what he said blew me away, "This is so strange, I had a dream last night a Mzungu was going to give me a Bible and tell me my story. I was not going to come to this place today, but my appointment at another place canceled on me." At that, Sheeba allowed me to share the gospel message with him and he confessed his sinfulness and prayed to put his faith in Christ.

Before Sheeba showed up, I thought the mission was basically over. What that taught me is God doesn't simply want us to *go* on a mission trip, he want us to constantly be on mission. I should have known. When Jesus gave the great commission saying *"Go make disciples of all nations,"* we most often translate that word *"Go"* as *"Go"*. Seems pretty simple, but that word *"Go"* in the original language is an imperative participle. As I learned in one of my New Testament Greek classes, it is probably better to translate it *"As you are going make disciples . . ."* or *"Conduct one's life making disciples . . ."*. In other words, don't just go on a mission, live your life on Mission for Jesus." I believe Jesus also strongly commands we gotta get up off our rear-ends and *"Go"* too.

At this point in our spiritual journey we should have a strong sense that everything we have and are is God's. While the Apostle Paul was heading home to Jerusalem from his third mission trip, he really got it, saying, *"But my life is worth nothing to me unless I use it for finishing the work assigned me by the Lord Jesus—the work of telling others the Good News about the wonderful grace of God"* (Acts 20:24 NLT). And he knew that *"jail and suffering lie ahead"* (Acts 20:23b NLT) Paul lived his life on mission, no matter what. So should we.

Jesus said to his disciples, *"You will receive power when the Holy Spirit comes on you and you will be witnesses in Jerusalem, and in all Judea and Samaria, and to the ends of the Earth"* (Act 1:8 NIV). I could do a whole message on this one verse, but in effect Jesus was saying, "Wherever you are, it's not about you anymore, it's all about me. Be on mission for me from now on."

The following are three ways you and I can be on mission. There are probably more, but here's what the Lord put on my heart.

**Own the Mission:**

This is where what you do vocationally or outside your local church individually is on mission for Jesus. My wife, Ann is an artist. Her primary medium is clay. She loves to create ceramic wall sculptures that depict and interpret a Bible story or truth. One of my favorites is her "I AM" piece. That's what God told Moses his name was when he appeared at the burning bush. As you look at the sculpture, you see the words "I AM AM I", written in gold lettering across the top. The "AM I" basically asks the viewer a question from God. "AM I *your* I AM"? I love that.

He certainly is for Ann. Apart from making art, she teaches fine art to all ages—from basic drawing to oil painting, wheel throwing and sculpture. She has her own art studio across the street from our house where she takes students in to "Discover The Artist In You." Many kids she teaches are seeking to grow in their creative expression. She knows this comes from their

Creator whether they know him or not; "In the beginning God created." Some students who come through the doors aren't very sports active and are simply trying to fit in somewhere. She often will describe some with obvious low self-esteem as having "broken wings". She recognizes them because she herself had great emotional pain and struggled with low self-esteem when she was a young teen. At times she will come home from her studio beaming saying, "God brought another bird with a broken wing to me today!" So excited God would entrust her with these precious little souls. And it's amazing how with all those "broken wings", over the course of a few months, their whole demeanor changes and their self-esteem begins to soar as she engages the creativity that lies within them. Some end up coming to our youth group or children's ministry. A few high school students have advanced so much they are art interns for her in her studio, beginning to minister to the younger artists, sharing their own personal creativity and encouragement with the next generation. That's owning the mission! Ever since I've known Ann, she's loved art and has loved on teens. Henry Nouwen wrote a book called "The Wounded Healer." When The Lord heals us from our deepest wounds, God uses us and our experiences as our greatest primary mission to heal others. We become the wounded healer. Ann's mother was an artist. But her mother exited her family when Ann was a teenager. It's no coincidence this is the mission God has given Ann. He redeems everything, even our deepest wounds. She joyfully looks forward to supporting Vietnam Church Planting and EPIC Global Missions church planting with her profits, investing seeds and sending ripples out beyond her little 450 square foot studio.

Melva is a widow and has lamented to me that she really doesn't serve anywhere in the church on Sundays, as she has her aging mother to care for and brings her along to when possible. Melva is remarkable, and has owned the mission for many years. While retired, currently she serves the elderly at a local assisted living center. One day I was out to lunch and happened to notice the name tag of the director of that center. So, I engaged in conversation exchanging pleasantries, then asked, "You must know Melva?" "Yes," she beamed! "How do you know Melva?" she asked. "I'm her pastor." Then she started telling me how amazing Melva was and how her presence brings such joy to the center. I love that! I recently spoke with Melva and she shared with me, "Every morning I wake up and ask God what he wants me to do today." Can you imagine? That's owning the mission! I told Melva, "I know you want to figure out a place to serve at the church on Sunday morning, but Melva, you are the church when you go serve at that center." She brings them worship, a hand of friendship and a heartwarming smile.

Andrea and Kaleo moved to Maui a few years ago so Kaleo could be a principal at a school there. Andrea was my assistant for many years and I almost thought it was sin that they'd move away, especially to Hawaii. However, since showing up, their presence is changing the spiritual culture of that school. They are on mission.

I could speak of Tim, a local principal who attends our church and serves in the youth ministry, but his primary mission is to be light in the public school arena. I could share how Bob has served faithfully in our children's ministry for over fifteen years, but his day job mission is to provide Godly financial advice to many people who need guidance dealing with their personal finances. On mission? Absolutely! Sometimes we get confused. Yes, I want to teach young believers it's important to learn your spiritual gifts and serve in the church as I stated in Milestone 1.3, but that's simply the training ground. One of my favorite Bible verses is Colossians 3:23, "*Whatever you do, do your work heartily as for the Lord rather than men.*" Whether you're a teacher, salesperson, barista, lawyer, truck driver—whatever, do your work for God first and, like Melva, ask him how he can use you each day. Own the mission!

**Support Missions**

As a guy who has gone on a lot of mission trips and leads a small mission organization called EPIC Global Missions, I know one thing for sure, to do mission trips effectively, they take all sorts of support. Just like a local church is a body that needs to work together to achieve its full redemptive potential, missions need people at home keeping things together as well as team members out in the field. I couldn't operate our missions' organization without Andrea, my now Hawaii based, administrator (she can move away but she can never leave!). Our finances would tank without Lorie, our servant missions bookkeeper. I have a board advisor who is a voice of calm and wisdom. Every one of these people are 100 percent volunteer servants, and they do their part joyfully to advance the kingdom of God.

One key area of support is supporting missions financially. Again, this is so huge. Many people cannot go out on a mission trip for various reasons, but they can support missions financially. Currently, a team member who goes on our two week Africa mission trip needs to raise $4300. That's a lot of money for a college student, a retiree or a single mom. It's a lot of money for just about anyone. I'm convinced God wants his people to go on mission trips as stated in Milestone 2.3, so I say, "Where God guides, God provides." He always does. I'm amazed at the generosity of donors to our team members. Their financial support for that individual not only helps to pay for the trip, but those missions supporters are playing a huge role in helping individual team members grow in their faith. I can't tell you how encouraging it is for team members to see their mission monetary goal being reached. Through financial supporters, they see the hand of God on their lives.

In addition to team members raising individual support to pay for their airlines tickets, on the ground travel, food and lodging, every time we plant a church in Africa it costs us around $25,000 to $30,000, including leasing the land for a year, building a "temporary" building, buying a sound system and generators and other necessary miscellaneous expenses. That's the dollar amount I need to raise. It's actually pretty cheap to start a church in Uganda compared to starting one in the states, but it's still stresses me out at times. That's where key supporters who live life on mission come in. They get it. During any one mission trip to Africa we often share the Good News at 15 to 20 different schools, a few hospitals, a prison and many businesses and homes. On average, over a two-week period, around 4000 individuals hear the gospel message—and it's not uncommon for about 1000 people to put their faith in Jesus for the first time. Do the math: A brand new church for $30,000. Say, 10 team members going to Africa for $4300 each. Let's round up—that's $75,000 total. And so far, every one of the churches we have planted is not just surviving, they're thriving! Who wouldn't want to invest in that?

If you're a small church or part of a small church, say even around 100 people, you can still have a global impact for Christ. For many years, we were a church of 130 to 300 people on Sundays. We supported my good friend, Pastor Cam Tu Le, who raises up young pastors and plants churches in Vietnam. To date, we have helped him plant around twenty-five churches there, where over 3000 worship on Sunday morning, the majority new to the faith. Why do we do that? As a church, we are on mission!

**Lead a Mission Trip**

Sometimes I wonder about people. I actually think at times they must be nuts. One such time was six months after I went on my first mission trip, my church in Seattle asked me to lead a mission trip back to the jungles of Costa Rica. I was engaged to be married to Ann at the time. So, after I naively said yes to our church leaders, I asked Ann if she would help me lead the trip. Now, I know, if you're a pastor, if you like this book and want to give it to some young singles folks to read, go ahead and rip out this page first. It's okay. But, we had great boundaries and no hanky-panky—so chill out! Even crazier than me accepting the challenge to lead, Ann not only said "yes" to marrying me, she said "yes" to helping me lead the trip. What's ludicrous is we both had no clue what we were doing. We did listen intently to what our pastors told us and totally trusted God. Well, everyone came back alive. Ironically, that's what I tell all my teams now, "The primary mission of NASA moon launches was not to get to the moon; it was to get the astronauts back to earth alive. Our primary goal for this short-term mission trip to get everyone back alive!" Really, God normally shows up and directs all the plans and everything else, but like I said in 2.3, people who go are never the same. Neither are the leaders.

Not everyone is called to lead a mission trip. However, I do believe we ought to give more opportunities for people with the gift of leadership to exercise it on a mission trip. I could never have guessed how it radically changed my life when my church leaders trusted me to lead back then. Without their trust, I doubt I would have become a leader or pastor. I doubt I'd be so sold out to missions. Literally tens of thousands have been touched with the gospel just with the missions I've been part of. It's multiplying Christ-followers globally and it's really about being on mission! Imagine what would happen if every church took the risk to let young people lead. Yeah, it would be messy. Church just is, but it would not only be good, it would be great!

At Milestone 3.3 we are increasingly not simply doing the mission, but are on mission. It's not what we do, it's who we are. When I wake up in the morning, like Melva I pray, "Use me today, Lord."

What do you think? Ready to be on mission as a lifestyle? Read the statement below and score yourself.

### 3.3–Be On Mission

I am on mission. My vocation is my mission and/or I also support or lead missions. I have a passion to multiply Christ-followers both locally and globally.

| WEAK | 1 | 2 | 3 | 4 | 5 | STRONG |

**Memory Verse: Acts 20:24 (NLT)** *"But my life is worth nothing to me unless I use it for finishing the work assigned me by the Lord Jesus—the work of telling others the Good News about the wonderful grace of God."*

## Questions for Further Reflection and Discussion

1. Reflect on or discuss the difference between going on a mission trip versus being on mission.

2. Consider the translations of Matthew 28:19a—"Go make disciples" and "As you are going make disciples" and "Conduct one's life making disciples."

3. How can you "own the mission" in your current station in life, be it in a job, at home, or as a student?

4. How can you support missions?

5. Do you feel you could lead a mission trip? Why? Why not? What might people who know you think?

6. What dreams to you have to live your life on mission?

# 3.4 Kingdom Giving

H ave you ever won the lottery? Me neither, but I know how it feels. Pretty cool! It was the summer right before we started Sunday church services in our new church plant. We just had a major outreach to the community and had about $84.42 left in our church bank account. All I could think was wow, we really connected with the community. If we're going to die before we even start, it's a good way to go.

A few days later there I was sitting in a gathering of fellow pastors and my cell buzzed. It was my associate pastor Jerry, "Brad, guess what?" "I give up." "We just got a check for $50,000 in the mail." "$15,000?" I whisper. "No, FIFTY thousand dollars." "Are you kidding me?" trying to keep my composure. "Brad, are you sitting down?" "Why?" I ask. "We got another check for "$50,000!" "No way!" "Yep!" "Take a picture of those checks and get them in the bank right away" I emphatically proclaimed. "Okay." "Hallelujah!" It was an old small group buddy of mine. I called him up, "Jeff, what prompted you to give us such an incredible donation?" He found out I was planting a church and said in his very unemotional monotone Jeff-speak, "God told me to send you $100,000, so I did." That's it. I'm so glad Jeff obeyed the voice of the Lord, because that was seed money to help get our church off the ground years ago, without which, it never would have happened. Many, many people have found Jesus through that church and many, many people have grown and become fully devoted followers of Jesus through that church. That extravagant donation advanced the Kingdom of God far beyond what anyone could have conceived back when we received it. It's helped to transform many people's lives over the years. There's a ripple effect!

In Luke's gospel, Jesus tells a parable of ten minas. One mina was considered three months' wages. It was really all about making investments to advance the kingdom of God, to save more lives. As always, the context is important. Zacchaeus, a short, despised tax collector hears the commotion of a crowd around Jesus and climbs a tree, looking for Jesus to approach. Jesus sees him up in the tree and says, Zaccheaus let's go catch up at your house. Well, Jesus gets flak from the people for connecting with Zac and they begin to mutter, *"He has gone to be the guest of a sinner"* (Luke 19:7 NIV). That day spent with Jesus caused Zacchaeus to have an extreme soul makeover and he tells Jesus, I'm going to make restitution–says he'll give half his possessions to the poor and if he's cheated anyone he'll pay back four times the amount. Can you believe that? Zac virtually instantaneously becomes a Kingdom Giver. Putting your money where your faith is really is where the rubber really hits the road. Then *"Jesus said to Zacchaeus, 'Today salvation has come to this house, because this man, too, is a son of Abraham. For the Son of Man came to seek and to save what was lost"* (Luke 19:9-10 NIV). A son of Abraham would mean in no uncertain terms that Zacchaeus exercised extreme faith, because it was by faith that Abraham became the father of the Hebrews. I imagine at that point Zacchaeus might have even funded a brand new local synagogue. That's the context for Jesus' parable that follows:

> "*While they were listening to this, he went on to tell them a parable, because he was near Jerusalem and the people thought that the kingdom of God was going to appear at once. He said: "A man of noble birth went to a distant country to have himself appointed king and then to return. So he called ten of his servants and gave them ten minas. 'Put this money to work,' he said, 'until I come back'* (Luke 19:12–13 NIV).

That last line, "Put this money to work... until I come back" is a command, not a request. Question: Whose money was it? It was the nobleman's money. All of it. It wasn't theirs; it was his. This is the first principle Kingdom giving. It's a bit of review from Milestones 1.4 and 2.4.

## Everything We Have Is God's

Everything we have—including the air we breathe—it's all from God. This is a tough thing to understand, until you do. Did you come into the world fully clothed? Were you born with rings, tattoos, and an iPhone? Did you have the keys to a Mercedes or a house on your toe in the womb? Even if all that was given to you or accumulated by you over time, know this: everything we have comes from the natural resources God put on this earth. Houses are from trees and rock, copper, sand, rivers and streams, etc. The same with your food and clothes. It all came to you indirectly from the hand of God. It's all his.

Often people think, "I'm not gonna give to no church— all they want is my money." Problem with that statement is one word—MY—if you think it's all yours, you're not ready to use it to go advance God's Kingdom. Sometimes it's spiritual immaturity or simply a learning issue, but sometimes, like the people in Jesus' parable, it's a bad attitude—they didn't want that nobleman to be king. Maybe they didn't like his views on money. Here's a truth: What we think about money and who's it is says a lot about what we think about God. Regardless of what the people desired, that nobleman was made king and came home. Then *"He sent for the servants to whom he had given the money, in order to find out what they had gained with it."* (Luke 19:15 NIV)

Just like the nobleman who went away and became king, Jesus was made King of all heaven and earth when he died and rose again from the dead. And even though he resides at the right hand of God the Father right now, he's coming back as King someday. But while he's gone, he's given us resources, and Ahe wants us to invest and take risks to advance his Kingdom, for which we will be held accountable. So, here's the second principle of Kingdom giving:

### God Want Us to Take Risks to Advance His Kingdom

As the king called his servant in, "The first one came and said, 'Sir, your mina has earned ten more'" (Luke 19:16 NIV). That guy took a risk. He made 10 times what was given to him! I love that! Faith is spelled R-I-S-K.

I love that that our church is full of Kingdom givers who take risks and give to people and missions all over the world. One ministry is Vietnam Church Planting. Back around fifteen years ago, as a small church, we began giving $150 a month and really believed in Pastor Cam Tu Le's vision for raising up young Vietnamese pastors and supporting them. It takes $50 a month to support a pastor in Vietnam. That's a pretty good bang for the buck. In 2008, when the economy in the US tanked, a number of churches decided to opt out. We prayed and decided to take a greater risk and upped our ante to $500 a month. That year, a new church was birthed in Vietnam because of our giving. That one church has since birthed ten more churches. As of today, we have helped to launch some 25 churches in Vietnam. I just a received our year-end statement from Pastor Cam. He wrote,

"Thanks for your generosity! Our church planting ministry in Vietnam has brought thousands of new souls to God's salvation in the past year. Praise the Lord!" I do too! What a privilege!

At our multisite church, we are heavily involved in starting indigenous-led churches in Africa (where we've started six new churches in four years) and as I stated in the previous chapter, we take teams there to launch those churches. Tens of thousands have heard the gospel, and close to 5000 have put their faith in Jesus, just in the past five years. In India, just last year we contributed $50,000 to create a safe house for women freed from human trafficking. Last year, in Turkey we also contributed close to $50,000 for a Christian prayer house, in the midst of a Muslim stronghold. Over the past five years we've contributed around one million dollars in Cambodia for church buildings and safe houses. All in addition to supporting many missionaries around the globe. We have a yearly fundraising program called Kingdom Builders to advance God's Kingdom locally and globally. Whether it's $20 or $20,000 or somewhere in-between, every cent of that comes from faithful Kingdom givers in our church who are giving above and beyond the tithe and are advancing the Kingdom of God.

I get pretty excited about the generous givers in our church. Honestly, I believe it should be the norm for all Christ-followers. You know what I want to hear and what I want all of us to hear when we stand before God and give an account? The same thing that the first servant in Jesus' parable heard:

> "'*Well done, my good servant!' his master replied. 'Because you have been trustworthy in a very small matter, take charge of ten cities.'*" The next servant got similar treatment from the king: "*The second came and said, 'Sir, your mina has earned five more.'*

*"His master answered, 'You take charge of five cities.'"* (Luke 19:17-19 NIV)

God promises us such blessing if we believe him when it comes to Kingdom giving. Jesus said *"Give, and it will be given to you. A good measure, pressed down, shaken together, and running over, will be poured into your lap. For with the measure you use, it will be measured to you"* (Luke 6:38 NIV).

The faithful servants in the parable had that happen. The first servant turned one mina into ten. Then he's rewarded ten cities! The next guy turns one mina into five. He gets five cities! Not a bad deal. Wow! That's running over. Why? With God there is a huge FAITH risk/reward factor. It needs to be said again, I'm not a health and wealth prosperity gospel guy. I'm not. But I've seen God do some crazy things.

My friend Bob, decided he's was just going to be an extravagant Kingdom giver all the time. He's started giving 15 percent of his income regularly. That's 5 percent above and beyond the tithe. Well, the way he gets paid is a bit different than normal in his industry. So, he based his giving on what he made the previous year. Toward the end of his 15 percent giving year experiment, he added his income up and low and behold, his income increased close to 50 percent, so he ended up "only" giving 10 percent of his income after all. He was amazed! You cannot out give God!

My wife and I led a building campaign for our church years ago. We were really excited and wanted to show a little faith so we decide to go out on a limb and pledge $5000. Prior to our actual pledge night, we took off and spent some time alone, reading and praying. God spoke to both of us and it was very clear that our pledge was way too low. I'm normally the guy who wants to give it all away; my wife is normally the practical one when it comes to giving. We prayed. Then she comes to me, "Brad, we need to change our pledge." "Yeah, Ann, I know. What are you thinking?" I asked her. She says, "$18,000." I say,

"Yep, that's exactly what I'm thinking." And we just laughed thinking that is totally hilarious. How could we ever afford to give that much? I love it that *"God loves a cheerful giver"* (2 Cor. 9:7b NIV). That word "cheerful" in the original Greek language is the word *hilaros*. We get the word *hilarious* from the word. Our giving should be hilarious when it comes to advancing the Kingdom of God. *"The point is this"* Paul said, *"whoever sows sparingly will also reap sparingly, and whoever sows bountifully will also reap bountifully. Each one must give as he has decided in his heart, not reluctantly or under compulsion, for God loves a cheerful [hilarious] giver"* (2 Cor. 9:6-7 ESV).

We sold the home that tree was leaning on and downsized to a townhouse a few blocks away. Shortly after we paid our pledge, my artist wife had her eye on an old 500 SF 1901 vintage house in Old Town, where she dreamed of having her art studio. The home we sold had her studio in a little room off the garage. Our new townhouse had no room for studio space. She came home one night in a panic, "Brad, Brad, the lady moved out of that old house!" I said, "Is there a For Sale sign on it?" "No!" she gasps. "Well, write a note and stick it on the door telling whoever owns it we are interested in buying it." I had checked comps and knew that another lot of the same size in Old Town went for about $150,000. I told Ann, "I'd be willing to give them that." The owners call. They want to sell. Ann and I go meet them. We look around. There is not much to see or inspect; it's only 500 square feet, after all. I ask them, "How much do you want for it?" The owner replies, "We were thinking $90,000." I quickly retort, "That'll do!" And that's what it was. It's like God just handed us $60,000. And I don't think it's a coincidence. I call that a "woo-woo" God moment. It's freaky in a good way. I've just seen and heard too many stories like that. We don't ever give to get. We give to obey and advance the Kingdom of God.

Now, not everyone gets Kingdom giving like those first two servants or Bob or perhaps you. The parable continues:

*"Then another servant came and said, 'Sir, here is your mina; I have kept it laid away in a piece of cloth. I was afraid of you, because you are a hard man. You take out what you did not put in and reap what you did not sow'"* (Luke 19:20—21 NIV). Underline that word: *afraid.* That third servant chose fear over faith and it really messed up his whole perspective on God, which leads to the last principle of Kingdom giving:

### Chose Faith over Fear

Not fear over faith. Remember, there were ten servants given a mina in this parable, but we only hear from three. We don't hear a word about what the other seven did with their mina. What's with that? Well, maybe that's us. Maybe we are the intended audience. Maybe Jesus is asking us, "Who are you gonna be?" Are you going to be like one of the first two servants who took some risks to advance the God's Kingdom? Or, are you going to be the third servant, overcome by fear? Remember Milestone 2.5 Grow Up—Emotionally. Remember, Cain and how he was emotionally toxic. He was emotionally immature, therefore spiritually immature. The same thing is going on in this parable. "I was afraid" the third servant says. And his fear caused him to create a misguided list to justify his fear as follows: 1. You're a hard man. 2. You take what's not yours. 3. You reap where you do not sow. And, we might add: 4. I don't give to organized religion. 5. All the church wants is your money. 6. Why would I want to invest in foreign people who I will never see? We need to be putting it here. 7. All the church ever talks about is money. On and on. Ever heard or said anything like that? They are all based in fear. I know of very few—if any—churches who simply want your money. I don't know of any churches that talk only about money. Generally, a church may talk about money three to four times a year maximum. If you come to church only that many times a year, two things may be operative. First, maybe you need to hear and heed those messages. Second, you probably ought to show up for church more often.

If you're not ready yet to become a Kingdom giver, that's okay. You may still be at Milestone 1 or even Milestone 2. Just don't buy into fear-based lists.

If you're making excuses for not being a Kingdom giver, be very careful. Don't ever dissuade someone else from Kingdom giving because of your attitude. You will be missing the blessing yourself and robbing someone else of the blessing. Honestly, a healthy fear of the Lord is important in the matter of Kingdom giving. Look what the master says to the third servant in the parable:

> *"His master replied, 'I will judge you by your own words, you wicked servant! You knew, did you, that I am a hard man, taking out what I did not put in, and reaping what I did not sow? Why then didn't you put my money on deposit, so that when I came back, I could have collected it with interest?' Then he said to those standing by, 'Take his mina away from him and give it to the one who has ten minas'"* (Luke 19: 22–24 NIV).

Jesus makes no bones about it; there are no excuses or lists that justify us not investing in his Kingdom. And it may really mess with us when we see what the King does with those who don't invest. It did with those in the parable when the king took away the mina from the third servant who didn't invest and gave it to the first servant who had ten.

> *"'Sir,' they said, 'he already has ten!' He replied, 'I tell you that to everyone who has, more will be given, but as for the one who has nothing, even what they have will be taken away"* (Luke 19:25-26 NIV).

Why would the king take away the one mina from the third servant and give it to the one who had 10? Because God really desires to save as many people as possible and he wants to flow his resources through people who are willing to take risks to advance his kingdom.

If your church is having a capital campaign, know that most pastors so want to advance God's Kingdom and know it's absolutely necessary to raise money to do so. Also know, most pastors don't ever want to be perceived as "always talking about money." However, someone has to lead the charge and someone has to talk about it and he should be applauded by stepping out in faith and taking a risk to advance the Kingdom of God through your church. Be a blessing to your pastor and let him know right away, you are on board. Tell him, you want to take some risks and be a Kingdom giver. That will be such a huge blessing to your pastor, and you will be blessed as a result.

There are many ways to be a Kingdom giver; supporting a Compassion child, contributing to drill a well in Africa, supporting missions teams and church plants locally and globally. I love initiatives that help the poor of the world. It seems God has a bent toward the poor. *"If you help the poor, you are lending to the Lord—and he will repay you!"* (Proverbs 19:17 NLT).

Matt and Tammy are teaching the values being Kingdom givers to their young children. Their twelve-year-old Katie desired to fund the building of a Compassion house in Uganda for orphans at the cost of $24,000. She willingly asked people not to give her birthday gifts so they might give to her project. Amazingly, when people found out about it, people gave generously and she accomplished her goal. Now her little brother is getting in on the act and raising money for another Compassion house. What a great example of giving up materialism for the purposes of loving the poor.

In the book of Acts, a number of people in the first church were extravagant Kingdom givers. Right after a great outpouring of the Holy Spirit ignited the early church, Luke writes, *"They sold property and possessions to give to anyone who had a need"* (Acts 2:45 NIV) The first church understood Loving God meant Loving People. To the first church, people were more important than possessions so much so they even sold their land! They desired to start building God's Kingdom and stop building their own.

God himself is an extravagant giver. He loved the world, that's you and me, so much, he gave his one and only son (John 3:16). Think about that one. One thing I'm sure of is that no one you and I know would be willing to give up their child. No one. But God did. The first church got this, which is why they were able to sell their property and give to anyone who had a need. Perhaps they actually saw Jesus hanging from the cross and God's love and passion became so real to them. They finally realized the worth God put on the souls of human beings, their souls, that everything else paled in comparison. Their property, their possessions, became totally secondary—just a bargaining chip for real lives and souls.

Reminds me of the movie *Schindler's List*, a true story of businessman, Oscar Schindler, in Nazi Germany. Oscar Schindler was a self-absorbed factory owner who was contracted by the Nazi regime to make pots and pans for the Army of the Third Reich. He employed mostly Jews in his factory, which increasingly came under Nazi scrutiny. As Schindler began to see the inhumane treatment of the Jews, it's like God got ahold of his heart, which enabled him to become a shrewd advocate for the Jewish people. At times, Schindler would bribe Nazi officers in order to keep Jews under his employ and out of concentration camps. Suddenly, his money was being used for a far greater purpose than self-indulgence and building his own empire. At the end of the movie, the war is over and Schindler must flee his factory and the Jews he has grown to love, because he is in danger of being tried as a Nazi war criminal. In the most poignant scene in the movie, the Jews he helped gather around him and give him a ring as a token of their gratitude for saving so many lives. On the ring is a Hebrew word that means, "Whoever saves one life, saves the world entire." Oscar breaks down emotionally, and says, trembling, "I could have got more out." And he begins to look at the material possessions he still has, "This car could have saved ten people... This lapel pin could have saved two, at least one." In that moment, he realized what was most important—people, not possessions! He actually fell in love with the very people he once just saw as slaves to help him to fulfill his self-centered lifestyle. His life was radically transformed.

Jesus is pretty clear; he wants people taking risks to advance his Kingdom, and to redeem as many as possible. Are you ready to be or become a Kingdom giver? Are you one already? Read the following statements and score where you land.

### 3.4–Kingdom Giving

I am a cheerful giver. I regularly and gladly give above and beyond the tithe, because I understand God was so extravagant when he gave his Son for me. Therefore, I am passionate about expanding God's Kingdom through Kingdom giving to redeem as many souls as possible.

WEAK    1    2    3    4    5    STRONG

**Memory verse: Acts 2:45 (NIV)** *"They sold property and possessions to give to anyone who had a need."*

# 3.5 Attaining Spiritual Maturity

Does your life ever feel like a drama? Do you ever get drained from it all? Ever known a person who is nothing but high maintenance and high drama? Is it you? Isn't it tiring? I imagine you just said "yes" to at least half of those questions. We live in a high drama, spiritually immature world. But here's the deal. Sometimes we think we're spiritually mature. We know the Bible, and we sing worship songs with all our heart. We even write clever spiritual posts on our social media pages, but we also create or are party to a lot of drama at home, at work, at school, and in our neighborhood. That simply means we're emotionally immature. Peter Scazarro points out this profound yet simple truth: "Emotional health and spiritual maturity are inseparable. It's not possible to be spiritually mature and while remaining emotionally immature." As I stated earlier, spiritual maturity and emotional maturity go hand in hand. So, how do we minimize the drama in our lives, shore-up the emotional drain, and truly become spiritually mature? Well, I'm glad you asked.

On Good Friday March 24, 1989, it was high drama up in Alaskan waters when the Exxon Valdez ran ashore and spilled 11 to 38 million gallons of crude oil into Prince Williams Sound. It was one of the worst man-made, preventable environmental disasters in history. Why did it happen? The captain was drunk and not even in the ships wheelhouse. Can you believe it? The third mate was in the wheelhouse, while the captain was in his bunk sleeping off a bender. Worse yet, the ships radar was broken. It was the perfect storm.

One thing I have learned over the years is to put the right things in my spiritual wheelhouse and keep the wrong things out. What's in your wheelhouse? I think this is at the heart of spiritual and emotional maturity. Here's my wheelhouse scripture:

*Lord, my heart is not proud;*
*my eyes are not haughty.*
*I don't concern myself with matters too great*
*or too awesome for me to grasp.*
*Instead, I have calmed and quieted myself,*
*like a weaned child who no longer cries for its mother's milk.*
*Yes, like a weaned child is my soul within me.*
Psalm 131:1 (NIV)

Often, I see people concern themselves with things that are simply none of their business. It's busybody stuff. And I know a busybody is not spiritually mature. My new phrase to my wife, to my kids, even to fellow pastors and my assistant when something comes up that I just can't do a thing about is, "I'm not going to put that in my wheelhouse."

"Brad, the state of Oregon now has a bisexual governor." What can I do about it? Not in my wheelhouse. "Brad, a person who left the church a year ago and is going to another church said some bad things about you and the church." Not in my wheelhouse, God bless them. "Brad, the President is not responding properly to terrorism!" Let's pray for him. Otherwise, I just can't fit it in my wheelhouse. "Brad, there's a church down the street that is doing a great job feeding the poor with their food pantry, can't we start one too?" Why? Let's support them. I only start new ministries that God brings a clear leader to lead. Otherwise, not in my wheelhouse. I could go on and on and on. So many things come our way that we simply just do not have to put in our wheelhouse. God has a handle on all those things, and has people way more qualified than me to deal with them.

Honestly, I really like to have a calm and quieted heart. The whole idea of being a weaned child in verse 2 is about being a spiritually and emotionally mature person. So, I just keep a lot of stuff that I have no control or influence over out of my wheelhouse.

We love drama. It sells news, movies, and often destroys politicians. It also drains. Here's something to consider: The following diagrams are how we can live our lives. The Drama is spiritually and emotionally immature. The Dance, on the other hand, is very mature!

There are three roles people place in the drama: The Victim, The Persecutor, and The Rescuer. The dance has three roles as well: The Father, The Son, and The Holy Spirit.

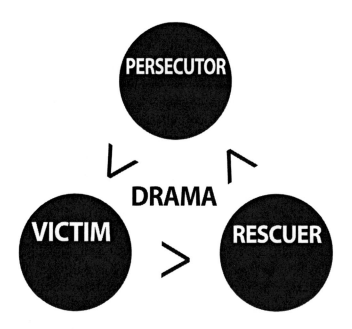

Adapted from Stephen Karpman 1968

Let's tackle The Drama first. We often grow up in homes filled with drama and we unwittingly and gladly play the roles. I had five brothers and a sister. My older brothers beat on me at times. What would I do? Well, I'm the victim. They were the persecutors and my mom was the rescuer. "Mom, Barry is beating on me!" I'd cry out. If she heard me, she'd come in and stop him—she'd rescue me. I had younger brothers too. So, guess what? I'd beat on them. Then I'd be the persecutor. And mom or one of my older brothers or my sister would be the rescuer. That's typical in most homes. Not a big deal. But it was drama! That's where we learn it. Generally, everyone plays a few roles.

Victims need to be rescued from persecutors. It makes for great movies. All of Marvel's superheroes play great rescuers. The whole earth is victimized by villains or persecutors from another planet and here comes Captain American or Ironman! Honestly, I love it in movies. However, when The Drama happens in our homes, our schools, our places of employment, in marriages, and even church, it's very painful and totally spiritually immature. And, get this, the devil is behind The Drama. He loves it. And he eggs us on to play some role, any role. It takes all three roles to keep the Drama spinning and draining us. The Drama is attached to our sinful nature, compliments of old red legs himself.

*"The acts of the sinful nature are obvious: sexual immorality, impurity and debauchery, idolatry and witchcraft; hatred, discord, jealousy, fits of rage, selfish ambition, dissensions, factions and envy; drunkenness, orgies, and the like"* (Gal. 5:19-21a NIV). Look at that list. It's all drama. I call that list *The Vice List.* Every one of those behaviors are spiritually immature and emotionally toxic, sinful behaviors. Which ones have you engaged in? Which ones have you seen others do? Which ones have been done to you? Drama! It's draining. The devil loves to wear us down emotionally so we will live a life of drama and sin. That kind of life is never a fruitful life. It's always sad and depressing.

Paul says, "The acts of the sinful nature are obvious." Obvious! Let's take sexual immorality. Question: Is pornography obviously sinful? Sure! It's from the pit of hell. Do you know why many men and now increasingly women engage in pornography? It's an attempt to fill an emotional void in their lives and a spiritual void in their soul. They go to the internet feeling a need, they click on a porn site and while they are on it, it seems to fill the void; but like eating pure sugar, it has no nutritional value. Then, after they log off, they just need and want more. Maybe they're feeling worthless; it will do that. Maybe they're feeling shame; it will do that too. Both are victim mentalities where life or someone else is the persecutor. They need a rescuer to save the day. So, come on porn or drugs or alcohol or whatever. It's really, really unhealthy. The devil knows it. He loves it. He's gotcha trapped, imprisoned. That's how all addictions work. We end up believing a lie. I'm pretty well convinced that every sin we commit has some sort of negative emotional connection. We create factions in churches to support our drama desires. We have fits of rage in an attempt to control people in our lives who aren't giving us what we want. Ever known someone who seemed to be angry all the time? Pretty draining! All I know is I want to take the entire vice-list completely out of my wheelhouse and keep it out. But, sometimes it's difficult. We get wrapped up in so many things.

A number of years ago, there was a couple who felt their son was being ignored by our youth pastor. He saw his son as the Victim and our youth pastor as the Persecutor. The husband wrote a nasty email to our youth pastor and cc'd me in the message. He was looking for me to be the Rescuer. "Okay. This has to be dealt with." I concluded. So, I called the husband and his wife into my office, along with our youth pastor. I told them their accusations were way off. Our youth pastor even helped their son become a vocalist on our youth worship team. We all loved their son and were trying to help him grow both spiritually and emotionally. I also told them never to send a toxic email like that again and I strongly suggested they ask our youth pastor for forgiveness. Suddenly, the roles shifted. They saw themselves as the Victims and me as the Persecutor. In fact, they began to gossip and create more drama in search of a Rescuer. They were even able to suck one of our key leaders into the Drama to serve as their Rescuer. It was a mess. A strong faction formed around that and some other issues. They left and it almost blew up the church. Do you think that's of God? No! It's obvious that it's all the sinful nature—*hatred, discord, jealousy, fits of rage, selfish ambition, dissensions, factions, envy, and the like!* It was all there. I've gone over that scenario countless times in my mind and heart. What could have I done different? Honestly, I still don't know. But I do know there is a way to live life free of the Drama. It's called The Dance.

Adapted from Katie Skurja

Ah, The Dance! God invites us into The Dance, with the Father, the Son, and the Holy Spirit who've been dancing together for eternity. We get into The Dance initially through his Son Jesus, who entered our drama as a human being not to be a simple rescuer, but to be our Savior. Paul describes The Dance like this: *"But the fruit of the Spirit is love, joy, peace, patience, kindness, goodness, faithfulness, gentleness and self-control"* (Gal. 5:22a). Look at that list from a spiritual and emotional perspective. That's spiritual maturity at its finest. That's all I want in my wheelhouse. These, of course, are commonly known as the fruits of the Spirit. I also call them *The Virtue List*. God has made us emotional beings and becoming spiritually mature enables our emotions to be felt and displayed in a healthy, mature way.

You want to become more loving? Want to be loved more? Sure! We all do. Joy anyone? More joy? Absolutely! Do you know what we do though? We let things into our wheelhouse all the time that rob our joy. Things like politics. Wow, there's a joy robber! Nothing but drama. We let emotionally toxic people rob our joy. It could be relatives, co-workers, or fellow students—they come in every way, shape, and form. It could be us!

As I look at that list of nine fruits of the spirit, yes, I want them all—we all should. God began to deposit them into my life when I first trusted Christ. About a month after I was saved, God took drunkenness completely out of my wheelhouse. I'm so grateful. Been 100 percent sober since. That right there removes a ton of drama from my life and allows me to dance with God so much more. As I assess how I have been able to maintain sobriety, there are lots of factors, new friends, AA meetings, and steering clear of slippery places like bars. One primary fruit of the Spirit seems to be most responsible: self-control. There it is all the way at the end of the virtue list. Self-control doesn't get a lot of attention and press from most Christians, but it is so key to spiritual and emotional maturity.

Back in my drinking days, I used to be a happy drunk. I prided myself on never getting angry. No one could do anything to bait me and I was proud of it. Just a few months sober, guess what? Suddenly, I was getting angry. Anger would just well up like never before. I'd even think, "Where did that come from, Brad?" Shortly thereafter, I came to understand the alcohol and drugs I had been taking for so long were simply anesthetizing the emotional pain that I'd been suppressing since childhood. When I did some course work, thinking I was going to go into addiction counseling, I also learned that when a person starts doing drugs or alcohol and becomes addicted, they pretty much stop growing emotionally, until they get sober. It's like that with a lot of other addictions and compulsive behaviors. Wow! So, there I was a twenty-nine-year-old man with the emotions of a twelve-year-old. And I was pissed! It would be great if I could say I got this whole anger thing handled right after that, but it's been a process. You just can't make up 17 years of emotional growth in one day.

Fast forward 30 years. A few years ago, I realized, yes, I've grown a ton in the area of anger management. Thank God! But every now and then, I'd still have a little blow up on my wife or on my kids. Not good. So, I got down on my knees and I asked the Holy Spirit to give me the fruit of the Spirit of self-control over my anger. He did it with alcohol and drugs and I believed he could do it with anger. Guess what. He did! That is not to say at times I don't get a little miffed. I do. And at times I've even had little slips with my wife—I hate that. But, in those moments the Lord will make me immediately aware and I'll go to her directly and ask for forgiveness. Her grace is amazing! I've come to realize I just can't do it on my own. I need God's help. Sometimes I need him to do it and I just need to cooperate. I needed him to replace my anger with peace, patience and kindness.

This is all about replacing a vice with a virtue and continue to grow spiritually. In Eastern religions one of their key spiritual disciplines is emptying one's self. Christ-followers don't do that. Here's why:

> *"When an evil spirit leaves a person, it goes into the desert, searching for rest. But when it finds none, it says, 'I will return to the person I came from.' So it returns and finds that its former home is all swept and in order. Then the spirit finds seven other spirits more evil than itself, and they all enter the person and live there. And so that person is worse off than before"* (Luke 11:24-26 NLT).

Scary, huh! We don't empty ourselves. We add a good, to push out an evil. We replace a vice with a virtue. We bring in the good to push out the bad. Bring in the fruits of the spirit, push out the sinful nature, and ask for God's help. If we are not growing spiritually and emotionally, we are dying. Again, there is no status quo in the kingdom of God. You can know the whole Bible, and believe your spiritually mature, but still be emotionally immature. Solomon was the wisest person in the Bible, except for Jesus, but he had such an emotional fixation on women—he had to have them all—700 wives and 300 concubines. That's drama, folks! No self-control!

We all embrace the Drama in one form or another. There is a better way; get out of the Drama and into the Dance, emotionally, and attain spiritually maturity. This is where we need to walk the walk not just talk the talk. Paul said, *"Those who belong to Christ Jesus have crucified the sinful nature with its passions and desires. Since we live by the Spirit, let us keep in step with the Spirit"* (Gal. 5:24 NIV). Keep in step, meaning, walk the walk. Walk with the Father, the Son, and the Holy Spirit in the Dance daily.

Most people love the idea of the Dance. But they ask, "What if you're constantly connecting with people who love the Drama at work and in unavoidable places? It's a good question. I would say, work harder to avoid them. That said, at times you can't. Jesus couldn't. Actually, it was part of his mission and ours to walk right into the fray. To be light in darkness. As he was being tried, the whole Jewish leadership stirred the emotions of large crowds into tipping point drama. Everyone there was squarely in the Drama, except Jesus. Yes, he was by all definitions a total victim, but he wouldn't play the role. He was perceived as a persecutor and suffered persecution for it. The leaders and chief priests heard he was a rescuer, the Messiah, but they didn't believe it. What did he do? We know the gospels say he pretty much kept his mouth shut, said nothing. Peter, who was right there the whole time records, *"When they hurled their insults at him, he did not retaliate; when he suffered he made no threats. Instead, he entrusted himself with him who judges justly"* (1 Pet. 2:23 NIV). Why didn't he say anything? If he just explained himself, wouldn't they understand? Two answers: First, Jesus knew, the Drama has no winners no matter what role a person plays, it's all of the devil. He was there to save people from the Drama, not become part of it. Second, there's the term *Confirmation Bias*. When people come against you in the Drama, they have already become judge and jury. No matter what Jesus would have said at that point, or you or I could say, they will take each word and find any fault they can to confirm their predisposed bias. That's just is how it is. I've learned that when someone comes strongly against the leadership of our church and decides to exit the church, there is nothing I can say to them anymore that will help. They will just find fault in it, no matter how true it might be. At that point, they have become unteachable—at least by me. Why? Confirmation bias.

Sometimes the best way to get out of the Drama and into the Dance is simple: be quiet and pray. Once, I was blindsided by a couple who saw me as the persecutor and themselves as the victims. I was deeply hurting, so I called my friend Dixon again in Texas. Get this about Dixon. He's a gent who went from being a NASA Rocket Scientist to Christian Psychologist. He says in his old southern drawl, "I went from outer space to inner space." So, he answers the phone, I tell him what happened, looking for an ally. He listens and then slowly and succinctly says, "Brad, have you thanked God for it?" *What? What do you mean? Are you insane?* I think to myself. I say sheepishly, "Uh, why no, not yet." He says, "Brad, we're supposed to be thankful in all things the Bible says." *Sure, Dixon*, I think. *Wow, I've gotta grow up! Thanks Dixon,* who, by the way, is fully in the Dance, not in the Drama. We will all struggle with this on some level until we leave for heaven. Jesus, on the night he was betrayed, took some bread and lifted it to heaven and gave thanks! Thanks for what he was about to do for you and me! Wow! There's the ultimate in spiritual maturity. In the middle of the greatest drama ever concocted by the devil, there was Jesus, fully in the Dance, loving God and loving people.

A few years ago, I learned something about myself while Christmas shopping that had plagued me all my life, but it was actually a good thing. See, I hate malls. I've known I hated malls and only frequented them once a year to get my wife and kids something for Christmas, because malls literally make me nauseous. This time, we all went as a family. By the way, women shop, men hunt! I need to get the kill early and easy, which makes for a successful shopping trip for me. There I was, done with my list, sitting in the mall corridor, and feeling nauseous. Feeling nauseous at the mall was not new to me. After about 30 minutes there, it just always happens. This time, however, I figured it out. I was bored. Bored! I'm never bored! That's what made me nauseous. Really, it's not that I live the life of a thrill seeker or that I'm a jet setter or I'm just such an exciting guy. No, I believe I'm rarely bored because I serve a God who is more exciting than a supernova or the biggest fish you can ever catch or watching a humpback whale breach from 100 yards. Somehow, growing closer to Him, living in the Dance on a daily basis brings a maturity and contentment that is what we all long for.

While in prison, the Apostle Paul wrote, *"I have learned the secret of being content in any and every situation, whether well fed or hungry, whether living in plenty or in want. I can do all this through Christ who gives me strength"* (Phil. 4:12b NIV) Can you imagine being content in prison? Can you imagine Paul was virtually never bored? Can you imagine being content—having a deep sense joy no matter what's happening in your life? That's what growing to be spiritual mature is all about.

God has a vision for each one of us, it's maturity. Paul wrote to the church in Colossae, *"We proclaim him, admonishing and teaching everyone will all wisdom, so that we may present everyone fully mature in Christ"* (Col. 1:28 NIV). Fully mature. That word *mature* in the original Greek language is *telios*, and it's often translated as mature, perfect, or complete. The word telescope is derived from *telios*. It's like God invites us to look through a telescope and see us how he sees us, off in the distance, where we are fully grown up and mature in Christ. Walking with Jesus daily as he leads us there is the way, the truth and the life. The ultimate goal of spiritual maturity is to love like Jesus loved. That's what the next chapter is all about.

What do you say? Where are you–in the Drama or the Dance? Read the following and score yourself below. Go before God and ask him to replace a vice with a virtue and work on those things with God.

### 3.5–Attaining Spiritual Maturity

I find myself growing to become both spiritually and emotionally mature. I have a deeper love, respect, and understanding of others. I'm rejecting the Drama more and more and learning to live in the Dance with God. I'm growing in giving grace rather than judgement and am actively seeking to love people as God first loved me.

| WEAK | 1 | 2 | 3 | 4 | 5 | STRONG |

**Memory verse: Galatians 5:24 (NIV)** *"Those who belong to Christ Jesus have crucified the sinful nature with its passions and desires. Since we live by the Spirit, let us keep in step with the Spirit."*

### Questions for Further Reflection and Discussion

1. What do you do with drama in your life?

2. Can you see the connection between spiritual maturity and emotional maturity? How?

3. Look at Galatians 5:22 and 23. What fruit of the Spirit do you need to go to God and ask for most? Why?

4. Share your thoughts on confirmation bias. Has it ever happened to you? Have you ever had it against someone? Why?

5. Think about Jesus being the most spiritually and emotionally mature person who ever lived. How can we emulate how he remained in the Dance, no matter how much people want to drag us into the Drama?

## 3.6 Purity & Holiness

This morning I woke up to eight inches of fresh snow in my neighborhood. It's a veritable winter wonderland outside. Everything is white and clean. I couldn't help but think, that's what God did to me. But He did an inside/out job on me.

Back in my BC—Before Christ days—I was one of those guys who was a man's man. Still am! I loved to shoot the bull with the guys. Still do! However, it wasn't uncommon for me to swear or drop an f-bomb in every other phrase or sentence. Then, I accepted Christ, and suddenly it's like God began to edit out all that stuff, almost without any effort on my part. My foul mouth got cleaned up almost immediately after I gave my life to Christ. The crazy thing is, even these days, I can still have a great conversation with the boys, exempt of profanity and they don't seem to care. Honestly, I love humor and jokes. And yes, some foul ones are still funny to me (let's just admit it and not try to be too holier than thou!). I've learned I just don't have to repeat them (see Ephesians 5:4). I've also observed that people who have to use profanity in an attempt to be funny, aren't really very clever. I find clean comedy much more intriguing and witty. God has a deep desire for us to be pure. To be holy. *"Be Holy as I am Holy"* (1 Peter 1:16). He knows it's best for us. How could I go from being a foul mouthed profane guy to 99 percent not, almost instantaneously? Here's the theological word for God making us holy: Sanctification. It's both an instant event when we surrender to Christ and it's an ongoing process. I've seen it happen in myself and in many others. Most profound is when it happened to Willie.

At about sixteen years old, my son, Willie, started doing things he shouldn't have been doing. He unwittingly decided to, slowly but surely, move away from God. I kept on thinking, and sometimes would say to him, "Willie, you don't need to have a testimony like mine. Some of my old friends didn't make it. Alcohol and drugs killed them." Honestly, it made me a little crazy. I loved him so much. It took about five years for God to finally get a hold of him. It was early August and I had just left for a mission trip to Africa. I knew Willie was planning to move to Idaho to hang with a buddy and pursue music. I wasn't on board with it, but I knew we had to let him go. I mean, he was twenty-one years-old. His move date was scheduled. He left while I was gone. I prayed at some point that God would do a prodigal son act on him. The sooner, the better—maybe a year. "Please not ten, Lord." Well, unknown to me three days after he got to Idaho he went into a drug induced panic attack and five days later I called home and Ann was in Idaho boarding a plane with Willie to bring him home. Just three days after leaving home he had gone out with a buddy drinking all night, got into some street drugs that were not as advertised, and he ended up in the emergency room. I'm clueless; I'm off the grid in Africa. He called Ann, tells her what happened. He says to his mom, "I prayed to God to take the pain away and God said, 'Willie, if you throw those drugs away I will.'" Ann starts to weep as she had just been praying 30 minutes earlier pleading for God to take away Willie's pain, that it was too much for him. As he's recounting all this with his mom on the phone from Idaho and asking her if God is real, he tells her he doesn't know if God is real anymore. Ann says, "Willie, if God's not real, who told you to do that?" Willie acknowledged it could only have been God's voice he heard. And Willie prayed a prayer of repentance and asked Jesus to take over his life right there and then. Willie says, "In that moment, it's like God gave me a spark of purity." And from that moment on, we got our son back and he is walking closely with the Lord every day now. It is all we ever dreamed. So good!

Spark of purity. I love that. It's so real. As a student of the Bible, I love it when theological truths show up in real lives, especially in the lives of my children. That spark of purity Willie described is called Sanctification. It means to be made holy. Again, God tells us to *"Be Holy as I am Holy"* (1 Pet. 1:16). We are not naturally holy. Naturally, we are very much unholy. We can only be holy if God has acted on our behalf in a supernatural way. At a conference in Hawaii a few years ago, Wayne Cordiero said, "You will never know or have the opportunity to be holy, unless you know or have had the opportunity to be unholy." Wow! If we think we're pretty holy, there's a great chance we're simply not. When I think of holy people, I think of Mother Theresa and Billy Graham.

What makes us holy? One thing and one person. Repentance and Jesus. In our natural state we have no choice but to walk away from the God of all life and the further we get away from Him, the more unholy and sinful we become. When we repent and turn to our holy God who gives life, holiness is the result. That's what happened to Willie and that's what happened to me and it can happen to you too. It's instantaneous when we turn to Jesus, confess we are sinners and desperately need a Savior. When that happens, a spiritual transaction takes place where God cleans the slate of our hearts and make us holy, so we can enter His presence. As has been said, then, we are good to go! That's immediate holiness, but it's also ongoing too.

Two key steps in Alcoholics Anonymous' 12 steps that enable people to stay sober are steps 4 and 5. They are also key to our ongoing sanctification and holiness as Christ-followers.

***AA Step 4: Made a searching and fearless moral inventory of ourselves.*** To keep it simple, when I did this, I went back as far as I could remember, back to about four years old, and wrote down all my major sins that I could remember. Everything. You can imagine by what I've shared to this point in this book, it took me hours. The key word in AA's Step 4 is *fearless*. Write down anything and everything. You may think some things or sins you committed are so unique to you. That's simply not true. I've learned what we believe to be most particular to us, is most general to the rest of humanity. It just is. So write it all down. That's the easy part. Next . . .

***AA Step 5: Admitted to God, to ourselves, and to another human being the exact nature of our wrongs.*** This is confession and repentance. It's sharing the list of Step 4 with someone who is a very mature Christ-follower. It's the single scariest and most cathartic thing I've ever done in my life. My monk friend, Father Francis, encouraged me to do this about 10 months into my Christian journey. I met him at a singles retreat up near Seattle and I hadn't known him long. When he spoke, it's like The Holy Spirit prompted me to go talk with him. Shortly after I met him, I ended up sharing the deepest darkest secret of my life. It was like God just wanted that out of me. Being familiar with AA, Francis then ask me to go home and write up Step 4 and schedule to meet with him so I could share all my sinful baggage in step 5. In a divine appointment, I met with him with ten pages of cliff notes of all my sins, which took me three hours to share. After I was done with the marathon sin dump, he was so gracious and told me, "Brad, any man can share all their accomplishments and the great things they've done in their life, but it takes God working in a man to share their mess ups and do what you did." It was amazing! When King David wrote, *"Wash away all my iniquity and cleanse me from my sin. Cleanse me with hyssop and I will be clean; wash me, and I will be whiter than snow"* (Ps. 51:2, 7 NIV), I totally felt that. Never before had I felt so clean and free. No longer did those old sins have any hold over me. No more guilt, no more shame. It was then I realized and appreciate more than ever before what Jesus really did on the cross for me. His blood paid the price for every one of my sins. I got it.

Sometimes, when one of those old sins comes to mind, an old tape plays in my mind and the Devil tries to still shame me because of it. But I'm not buying! No! Jesus died for every single one of those sins. For me to take them back on is to say, "Jesus died in vain." That's what the Devil would have us believe. But He didn't die in vain. Sorry Devil, "In the name of Jesus, go straight back to hell where you belong!" That's a little battle prayer I've adopted over the years. It works!

It's my strong conviction, that if churches and individual Christ-followers would embrace the principles of AA's Steps 4 and 5, we'd be a much holier church. We'd be a much more attractive church. If we didn't pretend to be holy and agreed with the Holy Spirit to make us holy because were not, I'm convinced people would really want what we have. Once we get our sins out of our hearts and minds and on the table into the light, they cease to control us and we act much more like Jesus. And God heals us. *"Confess your sins to each other so that you will be healed"* (James 5:16a NIV). Yes, these AA steps came right out of the Bible.

After we do a big sin dump like that, it's much easier to grow and be holy. Just keep a short list of your sins. Meaning, don't let the sin list grow without confessing it to God and/or a friend. It's called ongoing repentance. I heard it said of Billy Graham, when asked how he made it through all the minefields of being on a stage a great deal of his life and was able to maintain his integrity while so many others failed, Billy had one answer, "I've tried to live a life of ongoing repentance." What? Billy Graham? Why? How come? Some say the closer you get to the light the easier it is to see the flaws. I totally get where Billy is coming from.

We are asked by God to *"Take every thought captive to obey Christ"* (2 Cor. 10:5 ESV). We act out our sins after we have processed them in our brains. So, if we can arrest those thoughts right when they are happening, all the better. Sometimes I have bizarre thoughts, sometimes dark ones. Sometimes I'm lying in bed, eyes closed and my mind is wandering and a weird old sinful thought will come to mind—like doing drugs or something else. In those moments God gives me the grace to immediately open my eyes and pray, "Help me Lord. remove that thought and help me to dwell on your goodness and love and all you've done for me, my awesome wife and kids and amazing friends." That practice has taken captive and killed many a dark thought.

Paul wrote to the Corinthian church a list of ten sins that if a person persisted in, they were in danger of being omitted from heaven and instead headed for hell. He says, *"Those who indulge in sexual sin, or who worship idols, or commit adultery, or are male prostitutes, or practice homosexuality, or are thieves, or greedy people, or drunkards, or are abusive, or cheat people—none of these will inherit the kingdom of God"* (1Cor. 6:9b,10 NLT). I look at that list and I think, holy cow! I used to do seven or eight of those things before I met Christ. Guess what? That's the next verse! *"Some of you were once like that. But you were cleansed; you were made holy; you were made right with God by calling on the name of the Lord Jesus Christ and by the Spirit of our God"* (1Cor. 6:11 NLT). Think about these verses and the grace of God. that *but* is big! *"But you were cleansed, you were made holy."* In other words we were toast, headed for hell, BUT! But God, in his love for us made us holy. That word holy is often translated sanctified. It was done to us by the Holy Spirit, through the blood of Christ when we repented. Once again, amazing Grace. Listen, well intentioned Christ-followers often point out and focus on homosexuality as he ultimate deal breaker with God. But, look at that list of sins above. It's just one of many. This is not to give a pass on any sin God's word clearly states is sin. Just realize we all have our issues. Be careful in your judgement of others that you are not the one in peril. And be thankful that Jesus made you holy.

Every day I try to go before God and I often write in my journal, "Lord, show me. Show me my sins." Some days he does very clearly. It's painful sometimes. Often it's little stuff and I repent. "Lord, I was insensitive to that barista today, please forgive me." "Lord, I got a bit off when I was driving in all that traffic." "Why, Lord, why did I say that terse word to Ann?" "Lord, I was a little rough on Nathan or Sarah or Elliot or Willie—I love them more than anyone. Lord, I asked them for forgiveness, now I come before you Lord, please forgive me." That's why Jesus said, "*So if you are presenting a sacrifice at the altar in the Temple and your suddenly remember that someone has something against you, leave your sacrifice there at the altar. Go and be reconciled to that person. Then come and offer your sacrifice to God* (Matt. 5:23-24 NIV). The context of that verse was broken relationships caused by our sinfulness. Jesus so valued loving relationships, He essentially was saying here, don't come posing as holy, offering sacrifices if you have hate in your heart towards someone. No, that sacrifice is all about loving God. And, "*If we say we love God but hate our brother or sister, we are liars*" (1 John 4:20 NIV). And liars certainly are not holy.

There's a verse that nailed me early on in my Christian journey. I was so in love with God. This new life he gave me was incredible. But there I was, reading my Bible one night, and I came across 1 John 4:20. It hit me like a ton of bricks! I hated my brother Boyd. I hated him for shaming me and our family by being a homosexual. As far as I was concerned, "To hell with him!" Right there and then, the Holy Spirit did an act of ongoing sanctification on my heart and soul. It became very clear to me that I hated Boyd not so much because he was gay, but because I was most concerned about what people would think of me, knowing I had a homosexual brother. It was all about me and my self-centeredness. It had been years since I had spoken to Boyd. Well, I had to repent. So, I called him up and shared with him what God revealed to me and asked him for forgiveness. We both cried on the phone. He, too, repented of his lifestyle and confessed Christ as his Lord and shared with me how difficult it all was for him. A year or so later, Ann and I got married and he stood up in our wedding. He still struggled with his lifestyle. He was also a pretty good con artist, with lots of crazy stories. In spite of it all, God gave me a holy love for him. When he died of AIDS a few years later, I was able to share what Boyd meant to me and how I knew he was now free from all that plagued him. And, of course, I was totally confident he was finally holy, with our holy God.

It seems to me that's what God means for us to be holy; to love the unlovable. Jesus did. In spite of our unholiness, he loved like no other. We get it all mixed up and messed up. We often believe for us to be holy is to attain moral perfection. Maybe in the next life, if not this one. Certainly, our morals ought to get an extreme upgrade as we grow in Christ. And our behaviors must increasingly align with what God has declared in his Word, the Bible. Just because the world says this or that is not a sin anymore, that doesn't mean we change God's Word to align with our sinful behavior. It's above anyone's pay grade on this planet to change what God has deemed sinful. I know, I know, if I say homosexuality is a sin, then I'm deemed a hater. It's really the most ridiculous argument. God truly gave me genuine love for my brother, even though he continued to engage in the gay lifestyle. Just because I don't and can't agree with someone's behavior, doesn't mean I can't love them. Anyone who says so must never have had kids. There have been countless times over the course of raising our three children that I've totally disagreed with their behavior, but still loved them desperately. Like when our holy Heavenly Father looks down at us and still loves us enough to send his only Son. Holiness has everything to do with our ability to still love those that, on the surface, don't deserve it and are really hard to love. Think about it. A cuddly little baby is so easy to love. But when those poopy diapers come, it's a little bit harder. What about the really messy people on the streets? Or the abusive husband or wife, father or mother? What about the friend who just goes off on you? God asks us to be holy as he is holy. Jesus also said, "They will know you are Christians by your love." That's our brand: love! Nothing else! Love God, Love Others.

We forget, don't we? Often "mature" Christians begin to act like the moral police. That's what the Pharisees did. It wasn't pretty. Never is. Many Christians somehow believe that people who don't know Christ should somehow act like they do. Think about that one. That's insanity. I sure couldn't! People who are still under the power of this world and the ruler of this world are only acting according to their depraved sinful nature and are going do everything in their power to protect it. We should expect no less.

**Holiness**—Here's my definition: The most holy person in the room is the person who can truly love the most unlovable. Again, that's what Jesus did. We have this idea that holiness is simply moral purity. But Christianity is not moralism. Holiness devoid of love is nothing, empty. The most holy person is the person who truly does love God with all their heart, all their soul, all their mind and all their strength. And, they truly do love their neighbor as their self. The most holy person covers over a multitude of other people's sins (1 Pet. 4:8). Mother Theresa, when asked how she can spend so much time with the wretched decrepit people in the slums of Calcutta, India responded, "I see Jesus in the eyes of the poor." They say, you are who you hang with. So, yes, we become more moral and more holy as we walk with Jesus and love the unlovable, I'm sure that's what Mother Theresa did.

In my seminary days, I had the extreme privilege of taking two guided courses on evangelism and discipleship with Dr. Robert Coleman, the author of The Master Plan of Evangelism. It's like the defining work of our age on Discipleship. Get it and read it. It was pretty cool to do a course, meeting with him a few times a week for an hour, just one-on-one, him and me. He was a holy man! One day I came in troubled by an issue in my life and shared it with him. He said, "Well, Brad, let's pray." Then, right there at his desk, he got down on his knees, closed his eyes and began to pray. I was dumbfounded. I didn't know what to do. It was clear that I had no business taking the same position as this holy man took. So, I simply bowed my head in my chair and listened as he prayed. Really, I felt like I should take off my shoes, I was on Holy Ground. Dr. Coleman was and is the real deal. I knew, he had something I wanted. It's called holiness. Jesus offers it to all who realize they don't have it. Do you?

Read the following statement and score yourself. Make some notes about what God is prompting you to do to cooperate with him to make you holy.

### 3.6–Purity and Holiness

I desire to live a life of repentance and therefore confess my sins before God regularly and, when necessary, to a spiritual mentor. As I grow closer to God, I find myself longing for his Spirit to purify me so I can be holy as God is holy.

| WEAK | 1 | 2 | 3 | 4 | 5 | STRONG |
|------|---|---|---|---|---|--------|

**Memory verse: 1 Peter 1:15-16 (NIV)** *"But just as he who called you is holy, so be holy in all you do; for it is written: 'Be holy, because I am holy.'"*

## Questions for Further Reflection and Discussion

1. What is your biggest take-away from this chapter?

2. Read the above verses. What does it mean to be holy?

3. Reflect on your process of sanctification. Share where God has done some great work in you.

4. How can you be more holy in your relationships and love the unlovable?

5. What can you do to cover over someone else's sins and be holy?

## 3.7 Disciple-maker

We have a Great Commission. Commission simply means, with-mission. Sometimes in the Christian life we get confused about what that's all about. This is what it's about "Making Disciples!" Not of us, but of Jesus! Got it?

In Jim Collin's book, *Good to Great,* the first line of the first chapter states, "Good is the enemy of great." As I've observed many churches in America, I notice a troubling trend. Many do a lot of good, but they don't do what's great—make disciples. Funny, real disciples make disciples. It's just what they do. As I said in chapter 3.3, it's who we are!

Back in the early years of our marriage, as young Christ-followers, my wife and I led a group of 80 volunteers to completely renovate an elderly woman's home all in one day. That was the stated goal. Her name was Irene. Actually, both Ann and I spent some significant time leading up to *The Day,* getting to know Irene and her grandkids. See, her daughter was a drug addict and Irene's husband was deceased, but Irene had taken custody of her 3 grandkids, raising them on her own. We met with Irene who owned a modest home in Seattle that fell into disrepair after her husband died. We had to do get some drywall, electrical and plumbing work completed prior to the big day, which allowed us to get to know Irene. Well, *The Day* came, 80 volunteers converged on Irene's home, we painted it inside and out. We re-carpeted the entire house. We put new kitchen cabinets in, landscaped the front and back yards. We filled a 20 yard hopper with junk and debris, put new linens on all the beds and new drapes in every room and much more. It was Extreme Home Makeover before the show ever existed. Irene and her grandkids were gone all day. Then, as we were wrapping up, home they came. They were shocked. They wept! The kids were in awe. It was good. So good! Man we did good!

The problem is it wasn't great! Years later, reflecting on that good work, knowing what I know now, I see that day as discipleship failure. See, we never shared the gospel with her and her grandkids. We never even thought of carrying that relationship on after that day to perhaps disciple them. It would have been so easy. I'm sure, if my wife and I would have sensitively presented Jesus as their Savior and Lord, they would have put their faith in him. We didn't. We didn't disciple them. Never even thought of it. If we would have, it would have indeed been great, not just good.

Often, we settle for the good commission, and not The Great Commission. Missions organizations do it all the time: they build stuff, they drill wells, they provide health care. I love all of that! I've been to Africa many times and I know how desperately Africans need clean water. I love how many organizations, both Christian and secular, are now drilling clean water wells, which helps immeasurably with so many disease and learning issues. That's all really good! But if you're a Christian, why not share the Good News and plan to disciple and make it great? We are called to *great*, not just good. Oh, I know Francis of Assisi, who allegedly said, "Share the good news, use words only when necessary." Meaning, good works is what's most important, and only as a last resort should we share the gospel message verbally. That sounds so good, so spiritual. It's quoted all the time, but there is strong evidence he never said it. The idea that, as people watch me be so awesome and holy, they are just going to line-up and fall into the Kingdom of God because of my goodness, seems pretty absurd to me. Now, I know Jesus said, *"In the same way, let your light shine before others, that they may see your good deeds and glorify your Father in heaven"* (Matt. 5:16 NIV). Read the context and go back to Matthew 5:12. Jesus was talking about being persecuted, he says, *"In the same way they persecuted the prophets who were before you."* The prophets were persecuted specifically because they were mouth-pieces for God. People persecuted them because of what they said and the people did not want to hear it.

When we were living in Illinois, we had some great next-door neighbors, Sara and Paul. Sara was an incredible gardener and planted an amazing garden every year, with tomatoes! One day, I was kicking the ball around in our backyard with my kids and the ball sailed over the fence into Sara and Paul's backyard. They were out of town, so I went over to fetch it. As I leaned over to get the ball, a huge ripe tomato caught my eye, just dangling there on the plant. I love fresh, ripe garden tomatoes, but it didn't feel right to pick it while they were gone. My intrigue with that tomato however, prompted me to go over and gently put my hand under it and give it a slight squeeze. No sooner did I barely touch it that it plopped right into my hand. Yikes! What to do? Well, I took it home and ate it and knew I had to go and confess my sin when they got home. I did. They laughed. A few weeks later I got the opportunity to share the gospel message with Sara. I was able to use garden analogies to help her understand how much God loved her. When I asked her if there was any reason she wouldn't want to put her faith in Jesus, I'll never forget her response. Tears came spilling out of her eyes and ran down her face as she said, "Who wouldn't want a relationship with God?" And she prayed right there to put her faith in Christ. She was as ripe as that tomato to hear the gospel. She went on to be a leader in our parenting ministry at Willow Creek, worked towards a theology degree, and continued to invite unchurched neighbors and friends into her home for evangelistic Bible studies. What if I never shared the gospel with her? The fields are ripe for harvest. Jesus said, *"The harvest is plentiful, but the workers are few."* I think of so many churches and Christians that have done such fine good works. The fields are prepared, but they never ever check the fruit by sharing the gospel message. It would be so easy.

The fact is, I fear that by simply doing good works, perhaps we communicate a different gospel than the gospel of grace alone. Perhaps we're modeling a gospel of good works, not a gospel of grace. Good works lend significant credibility to our words. And certainly, there are great kingdom-advancing strategies to love people and show them you care that lay the groundwork for opportunities to share the gospel message. Marketplace evangelism that helps people see high-integrity business practices that build bridges is awesome.

At our church in Oregon, we build key relationships with public schools through community care, where we provide large barbecues for all the parents and students for Back-to-School Night. We also participate in reading, mentoring and lunch buddies programs. Do we share the gospel there? No. But, when a family or student going to that school has a crisis, often times they will seek out our church, and then we have all the freedom in the world to share Jesus. It's a great strategy to be good news before you share the *good news.*

Make no mistake, I'm for good works, just not devoid of a plan for the proclamation of the gospel message of grace and discipleship. You really want to grow? Go share the gospel message with your neighbor or co-worker or boss. That will put you on your knees. Jesus shared the good news with words constantly. Before becoming a Christ-follower Paul was into works—arresting and killing Christians. Then once he became a Christian, words about Jesus were all that mattered. Words matter! God spoke creation into existence with words. Jesus was the Word who became flesh!

So, let's stop with this self-serving nonsense that we can't talk about Jesus and lead people to him and make them disciples. Jesus commanded us to do it. He said, if you do, "I will be with you always" (Matt. 28:20 NIV). When his mission of making disciples is our mission, he's there. If that's really not our mission, I doubt we should count on him.

If you look at Jesus' ministry, yes, he healed the lame and sick and blind! But he never built anything, except perhaps some furniture with His dad. *"Jesus traveled about from one town and village to another, proclaiming the good news of the kingdom of God"* (Luke 8:1 NIV). Amazingly, in that same chapter, we see *"The twelve were with him and also some women who had been cured of evil spirits and diseases"* (Luke 8:2a NIV). He took these folks with him on his journey to make them disciples. He spent time with them. He did life with them. He taught them to obey everything he commanded. Making disciples just takes time. It takes way more than an hour church service on Sunday. It takes doing life together. It just does.

When we get to heaven I don't think God is going to ask how many people came to your church. I think he's going to ask all of us, "How many disciples did you make?" It's a scary thought. Jesus, in three and a half years, perhaps made seventy-two disciples and change. We know there were 120 in the upper room so let's give Him those too. I love large mega-churches and they often have the fire-power to do great things, but they are a small percentage of the overall church. So, rather than focusing on church size and how many attenders a church has, most important is a bona fide plan and structure to make disciples of those who come to your church—to "turn pagans into missionaries" sold out to Jesus. To use the gardening analogy, growth is measured in deepness of roots of each individual disciple.

When asked, how is your church growing? Hopefully your first response describes growing disciples in Christ.

Sometimes I hear Christians and even pastors say, with all sincerity, "If my life or our church can help just one person find Jesus then it's all been worth it and we've been successful." I understand. That's nice. I used to say it. I don't anymore. I'm convinced more often than not, Jesus wants to touch way more lives than one with my life and yours too. When he talked about fruit, he never said one grape. He never said add one more fig or olive. He did say, leave the 99 to go after the one. But that makes 100. Sure, some will have a capacity for more, some less. Jethro, the father-in-law of Moses imparted some great wisdom to Moses regarding a person's discipleship bandwidth: *"Select from all the people some capable, honest men who fear God and hate bribes. Appoint them as leaders over groups of one thousand, one hundred, fifty, and ten"* (Exod. 18:21 NLT). This was a plan to settle disputes among the Israelites, but it was also a plan to take the load off Moses. It does show clearly that some can handle more, some less.

**Leadership or pastor tip:** If you have a plan to make disciples, great! If you don't have a plan, use this book as your guide. See the Appendix A for how to implement GROW discipleship classes on a quarterly basis or just use this book and offer it as a small group guide.

It goes back to the parable of the farmer sowing seed. Sure, some will be wasted. Some will appear to grow, but fade. Sadly, I've seen it happen hundreds of times. But some really grows and produces big time. Who are you sowing into? Who are you helping to learn how to till the soil of their hearts? Are you tilling the soil of your heart with his Word, in meditation and by persevering? Then you're good soil, ripe for a crop! Jesus said, *"But the seed that falls on good soil stands for those with a noble and good heart, who hear the word, retain it, and by persevering produce a crop"* (Luke 8:15 NIV) A crop! Not just one more. A whole crop! I love that. Don't you want to have a fruitful life for Jesus? I know he wants it for you. In fact, in the preface to the Great Commission Jesus gave is, *"All authority on heaven and earth has been given to me"* (Matt. 18a NIV). That just added enormous weight to what he was about to say! So, what did he command his disciples after he said that? The same thing he commands of you and me: *"Go and make disciples (plural) of all nations, baptizing them in the name of the Father, and of the Son and of the Holy Spirit and teaching them to obey everything I commanded"* (Matt. 28:19—20a NIV). And if we do that, *make disciples,* and be laser-focused on that, look what Jesus says, *"And surely I am with you always, to the very end of the age"* (Matt. 28:20b). Think and pray hard on this. I have. This isn't just a passing thought Jesus gently encouraged his followers to consider as a good option. It was a command with the weight of heaven and earth attached to it. Seems like we better start taking it very seriously.

Finally, disciples are not into addition. They are into multiplication. Jesus sure was. It starts small, but in a short amount of time, it can explode if we just obey The Great Commission and be disciple-makers. It was the most brilliant network marketing scheme ever concocted. No, we may not get the pink Cadillac or the golden Rolex in this life. But Jesus promised his true disciples great rewards in the next. All for his glory!

Ready? Are you a disciple-maker? Do you want to become one? Just follow the plan in this book and it will happen. Score yourself.

| WEAK | 1 | 2 | 3 | 4 | 5 | STRONG |

### 3.7–Disciple-maker

I'm called and commanded by Jesus to make disciples. I take that seriously and by leaning into him and his Word, I can't wait to see what he will do in me and through me to accomplish the Great Commission.

**Memory verses: Matthew 28:18b-20 (NIV)** *"All authority in heaven and earth has been given to me. Therefore go and make disciples (plural) of all nations, baptizing them in the name of the Father, and of the Son and of the Holy Spirit and teaching them to obey everything I commanded you. And surely I am with your always, to the very end of the age"*

## Questions for Further Reflection and Discussion

1. How much of a disciple-maker are you?

2. Read the above memory verses which are the Great Commission. Discuss it in depth based on thoughts in this chapter.

3. Why can doing good get in the way of great?

4. What's your plan to make disciples?

5. What action are you going to take today or tomorrow to be a disciple-maker?

## 3.8 Sell-out to Reconciliation

Both my wife and I come from families where our parents divorced when we were fourteen-years-old. My wife seemed to be impacted harder than me, but she's also much more sensitive and merciful than I am. Often, I just move on. I do distinctly remember that after my mom and dad divorced, dad called all of us seven kids over to the house and told us he was disowning us all. Disowning us! Can you believe that? I think my five brothers and my sister may have blown most of his rhetoric off, but I took him very seriously. I wasn't even a Christian then, but I thought, "Who does that? What respectable father says that to any of their kids?" Well, at the time, my dad was not even close to respectable. From that point on, I just hardened my heart against him and didn't talk to him for three years. Then he got in a car accident my senior year in high school and almost died. Jolted by the fear of losing him, a little love for my dad began to surface again, and, eventually, we were able to have an okay relationship. However, it wasn't until I put my faith in Jesus some twelve years later that I began

255

to really love him in spite of all his shortcomings. He came to Chicago for my college graduation in 1997. (Yeah, I graduated from college twenty-two years after I barely graduated from high school, even got a master's degree two years later! Proof positive there is a God!) I was really sad when he died in 1999, just a few months prior to my master's degree commencement ceremony. The crazy thing is, if I could have one thing in the world for just one day, it would be a day with my dad.

As I have spent a lot of time with Jesus and his Word, I'm absolutely sold out to reconciliation. Jesus was, all the way to the cross! My dearest life and ministry passages are found in 2 Corinthians chapter 5. Read it. Meditate on it. SOAP on it.

*If we are "out of our mind," as some say, it is for God; if we are in our right mind, it is for you. *[14]*For Christ's love compels us, because we are convinced that one died for all, and therefore all died. *[15]*And he died for all, that those who live should no longer live for themselves but for him who died for them and was raised again.* *[16]*So from now on we regard no one from a worldly point of view. Though we once regarded Christ in this way, we do so no longer. *[17]*Therefore, if anyone is in Christ, the new creation has come: the old has gone, the new is here! *[18]*All this is from God, who reconciled us to himself through Christ and gave us the ministry of reconciliation: *[19]*that God was reconciling the world to himself in Christ, not counting people's sins against them. And he has committed to us the message of reconciliation. *[20]*We are therefore Christ's ambassadors, as though God were making his appeal through us. We implore you on Christ's behalf: Be reconciled to God. *[21]*God made him who had no sin to be sin for us, so that in him we might become the righteousness of God* (2 Cor. 5:13-21 NIV).

Some thoughts and convictions on the above passage: Verse 13: Yes, by now you know I am out of my mind for God. For you and your loved ones, reconciliation is the ball game. I've just seen too much damage by divorce, by adult children cutting their parents out of their lives, and friends and business partners terminating their relationships for petty misunderstandings and money. It's so painful. Why do I even write this? Verses 14 and 15 that's why: Christ's love for me, proven on the cross, *compels* me. His love for us should compel all Christ-followers to be sold out to reconciliation.

Verse 16 is so key: We regard no one as a throw away. All relationships are supremely valuable to God and even more so (verse 17), if they know Christ. As senior a pastor for sixteen years, I've experienced more relational termination than the average bear. It just seems to part of the mantle senior pastors get. People can leave the church and still be friends with anyone in the church, but somehow the senior pastor needs to be avoided like the plague. It's a weird phenomenon. But it's happening all over the planet. These are Jesus-believing Christ-followers who buy into irreconcilable differences. I can tell you this, anyone who ever has terminated me for any reason, I'd welcome back with open arms. Now, certainly there may need to be some repentance on my part and on theirs. I'm willing. Totally. I must be! Everyone and every relationship is redeemable while we have breath. That's the message of reconciliation.

Jesus came to us. Why? To reconcile us to himself because we had no ability to go to him. His absolute spiritual and emotional maturity compelled him to take the initiative to visit our planet for the purposes of reconciliation. And, get this, none of the relational breakdown was his fault. It was all ours. For many years I had an awesome assistant named Andrea. She also directed our children's ministry. She was a great team builder; when some of her team members would get upset, she took it very personally, and even cried because she loved those people so much. Every now and then, she'd come to me and say, "Brad, so-and-so said this or did that and it really hurt me." I'd console her and then ask, "Does that person feel hurt by you?" "Yeah, but I didn't do anything wrong!" She'd exclaim. "I know," I'd say. "What can I do?" She'd ask, wanting resolution. I'd say,

"The hard thing—go and ask them for forgiveness." "What? I didn't do anything wrong!" "I know, Andrea, but they are still hurt. The most spiritually mature person in the relational rift needs to take the initiative to reconcile the relationship. It's just how it works. That's what Jesus did, and if we are truly going to be Christ's ambassadors, that's what we need to do. So, go. I'll pray for you." "Brad," she'd say, "Okay, but it's going to be really hard." "I know. It was really hard for Jesus too." He sweat blood in the garden it was so hard, but he didn't waver. Why? Reconciliation. He was sold out to it.

When I first became a Christ-follower, as I shared earlier, I was also attending AA. Again, Alcoholics Anonymous has a few steps of their 12 that are exceedingly helpful for proper reconciliation.

Step 8 says: *Made a list of all persons we had harmed, and became willing to make amends to them all.*

Step 9 says: *Made a direct amends to such people wherever possible, except when to so do would injure them or others.*

In my first year of AA I made that list. I harmed a lot of people with my self-centeredness and drinking. I could justify it all in my own twisted mind too. No problem.

But when I found Jesus and when he directed me toward reconciliation I started to think more clearly. So I followed Step 9 and worked down my list—made phone calls and sometimes went to talk to people I'd harmed directly and asked them for forgiveness. I was amazed at most people's graciousness toward me. There would be those situations with an old girlfriend where it was just inappropriate for me to show up in her life; where that might cause more harm than good. So, I just left those situations alone.

One person I owed an amends to was an ex-boss, Dave, whom I worked for over six years. He was like a second father to me and his son Rick was my very best friend in high school. I had bought a vehicle when I worked for him and in order for me to secure a loan for it he co-signed. Well, that vehicle got stolen and the insurance company wouldn't pay it totally off and left me with $3000 owing. Shortly after that happened, I quit the company and left that $3K on him. Because he co-signed he paid it and, for six years or so, I totally ignored all inquiries to collect it from me. I made all sorts of justifications for not paying him. He owed me commissions. He didn't treat me right. He's a jerk anyway! It's funny how we justify our bad behaviors by pointing out our perceptions of other people's poor behaviors. That's simply our warped attempt at somehow reconciling the moral books of our life. My attitude and my actions not only destroyed my relationship with Dave, but it destroyed my friendship with Rick, my best friend.

Well, the Lord spoke to me when I made that list. So, I called Dave up and told him "I'm so sorry, please forgive me. I was so wrong. I'm completely at fault and I'm willing to make an amends to you. I know I owe you at least $3000, plus interest. I've thought of a plan, I can't pay it all back at once right now, but I can pay you around $300 a month until it's paid off." He said, "Brad, that's fine, let's just do that for ten months and it will be all paid. But Brad, I have to tell you, you have no idea how good this makes me feel. Thank you!" Rick, my old buddy, found out immediately and we, too, were reconciled. Not long after I became a pastor, Dave died and Rick called me to do his dad's funeral. They weren't churchgoers, but I got to share the gospel with a huge group of unchurched people. I was so honored. Same thing happened with his mom a few years later. Amazing Grace how sweet the sound that used a former wretch like me. Only God!

Reconciliation and repentance go hand in hand. Over the years I've learned true repentance often means restitution, which is huge when it comes to seeking reconciliation. John the Baptist was big on repentance. His sermon in Luke 3 was astounding.

He minced no words, *"Prove by the way you live that you have repented of your sins and turned to God"* (Luke 3:8 NLT) The crowd's response was equally amazing, *"What should we do?'* (verse 10). The tax collector asked, *"What should we do?"* (verse 11) The Roman solders, *"What should we do?"* (verse 14). Man, I wish just once, people in the crowd on Sunday would ask me that when I'm preaching! So good! That's the heart of repentance—to be so committed to reconciling that there's a heart of restitution. Realizing you've been heading the wrong direction away from God and turning around—then intentionally moving toward God to love God and love people. Each time John answers with strong suggestions of caring actions of restitution that would bring reconciliation to each group of people sinned against.

We must be sold out to reconciliation, and not sell out the devil and irreconcilable differences. He is so crafty. John 10:10— *The thief comes only to steal, kill and destroy.* Underline the word *only!* That's all he does. He's the author of irreconcilable differences. And all too often, Christ-followers buy his book of lies. Ronald Reagan was perhaps one of the greatest presidents of the 20th Century. No doubt. But I have often wondered, when he died and stood before God if that even came up in the discussion. From my viewpoint, I believe God might come down hard on Ronnie. When Ronald Reagan was governor of the great state of California, he was the forerunner—the first governor of any state in the union, to sign into law no fault divorce in year 1969, making it easy for couples to divorce. That caused a catastrophic domino effect as most other states quickly followed. What that enabled people to easily do is embrace irreconcilable differences. That's the primary reason cited on divorce filings— irreconcilable differences. It's so easy! Don't even attempt to work through your problems. Make no effort to try to reconcile. Just end it. Now, I know, the desire for divorce is often one sided and the husband or the wife wants to avoid it at all costs. But, that doesn't matter. Our government and world say, hit the eject button on the relationship quickly. It's okay. No one's fault. It happens. But the pain and hurt and devastation lasts a life-time, especially for the children who have no say. Divorce is so hard and so painful. For many who don't want it, it feels like the ultimate failure. The church needs to accept, care for, and love individuals who have been divorced. We need to help them through the pain and provide hope. That's a book in itself. Many churches offer Divorce Recovery groups to help meet this need. We have become a world sold out to irreconcilable differences. We even see it in the church.

When a Christian seems hell-bent on terminating a long-time committed relationship in their families, friends and church family, I sometimes wonder if they really know Christ in the first place. It takes forgiveness on each person's part to stay in a loving, long term relationship, and only when we've experienced Christ's full forgiveness of our own sins can we truly forgive another person. I wonder if they've truly been reconciled with God through Jesus Christ. Sometimes we need to just start with the gospel. Perhaps that's you. Do you really know Jesus? Have you asked him for forgiveness for all your sins? Really? If you're struggling to reconcile with someone, perhaps you need to go to Jesus and start or renew your relationship with him first. Stop reading right now and do that. Nothing is more important. Ask Jesus to help you be willing to forgive the unforgivable. Watch him work the miracle of forgiveness and see your life set free from the imprisonment of unforgiveness and irreconcilable differences.

But why broken relationships and irreconcilable differences? Jesus' answer: Hard hearts (Matt. 19:8). No one knows the hour or day Jesus will return, but I know for sure we are closer than yesterday. Jesus said a key indicator for the End Times will be, *"Sin will be rampant everywhere, and the love of many will grow cold"* (Matt. 24:12 NLT).

Why do people buy into irreconcilable differences? Their own sin or the other person's sin has hardened their heart with bitterness and resentment making their love grow cold. That may be well and good for others, but it's not okay for the

Christ-follower. Just about every time we use irreconcilable differences as an excuse for us to initiate the end of a relationship we are selling out to the devil. Don't do it!

Kids, forgive your parents. Only God is the perfect parent. Forgive your friends and co-workers and even church family members and seek reconciliation. I tell married couples especially, "Just take divorce out of the equation." Jesus said the only legitimate reason for divorce is sexual unfaithfulness, but even then, willing couples can do the very hard work of reconciliation. I've seen it; it's amazing. As much as you hate a person and even loathe them, God can give you love for that person again, because all love comes from him in the first place.

When Ann and I were friends, back before we were married, I began to have feelings for her more than "simply friends" feelings. I knew there was no way! She was stunningly beautiful both inside and out (even more so now). I, on the other hand, was beginning to show male pattern baldness, among other obvious flaws, and was not nearly as cultured as she was, but I could not get her out of my mind and away from the feelings I had for her. So, I took it to The Lord. "Lord," I prayed, "All love comes from you! We love because you first loved us. Lord, I cannot make Ann love me, but you can!" I cried out. And he did! In the same way, God can give you love for a person you are currently estranged to if you are willing.

I talked about perseverance, I spoke on forgiveness. All that needs to be employed to the greatest degree when it comes to reconciliation. I know deep gashes come into relationships and the only option seems to be irreconcilable differences and relational termination. I've seen it too often. I hate it. An old nursery rhyme is helpful here: *Humpty Dumpty sat on the wall. Humpty Dumpty had a great fall. All the king's horses and all the king's men, couldn't put Humpty Dumpty together again.* Nope, they couldn't do it. But God can! And he often will, if you are willing. Remember, God is love (1 John 4:8). Without love we have nothing (1 Cor.)! Why are we so willing to give love up then? It's everything! And when it comes to our spiritual journey, growing in love no matter what is the ultimate goal.

You may read this and say, "I know all this reconciliation business is true and right, but I still don't want to reconcile." I know. I've been there. I called Dixon in Texas. Again, in his slow southern drawl, "Can you just wanna, wanna for now, Brad?" Meaning, you may not want to right now, but try to just want to love that person again. Then God can begin to work in you and the other and soften hearts. Deal? Don't sell out to the devil. Be utterly sold out to reconciliation. Jesus was. That's what the cross is all about. The vertical member symbolizes being reconciled to God. The horizontal member symbolizes being reconciled to each other. Be a true ambassador for Christ and sold out to reconciliation in all you do.

Where are you at? Are you utterly sold out to reconciliation? Read the following sentences and score yourself.

### 3.8–Sell out to Reconciliation

I believe my primary purpose is to spread the message of reconciliation to a world that embraces irreconcilable differences. I am an ambassador for Christ first and foremost and therefore his love compels to see all people as redeemable – I'm sold out to reconciliation.

| WEAK | 1 | 2 | 3 | 4 | 5 | STRONG |
| --- | --- | --- | --- | --- | --- | --- |

**Memory verse: 2 Corinthians 5:18 (NIV)** *"All this is from God, who reconciled us to himself through Christ and gave us the ministry of reconciliation: 19 that God was reconciling the world to himself in Christ, not counting people's sins against them. And he has committed to us the message of reconciliation."*

## Questions for Further Reflection and Discussion

1. Read the above memory verses and talk about how they apply to you.

2. Share when and how you were reconciled to God.

3. Knowing God went to extraordinary lengths to reconcile you to himself, how does that impact you going to extra lengths to reconcile with someone who hurt you?

4. Make a list of people who you think you may need to make amends to. How do you feel about going to them and doing it?

5. Have you lost your love for someone and them for you? What can God do to restore that love? Have you asked him?

6. What does it mean to you to be an Ambassador for Christ? How sold out to reconciliation are you?

# 3.9 Rest—Reflect—Record

### 3.1–Practice Meditation and Solitude

I regularly meditate on God's word and periodically get away to a place of solitude to be recharged and filled up by God. I believe these are key spiritual practices that help me to develop and maintain an intimate relationship with the Father, Son, and Holy Spirit.

| WEAK | 1 | 2 | 3 | 4 | 5 | STRONG |
|------|---|---|---|---|---|--------|

**Memory verse: Mark 6:31b—32 (NIV)** *"Come with me by yourselves to a quiet place and get some rest. So they went away by themselves in a boat to a solitary place."*

### 3.2–Mentor Others

I regularly mentor others. I'm a mature follower of Jesus Christ and want to give away what God has given me to help others to also become committed, mature followers of Christ.

| WEAK | 1 | 2 | 3 | 4 | 5 | STRONG |
|------|---|---|---|---|---|--------|

**Memory verse: Hebrews 5:12a (NLT)** *"You have been believers so long now that you ought to be teaching others. Instead, you need someone to teach you again the basic things about God's Word."*

### 3.3–Be On Mission

I am on mission. My vocation is my mission and I lead and/or support missions with my own church and beyond. I have a passion to multiply Christ-followers both locally and globally.

| WEAK | 1 | 2 | 3 | 4 | 5 | STRONG |
|------|---|---|---|---|---|--------|

**Memory Verse: Acts 20:24 (NLT)** *"But my life is worth nothing to me unless I use it for finishing the work assigned me by the Lord Jesus—the work of telling others the Good News about the wonderful grace of God."*

### 3.4–Kingdom Giving

I am a cheerful giver. I regularly and gladly give above and beyond the tithe, because I understand God was so extravagant when he gave his Son on the cross for me. Therefore, I am passionate about expanding God's kingdom through Kingdom Giving to redeem as many souls as possible.

| WEAK | 1 | 2 | 3 | 4 | 5 | STRONG |
|------|---|---|---|---|---|--------|

**Memory verse: Acts 2:45 (NIV)** *"They sold property and posses-sions to give to anyone who had a need"*

### 3.5–Attaining Spiritual Maturity

I find myself growing to become both spiritually and emotion-ally mature. I have a deeper love, respect and understanding of others. I'm rejecting The Drama more and more and learning to dance with God. I'm growing in giving grace rather than judgement and am actively seeking to Love people as God first loved me.

| WEAK | 1 | 2 | 3 | 4 | 5 | STRONG |
|------|---|---|---|---|---|--------|

**Memory verse: Galatians 5:24 (NIV)** *"Those who belong to Christ Jesus have crucified the sinful nature with its passions and desires. Since we live by the Spirit, let us keep in step with the Spirit."*

### 3.6–Purity and Holiness

I desire to live a life of repentance and therefore confess my sins before God regularly and when necessary to a spiritual mentor. As I grow closer to God, I find myself longing for his spirit to purify me so I can be holy as God is holy (1 Pet. 1:15, 16).

| WEAK | 1 | 2 | 3 | 4 | 5 | STRONG |
|------|---|---|---|---|---|--------|

Memory verse: **1 Peter 1:15-16 (NIV)** *"But just as he who called you is holy, so be holy in all you do; 16 for it is written: 'Be holy, because I am holy.'"*

### 3.7–Disciple-maker

I'm called and commanded by Jesus to make disciples. I take that seriously, and by leaning into him and his word, I can't wait to see what he will do in me and through me to accomplish The Great Commission.

WEAK   1   2   3   4   5   STRONG

**Memory verses: Matthew 28:18b-20 (NIV)** *"All authority in heaven and earth has been given to me. Therefore, go and make disciples (plural) of all nations, baptizing them in the name of the Father, and of the Son and of the Holy Spirit and teaching them to obey everything I commanded you. And surely I am with your always, to the very end of the age"*

### 3.8–Sell out to Reconciliation

I believe my primary purpose is to spread the message of reconciliation to a world that embraces irreconcilable differences. I am an ambassador for Christ first and foremost and, therefore, his love compels me to see all people as redeemable (2 Cor. 5).

WEAK   1   2   3   4   5   STRONG

**Memory verse: 2 Corinthians 5:18 (NIV)** *"All this is from God, who reconciled us to himself through Christ and gave us the ministry of reconciliation: that God was reconciling the world to himself in Christ, not counting people's sins against them. And he has committed to us the message of reconciliation."*

# Epilogue

# Be Resolute

M y hope is that this book has been a turning point for you and your spiritual growth. A turning point in Jesus' journey to the cross came in the gospel of Luke when, *"As the time drew near for him to ascend to heaven, Jesus resolutely set out for Jerusalem"* (Luke 9:51 NLT). It was at this moment that the cross was in full focus for Jesus. He knew the cross was the only obstacle to ais ascension to heaven. So, he *resolutely* set out. True to form, immediately after this key moment, Jesus ran into one man who really wanted to follow him and stated, *"I will follow you wherever you go"* (Luke 9:57 NLT). Jesus warned the man what he was going to have to give up—even a place to sleep—to do so. Two others in the same chapter wanted to follow Jesus, but both gave excuses. One said, "Gotta go bury my father," meaning, "can't go until my dad dies—could be a few years, Jesus." The other, "Gotta go say goodbye to my family." Jesus tells him, *"Anyone who puts a hand to the plan and then looks back is not fit for the Kingdom of God"* (Luke 9:62 NLT). Sounds a little harsh, doesn't it? Jesus is simply being honest. That's the problem with many Christ-followers: we are simply not fit or not in good spiritual fitness. Certainly, we all could use getting into to better shape to first be a resolute disciple and then make disciples. Revisiting the spiritual exercises in this book on an ongoing basis is key. All the great saints of the past two millennia did them resolutely, and so did Jesus. That gives us a clue; we should continue to do them too.

Remember the ghost people in CS Lewis' *The Great Divorce?* The "ghost people" took a journey to the outskirts of heaven where they encountered the solid people in the foothills. The ghost people had the option of getting off the bus and going into the foothills to shed their flimsy selves and be transformed into one of the solid people. Some did, some didn't. The same is true for us. God gives us everything we need in his Word, his Spirit, in his Son Jesus and in each other to become fit and solid for Jesus—totally in love with God and people. Our job is to be resolutely determined to get there. The road signs have been marked out for you. Now the choice is yours. Don't let anything detour you in your spiritual journey of following Jesus! Be resolute!

As we walk with Jesus daily, we become more like him. One of my favorite stories in the early church is where James and John are arrested by the religious leaders. The religious high council doesn't know what to do with them because they were sold out to Jesus. Luke records, *"The members of the council were amazed when they saw the boldness of Peter and John, for they could see that they were ordinary men with no special training in the Scriptures. They also recognized them as men who had been with Jesus"* (Acts 4:13-14 NLT). They were just ordinary men doing extraordinary things for God. I love that! Wouldn't you want people to recognize you as someone who has been with Jesus? I sure do. My prayer, as you cling to Jesus by disciplining yourself for godliness, is that your life will bear fruit in the most amazing ways and God will use your life to multiply Jesus-followers everywhere you go! And he will be so glorified!

# Appendix A

# GROW SELF ASSESSMENT SURVEY

This self-assessment survey is for you to administer to yourself to see where you're at on a periodic basis. *"Be honest in your evaluation of yourselves, measuring yourselves by the faith God has given us"* Romans 12:3b (NLT).

**Milestone 1**

### 1.1–Attend Weekly Church Services
Attending a church service and joining in worship is an essential first step to help me grow in loving God.

WEAK    **1**    **2**    **3**    **4**    **5**    STRONG

**Memory verse: Hebrews 10:25** *"And let us not neglect our meeting together, as some are in the habit of doing, but encourage one another—and all the more as you see the Day approaching"*

### 1.2–Attend a Small Group

I regularly attend a small group or Bible study. Attending a small group is an essential first step to help me grow in loving people.

| WEAK | 1 | 2 | 3 | 4 | 5 | STRONG |

**Memory verse: Acts 2:42 (NIV)** *"They devoted themselves to the apostles' teaching and to fellowship, to the breaking of bread and to prayer."*

### 1.3–Serve at Church

I regularly serve in the church. I have discovered my spiritual gifts and am using them to serve the Lord in my local church. I believe doing my part and serving in the church is an essential first step to help me grow in serving the needs of others in this world.

| WEAK | 1 | 2 | 3 | 4 | 5 | STRONG |

**Memory verse: 1 Corinthians 12:27 (NIV)** *"Now you are the body Christ, and each one of you is a part of it."*

### 1.4–Give Regularly

I regularly give to God through the church. I believe that giving helps me become a more generous person and giving to the church really means giving back to God a portion of what he has so generously given me.

| WEAK | 1 | 2 | 3 | 4 | 5 | STRONG |

**Memory verse: 2 Corinthians 9:7 (NLT)** *"You must each decide in your heart how much to give. And don't give reluctantly or in response to pressure. "For God loves a person who gives cheerfully."*

### 1.5–Support Leaders

I wholeheartedly support and obey the church leadership. I am learning to resolve any issues I have with my leaders or others directly with the person involved in an emotionally healthy fashion.

WEAK   1   2   3   4   5   STRONG

]

**Memory verse: Hebrews 13:17 (NIV)** *"Have confidence in your leaders and submit to their authority, because they keep watch over you as those who must give an account. Do this so that their work will be a joy, not a burden, for that would be of no benefit to you."*

### 1.6–Be Real

I know I am a sinner saved by grace alone. Therefore, I am transparent, authentic and honest and not a spiritual poser. I keep a short list of my sins and confess any sin issues I have. With the help of God, I'm becoming the real me.

WEAK   1   2   3   4   5   STRONG

**Memory verse: Matthew 23: 5 (NLT)** *"Everything they do is for show. On their arms they wear extra wide prayer boxes with Scripture verses inside, and they wear robes with extra-long tassels."*

### 1.7–Reach Out

I am beginning to understand the church's mission of reaching out to people who don't know Jesus yet. I am excited to tell others about my church and about Jesus, even though they might think I'm crazy and, at times, say hurtful things about my faith. I pray for people in my life who don't yet have a relationship with God (1 Pet. 3:15-16).

**Memory verse: 1 Peter 3:15 (NIV)** *"But in your hearts revere Christ as Lord. Always be prepared to give an answer to everyone who asks you to give the reason for the hope that you have. But do this with gentleness and respect."*

WEAK   **1**   **2**   **3**   **4**   **5**   STRONG

### 1.8–Forgive

I am willing to forgive those who hurt me, even when it's hard. I understand that unforgiveness is unhealthy and toxic. Mostly, I believe that God has forgiven me and paid the ultimate price by sending his Son to die on the cross for all my sins. Therefore, I must forgive others and not hold resentments against them.

WEAK   **1**   **2**   **3**   **4**   **5**   STRONG

**Memory verses: Matthew 18:21, 22** *"Then Peter came to Jesus and asked, 'Lord, how many times shall I forgive someone who sins against me? Up to seven times?' Jesus answered, 'I tell you, not seven times, but seventy times seven.'"*

**TOTAL SCORE:**

**AREAS FOR GROWTH:**

**AREAS OF STRENGTH:**

## Milestone 2

### 2.1–Practice Daily Devotion

I practice a daily quiet time, giving God my undivided attention though prayer, Bible reading, and journaling is one of the most important steps to loving God and growing closer to him every day (Mark 1:35; Deut. 6:4-9).

WEAK    1    2    3    4    5    STRONG

**Memory verse: John 15:5** *"I am the vine; you are the branches. If you remain in me and I in you, you will bear much fruit; apart from me you can do nothing."*

### 2.2–Lead or Support a Small Group

I regularly lead, co-lead, or support a small group. I understand that it's great to be a small group participant, but now I also feel responsible to help others grow by leading, co-leading, hosting, or supporting a small group.

WEAK    1    2    3    4    5    STRONG

**Memory verse: Ephesians 4:16 (NLT)** *"He makes the whole body fit together perfectly. As each part does it's own special work, it helps other parts grow, so that the whole body is healthy and growing full of love."*

### 2.3–Go on a Mission

I love serving in mission opportunities, across town or out of the country. I have a passion to serve outside the borders of this church and be involved in expanding God's kingdom both locally and globally.

| WEAK | 1 | 2 | 3 | 4 | 5 | STRONG |
|------|---|---|---|---|---|--------|

**Memory verse: Luke 10:2 (NIV)** *"He told them, the harvest is plentiful, but the workers are few. Ask the Lord of the harvest, therefore, to send out workers into his harvest field."*

### 2.4–Tithe

I faithfully tithe to my home church. Faithfully giving 10 percent of my income is an act of worship that helps me grow my faith in God, who always provides all that I need (Mal. 3:8-11).

| WEAK | 1 | 2 | 3 | 4 | 5 | STRONG |
|------|---|---|---|---|---|--------|

**Memory Verse: Malachi 3:10 (NIV)** *"Bring the whole tithe into the storehouse, that there may be food in my house. Test me in this,"* says the Lord Almighty, *"and see if I will not throw open the floodgates of heaven and pour out so much blessing that there will not be room enough to store it."*

### 2.5–Grow-up Emotionally

I am not offended by others. I am learning to love people who hurt me, to give others the benefit of the doubt when I don't understand their actions, and to not pass judgment on them. I don't need to have my way (Rom. 12:17-21).

```
WEAK    1    2    3    4    5   STRONG
```

**Memory verse: Ephesians 4:2 (NLT)** *"Always be humble and gentle, be patient with each other, making allowance for each other's faults because of your love."*

### 2.6–Be Mentored Spiritually
I regularly meet with a special mentor or an accountability partner who is further along their spiritual journey than I am. I want to be held accountable and embody what it means to be faithful, available, and teachable.

```
WEAK    1    2    3    4    5   STRONG
```

**Memory verse: Proverbs 27:17** *"As Iron sharpens Iron, so one man sharpens another."*

### 2.7–Persevere
I am not a quitter. I am so glad Jesus did not quit on me and persevered all the way to the cross. I know suffering is part of life and, although I don't like it, I also know often that's where I grow most. Therefore, I'm committed to persevere to the end (Rom. 5:3b-5).

```
WEAK    1    2    3    4    5   STRONG
```

**Memory verse: Romans 5:3b-5 (NIV)** *"We know that suffering produces perseverance; perseverance, character; and character, hope. And hope does not put us to shame, because God's love has been* *poured out into our hearts through the Holy Spirit, who has been given to us."*

### 2.8–Obedience

I have an increasing desire to read, understand, and obey the Bible. I believe the Holy Spirit gives me the wisdom and power to understand and obey God's Word, and how to apply it to my daily life.

WEAK    1    2    3    4    5    STRONG

**Memory verses: 1 John 2:4, 5a (NIV)** *"Those who say, 'I know him', but do not do what he commands are liars, and the truth is not in them. But if anyone obeys his word, love for God is truly made complete in them'".*

**TOTAL SCORE:**

**AREAS FOR GROWTH:**

**AREAS OF STRENGTH:**

## Milestone 3

### 3.1–Practice Meditation and Solitude

I regularly meditate on God's Word and periodically get away to a place of solitude to be recharged and filled up by God. I believe these are key spiritual practices that help me to develop and maintain an intimate relationship with the Father, Son, and Holy Spirit.

| WEAK | 1 | 2 | 3 | 4 | 5 | STRONG |
|------|---|---|---|---|---|--------|

**Memory verse: Mark 6:31b–32 (NIV)** *"Come with me by your-selves to a quiet place and get some rest. So they went away by themselves in a boat to a solitary place."*

### 3.2–Mentor Others

I regularly mentor others. I'm a mature follower of Jesus Christ and want to give away what God has given me to help others to also become committed, mature followers of Christ.

| WEAK | 1 | 2 | 3 | 4 | 5 | STRONG |
|------|---|---|---|---|---|--------|

**Memory verse: Hebrews 5:12a (NLT)** *"You have been believers so long now that you ought to be teaching others. Instead, you need someone to teach you again the basic things about God's Word."*

### 3.3–Be On Mission

I am on mission. My vocation is my mission and/or I also support or lead missions. I have a passion to multiply Christ-followers both locally and globally.

WEAK    **1**    **2**    **3**    **4**    **5**    STRONG

**Memory Verse: Acts 20:24 (NLT)** *"But my life is worth nothing to me unless I use it for finishing the work assigned me by the Lord Jesus—the work of telling others the Good News about the wonderful grace of God."*

### 3.4–Kingdom Giving

I am a cheerful giver. I regularly and gladly give above and beyond the tithe, because I understand God was so extravagant when he gave his Son for me. Therefore, I am passionate about expanding God's Kingdom through Kingdom giving to redeem as many souls as possible.

WEAK    **1**    **2**    **3**    **4**    **5**    STRONG

**Memory verse: Acts 2:45 (NIV)** *"They sold property and possessions to give to anyone who had a need."*

### 3.5–Attaining Spiritual Maturity

I find myself growing to become both spiritually and emotionally mature. I have a deeper love, respect, and understanding of others. I'm rejecting the Drama more and more and learning to live in the Dance with God. I'm growing in giving grace rather than judgement and am actively seeking to love people as God first loved me.

WEAK    1    2    3    4    5    STRONG

**Memory verse: Galatians 5:24 (NIV)** *"Those who belong to Christ Jesus have crucified the sinful nature with its passions and desires. Since we live by the Spirit, let us keep in step with the Spirit."*

### 3.6–Purity and Holiness

I desire to live a life of repentance and therefore confess my sins before God regularly and, when necessary, to a spiritual mentor. As I grow closer to God, I find myself longing for his Spirit to purify me so I can be holy as God is holy.

WEAK    1    2    3    4    5    STRONG

Memory verse: **1 Peter 1:15-16 (NIV)** *"But just as he who called you is holy, so be holy in all you do; for it is written: 'Be holy, because I am holy.'"*

### 3.7–Disciple-maker

I'm called and commanded by Jesus to make disciples. I take that seriously and by leaning into him and his Word, I can't wait to see what he will do in me and through me to accomplish the Great Commission.

**Memory verses: Matthew 28:18b-20 (NIV)** *"All authority in heaven and earth has been given to me. Therefore go and make disciples (plural) of all nations, baptizing them in the name of the Father, and of the Son and of the Holy Spirit and teaching them* *to obey everything I commanded you. And surely I am with your always, to the very end of the age"*

### 3.8–Sell-out to Reconciliation

I believe my primary purpose is to spread the message of reconciliation to a world that embraces irreconcilable differences. I am an ambassador for Christ first and foremost and therefore his love compels to see all people as redeemable – I'm sold out to reconciliation.

WEAK   **1**     **2**     **3**     **4**     **5**   STRONG

**Memory verse: 2 Corinthians 5:18 (NIV)** *"All this is from God, who reconciled us to himself through Christ and gave us the ministry of reconciliation: 19 that God was reconciling the world to himself in Christ, not counting people's sins against them. And he has committed to us the message of reconciliation."*

**TOTAL SCORE:**

**AREAS FOR GROWTH:**

**AREAS OF STRENGTH:**

## GROW SELF ASSESSMENT SURVEY

This self-assessment survey is for you to administer to yourself to see where you're at on a periodic basis. *"Be honest in your evaluation of yourselves, measuring yourselves by the faith God has given us"* Romans 12:3b (NLT).

### 1.1–Attend Church
I attend weekly church services. Attending a church service and joining in worship is an essential first step to help me grow in loving God.

| WEAK | 1 | 2 | 3 | 4 | 5 | STRONG |
|------|---|---|---|---|---|--------|

**Memory verse: Hebrews 10:25** *"And let us not neglect our meeting together, as some are in the habit of doing, but encourage one another—and all the more as you see the Day approaching"*

### 1.2–Attend a Small Group
I regularly attend a small group or Bible study. Attending a small group is an essential first step to help me grow in loving people.

| WEAK | 1 | 2 | 3 | 4 | 5 | STRONG |

**Memory verse: Acts 2:42 (NIV)** *"They devoted themselves to the apostles' teaching and to fellowship, to the breaking of bread and to prayer."*

### 1.3–Serve at Church

I regularly serve in the church. I have discovered my spiritual gifts and am using them to serve the Lord in my local church. I believe doing my part and serving in the church is an essential first step to help me grow in serving the needs of others in this world.

| WEAK | 1 | 2 | 3 | 4 | 5 | STRONG |

**Memory verse: 1 Corinthians 12:27 (NIV)** *"Now you are the body Christ, and each one of you is a part of it."*

### 1.4–Give Regularly

I regularly give to God through the church. I believe that giving helps me become a more generous person and giving to the church really means giving back to God a portion of what he has so generously given me.

| WEAK | 1 | 2 | 3 | 4 | 5 | STRONG |

**Memory verse: 2 Corinthians 9:7 (NLT)** *"You must each decide in your heart how much to give. And don't give reluctantly or in response to pressure. "For God loves a person who gives cheerfully."*

## 1.5–Support Leaders

I wholeheartedly support and obey the church leadership. I am learning to resolve any issues I have with my leaders or others directly with the person involved in an emotionally healthy fashion.

WEAK　　1　　2　　3　　4　　5　　STRONG

**Memory verse: Hebrews 13:17 (NIV)** *"Have confidence in your leaders and submit to their authority, because they keep watch over you as those who must give an account. Do this so that their work will be a joy, not a burden, for that would be of no benefit to you."*

## 1.6–Be Real

I know I am a sinner saved by grace alone. Therefore, I am transparent, authentic and honest and not a spiritual poser. I keep a short list of my sins and confess any sin issues I have. With the help of God, I'm becoming the real me.

WEAK　　1　　2　　3　　4　　5　　STRONG

**Memory verse: Matthew 23: 5 (NLT)** *"Everything they do is for show. On their arms they wear extra wide prayer boxes with Scripture verses inside, and they wear robes with extra-long tassels."*

## 1.7–Reach Out

I am beginning to understand the church's mission of reaching out to people who don't know Jesus yet. I am excited to tell others about my church and about Jesus, even though they might think I'm crazy and, at times, say hurtful things about my faith. I pray for people in my life who don't yet have a relationship with God (1 Pet. 3:15-16).

**Memory verse: 1 Peter 3:15 (NIV)** *"But in your hearts revere Christ as Lord. Always be prepared to give an answer to everyone who asks you to give the reason for the hope that you have. But do this with gentleness and respect."*

| WEAK | 1 | 2 | 3 | 4 | 5 | STRONG |
|------|---|---|---|---|---|--------|

**1.8–Forgive**
I am willing to forgive those who hurt me, even when it's hard. I understand that unforgiveness is unhealthy and toxic. Mostly, I believe that God has forgiven me and paid the ultimate price by sending his Son to die on the cross for all my sins. Therefore, I must forgive others and not hold resentments against them.

| WEAK | 1 | 2 | 3 | 4 | 5 | STRONG |
|------|---|---|---|---|---|--------|

**Memory verses: Matthew 18:21, 22** *"Then Peter came to Jesus and asked, 'Lord, how many times shall I forgive someone who sins against me? Up to seven times?' Jesus answered, 'I tell you, not seven times, but seventy times seven.'"*

**TOTAL SCORE:**

**AREAS FOR GROWTH:**

**AREAS OF STRENGTH:**

## 2.1–Personal Devotional Time

I practice a daily quiet time. Giving God my undivided attention though prayer, Bible reading, and journaling is one of the most important steps to loving God and growing closer to him every day.

WEAK    1    2    3    4    5    STRONG

**Memory verse: John 15:5 (NIV)** *"I am the vine; you are the branches. If you remain in me and I in you, you will bear much fruit; apart from me you can do nothing."*

## 2.2–Lead or Support a Small Group

I regularly lead, co-lead, or support a small group. I understand that it's great to be a small group participant, but now I also feel responsible to help others grow by leading, co-leading, hosting, or supporting a small group.

WEAK    1    2    3    4    5    STRONG

**Memory verse: Ephesians 4:16 (NLT)** *"He makes the whole body fit together perfectly. As each part does its own special work,* *it helps other parts grow, so that the whole body is healthy and growing full of love."*

## 2.3–Go on a Mission
I love serving in a mission opportunity, across town or out of the country. I have a passion to serve outside the borders of this church and be involved in expanding God's Kingdom both locally and globally.

[

| WEAK | 1 | 2 | 3 | 4 | 5 | STRONG |

**Memory verse: Luke 10:2 (NIV)** *"He told them, the harvest is plentiful, but the workers are few. Ask the Lord of the harvest, therefore, to send out workers into his harvest field."*

## 2.4–Tithe
I faithfully tithe to my home church. Faithfully giving ten percent of my income is an act of worship that helps me grow my faith in God, who always provides all I need.

| WEAK | 1 | 2 | 3 | 4 | 5 | STRONG |

**Memory Verse: Malachi 3:10 (NIV)** *"Bring the whole tithe into the storehouse, that there may be food in my house. Test me in this,"* says the Lord Almighty, *"and see if I will not throw open the floodgates of heaven and pour out so much blessing that there will not be room enough to store it."*

## 2.5–Grow up—Emotionally
I am not offended by others. I am learning to love people who hurt me, to give others the benefit of the doubt when I don't

GROW

understand their actions, and to not pass judgment on them. I don't need to have my way.

( WEAK    1    2    3    4    5    STRONG )

**Memory verse: Ephesians 4:2 (NLT)** *"Always be humble and gentle, be patient with each other, making allowance for each other's faults because of your love."*

## 2.6–Be Mentored Spiritually

I regularly meet with a special mentor and/or an accountability partner who is further along The Spiritual Journey than I am. I want to be held accountable and embody what it means to be faithful, available, and teachable.

( WEAK    1    2    3    4    5    STRONG )

**Memory verse: Proverbs 27:17 NIV** *"As Iron sharpens Iron, so one man sharpens another."*

## 2.7–Persevere

I am not a quitter. I am so glad Jesus did not quit on me and persevered all the way to the cross. I know suffering is part of life and although I don't like it, I know often that's where I grow most. Therefore, I'm committed to persevere to the end.

( WEAK    1    2    3    4    5    STRONG )

**Memory verse: Romans 5:3b-5 (NIV)** *"We know that suffering produces perseverance; perseverance, character; and character, hope. And hope does not put us to shame, because God's love has been* *poured out into our hearts through the Holy Spirit, who has been given to us."*

### 2.8–Obedience

I have an increasing desire to read, understand and obey the Bible. I believe the Holy Spirit gives me the wisdom and power to understand and obey God's word, and shows me how to apply it to my daily life.

WEAK    **1**     **2**     **3**     **4**     **5**    STRONG

**Memory verses: 1 John 2:4, 5a (NIV)** *"Those who say, 'I know him, but do not do what he command are liars, and the truth is not in them. But if anyone obeys his Word, love for God is truly made complete in them.'"*

**TOTAL SCORE:**

**AREAS FOR GROWTH:**

**AREAS OF STRENGTH:**

### 3.1–Practice Meditation and Solitude

I regularly meditate on God's word and periodically get away to a place of solitude to be recharged and filled up by God. I believe these are key spiritual practices that help me to develop and maintain an intimate relationship with the Father, Son, and Holy Spirit.

WEAK   1   2   3   4   5   STRONG

**Memory verse: Mark 6:31b–32 (NIV)** *"Come with me by yourselves to a quiet place and get some rest. So they went away by themselves in a boat to a solitary place."*

### 3.2–Mentor Others

I regularly mentor others. I'm a mature follower of Jesus Christ and want to give away what God has given me to help others to also become committed, mature followers of Christ.

WEAK   1   2   3   4   5   STRONG

**Memory verse: Hebrews 5:12a (NLT)** *"You have been believers so long now that you ought to be teaching others. Instead, you need someone to teach you again the basic things about God's Word."*

### 3.3–Be On Mission

I am on mission. My vocation is my mission and/or I also support or lead missions. I have a passion to multiply Christ-followers both locally and globally.

```
( WEAK    1    2    3    4    5    STRONG )
```

**Memory Verse: Acts 20:24 (NLT)** *"But my life is worth nothing to me unless I use it for finishing the work assigned me by the Lord Jesus—the work of telling others the Good News about the wonderful grace of God."*

### 3.4–Kingdom Giving

I am a cheerful giver. I regularly and gladly give above and beyond the tithe, because I understand God was so extravagant when he gave his Son for me. Therefore, I am passionate about expanding God's Kingdom through Kingdom Giving to redeem as many souls as possible.

```
( WEAK    1    2    3    4    5    STRONG )
```

**Memory verse: Acts 2:45 (NIV)** *"They sold property and possessions to give to anyone who had a need."*

### 3.5–Attaining Spiritual Maturity

I find myself growing to become both spiritually and emotionally mature. I have a deeper love, respect, and understanding of others. I'm rejecting the Drama more and more and learning to live in the Dance with God. I'm growing in giving grace rather than judgement and am actively seeking to love people as God first loved me.

| WEAK | 1 | 2 | 3 | 4 | 5 | STRONG |

**Memory verse: Galatians 5:24 (NIV)** *"Those who belong to Christ Jesus have crucified the sinful nature with its passions and desires. Since we live by the Spirit, let us keep in step with the Spirit."*

### 3.6–Purity and Holiness
I desire to live a life of repentance and therefore confess my sins before God regularly and, when necessary, to a spiritual mentor. As I grow closer to God, I find myself longing for his Spirit to purify me so I can be holy as God is holy.

| WEAK | 1 | 2 | 3 | 4 | 5 | STRONG |

Memory verse: **1 Peter 1:15-16 (NIV)** *"But just as he who called you is holy, so be holy in all you do; for it is written: 'Be holy, because I am holy.'"*

### 3.7–Disciple-maker
I'm called and commanded by Jesus to make disciples. I take that seriously and by leaning into him and his Word, I can't wait to see what he will do in me and through me to accomplish The Great Commission.

**Memory verses: Matthew 28:18b-20 (NIV)** *"All authority in heaven and earth has been given to me. Therefore go and make disciples (plural) of all nations, baptizing them in the name of the Father, and of the Son and of the Holy Spirit and teaching them to obey everything I commanded you. And surely I am with your always, to the very end of the age"*

### 3.8–Sell-out to Reconciliation

I believe my primary purpose is to spread the message of reconciliation to a world that embraces irreconcilable differences. I am an ambassador for Christ first and foremost and therefore his love compels to see all people as redeemable – I'm sold out to reconciliation.

| WEAK | 1 | 2 | 3 | 4 | 5 | STRONG |

**Memory verse: 2 Corinthians 5:18 (NIV)** *"All this is from God, who reconciled us to himself through Christ and gave us the ministry of reconciliation: 19 that God was reconciling the world to himself in Christ, not counting people's sins against them. And he has committed to us the message of reconciliation."*

**TOTAL SCORE:**

**AREAS FOR GROWTH:**

**AREAS OF STRENGTH:**

# Appendix B

# Implementing GROW at Your Church

Y ou have likely already seen that this book is tailored for small groups. As you consider starting GROW Discipleship classes at your church, know that it's pretty simple. It's all based on the book. We recommend you take your church staff through the book first, to strengthen their spiritual journey in order to lead and guide the church family as they embark on The Spiritual Journey. Start each class with a surrendered commitment to the mandate of the Great Commission and know that Jesus will certainly be with you—as he promised—if you are consistent in your resolve to make disciples. Here's how we do it:

We recommend offering Milestone 1, Milestone 2, and Milestone 3 classes every quarter of the year—three times a year for each class. We make each class available every quarter, except in summer. Start with a New Friends Lunch for new people at your church.

**New Friends Lunch (NFL):** This is on ramp for GROW classes. Here we provide a lunch once a month after our last Sunday morning church service. In our NFL, we share what the church is all about, how we seek to meet the spiritual needs of each person who attends, and our aim to provide a community in which members can engage and grow. Essentially, we give a light "brochure" of what the church is all about. The final focus of the lunch is to encourage them to take the next step in their spiritual journey by attending the Milestone 1 class.

**Milestone 1 class:** We start with the Love God, Love Others, Serve the World icon

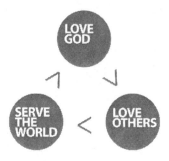

Then we share how that's what everything we do comes out of. Next, we share The Spiritual Journey Continuum as follows:

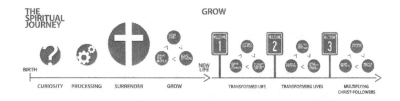

GROW is easy to teach; just follow the teaching in the book. We encourage those who are going to teach it to learn how to draw the above Spiritual Journey Map upside down on a napkin in a coffee shop, like you're actually using it to lead someone to Christ. Chances are that some people who take this class will not be Christ-followers yet and you'll have the chance to lead them to Christ. One-on-one conversations between trained leaders and class attendees with The Spiritual Journey Continuum can reveal areas people are "stuck" in, blocking them from making a focused surrender to Jesus Christ. Help them get their questions answered if they have some.

In this class, take some time for questions. When you get to the Cross/Surrender part, lead the class in a prayer of salvation and surrender to Christ. It's good for everyone to pray out loud to add strength to those who are praying to trust Christ for the first time.

After this, the key focus is Milestones 1.1, 1.2, and 1.3, which are highlighted in the following icon:

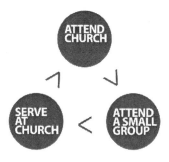

Use the book as much as you feel comfortable with, but also do what fits your church culture. One of the most important parts of the Milestone 1 class is the gifts assessments. Getting more and more people assessed and serving in their area of giftedness and passion will supercharge your church! It's amazing! It's key to making disciples.

After these three areas, pick and choose what you want to focus on regarding 1.4 through 1.8. You should give everyone a book to keep. That way, they can read and grow on their own. At some point, have them take the GROW Survey; copy it and have your class members write their names on it and hand it in with all their gifts assessment materials.

Note: All the materials they hand in are like *gold*! Please do your best to process it all quickly and call them back in to have a one-on-one coaching session with a pastor or ministry leader.

Then have them first visit potential ministry areas of interest, followed by getting them them plugged into a good fit serving position twice a month in your church for Sunday and/or mid-week serving teams. Remember, we were made for community–no one serves alone!

At the end of the Milestone 1 class, encourage everyone to read the GROW book and focus on building a solid foundation for their spiritual journey, but also come back for the Milestone 2 class.

Milestone 2 Class: The prerequisite for the Milestone 2 class is completing Milestone 1 in the book and in the class. As you teach this Milestone 2 class, again, focus on Milestones 2.1, 2.2, and 2.3 as the following icon indicates:

I highly recommend 2.5 for emotional growth. As you have already read, 2.1 Practicing Daily Devotion is pretty much the ball game. So, I emphasize that milestone the most. At this milestone, I would also talk about tithing. We have determined this is the place where we invite people to be members or partners in our church. As we wrestled with GROW and membership and where to put church membership in the process, one of the most brilliant statements came from our Senior Pastor, Stan Russell, "Membership is getting in the way of discipleship." I loved that! Often churches are so bent on membership and getting people to agree on things that don't matter that much that it clouds discipleship. We realized Jesus never said, "Go make members." It's something to seriously think about.

Get names of people who are willing to be mentored. Create a profile of who they are and where they are at in their spiritual journey. This way you can pair them up with people willing to mentor them from Milestone 3. If you have a mission opportunity for people to go on, this is a great class to gain interest and get sign-ups.

**Milestone 3 Class:** The prerequisite for taking the Milestone 3 class is completing the Milestone 2 class and reading Milestone 2 in the GROW book, scoring 3 to 5 on most milestones. There is a lot of great stuff in this particular section. Focusing on Milestones 3.1 to 3.3 as follows is a great start.

This is a great opportunity to get names of people willing to mentor others. Teach the guidelines in the class that are in the book. Follow up with those in Milestone 2 who are looking for a spiritual mentor. This is where you intentionally pair people up for a tryout. Learning The Drama and The Dance and drawing it on the white board for your class is also very powerful. Be vulnerable where you struggle in that yourself. Make sure you get to reconciliation. It is vital.

**www.thegrowjourney.com**

Log onto **www.thegrowjourney.com** for video training
and image downloads and quantity discounts on
the GROW book are also available.

For churches, we highly recommend using GROW as a discipleship sermon series emphasis, aligning all your church small groups with the sermon series. Continue to offer GROW small groups and quarterly classes as noted in Appendix A. GROW serves as an excellent discipleship plan and resource.

The key thing is you're really going to make disciples if you follow the book to a large degree. God bless you on your spiritual journey as you go for it!

# Appendix C

# SOAPING MODEL and Bible Reading Plan

---

S OAP is a great tool to use scripture to wash your soul. It's really simple. The following are some simple steps to help you embrace SOAPing:

Step 1—Pray. Something like this: "Jesus, you said in John 16 that your Spirit would guide me in all truth. So, I'm listening. Teach me today as I read the Bible.

Step 2—Find the Scriptures for today in the Bible Reading Plan on the next pages.

Step 3—Read the assigned passages. Note if you choose the "Milestone 1" plan, it will take you through the whole New Testament in one year. If you're at Milestone 2 in your Spiritual Journey, choose the "Milestone 2" plan. It will get you through the whole Bible in a year. If you are at Milestone 3 in your Spiritual Journey, choose the "Milestone 3" plan. It will get take you through the entire Bible in a year and the New Testament twice. Try to read the assigned passages daily, but if you miss a day don't sweat it. Just move on to the next day's assigned passages. Note for Pastors and Teachers: Your yearly journal can serve as a quick reference for interweaving personal testimony and reflections as you prepare sermons and presentations from different scriptures in God's Word.

Step 4—Choose one gem or verse that grabbed your attention as you were reading. I underline those passages in my Bible. Write it out in your journal as your "S" Scripture. That will be the passage you meditate on utilizing the SOAP tool.

## S.O.A.P.

- Write today's date.
- Write down the verse that caught your attention. **(Scripture)**
- Write down what you observe in the scripture, taking into consideration what was going on in the surrounding context. **(Observation)**
- Write down how you can apply that scripture to your life. What's God affirming in your life? What's God challenging you to change? **(Application)**
- Write out a prayer to thank God for his Word and to help you apply his word specifically to your life. **(Prayer)**

The following is an example of one of my SOAPs:

**SOAP Example**
**By Brad Brucker**

**Bible Reading for March 16th: Deuteronomy 30, 31, Psalm 40, and 1 Corinthians 1**

**Scripture: Deuteronomy 30:19, 20a (New Living Translation)**

"Today I have given you the choice between life and death, between blessings and curses. Now I call on heaven and earth to witness the choice you make. Oh, that you would choose life, so that you and your descendants might live! You can make this choice by loving The Lord your God, obeying him and committing yourself firmly to him. This (He) is the key to your life!"—*Spoken by God through Moses*

**Observation:**

Moses is clearly laying out before all the Israelites a choice they must make: follow God and live a great life full of blessings or do your own thing and—slowly or quickly, but certainly painfully—die from a life full of curses. He's saying *"Choose, choose"*—pleading with them to choose life. You can hear the pleading and anguish in his voice in the text. God's voice through Moses said, "Oh, that you would choose life and live!" Wow!

**Application:**

Every day we have a choice to make. God is the God of life—all life! And he longs for us to choose him, cling to him and his Word, as we pray and walk along the road. He promises if we do we will truly *live* and be blessed. He is the key to life. Jesus said, "Give us this day our daily bread." He didn't say, give us this week. Nope! Just this day. Yesterday, I got upset with Ann and said some things I shouldn't have. I actually chose a bit of death yesterday. Today, I will go to her and ask her for forgiveness and be a life-giver like God is to me. So, today, I choose life with God—today!

**Prayer:**

Dear Lord, it's amazing you actually give us a choice. You don't force yourself on us because you loved us so much. Help me to go to Ann and ask her for forgiveness. Holy Spirit, go before me and help her be receptive to my words and bring 100 percent reconciliation to our relationship. Heal her of the wounds I have caused her. Lord, help me to love you and others today with everything I have. I'm all yours, Lord. Do with me as you please. Help me to live today to bless you. Thy kingdom come, Thy will be done in my life today. In Jesus' name, Amen.

# BIBLE READING GUIDE

## JANUARY

| | MILESTONE 1 | MILESTONE 2 | MILESTONE 3 |
|---|---|---|---|
| 1 | Genesis 2:4-25 | Genesis 2; Luke 1:26-66 | Genesis 1-2; Luke 1 |
| 2 | Luke 2:1-40 | Genesis 3; Luke 2 | Genesis 3-5; Luke 2 |
| 3 | Genesis 6 | Genesis 6-7; Luke 3:1-22 | Genesis 6-8; Luke 3 |
| 4 | Luke 4:1-30 | Genesis 9; Luke 4 | Genesis 9-11; Luke 4 |
| 5 | Genesis 12 | Genesis 12; Luke 5 | Genesis 12-14; Luke 5 |
| 6 | Luke 6:37-49 | Genesis 15; Luke 6 | Genesis 15-17; Luke 6 |
| 7 | Luke 7:1-17; Psalms 3 | Genesis 18; Psalms 3; Luke 7 | Genesis 18-19; Psalms 3; Luke 7 |
| 8 | Genesis 22 | Genesis 22; Luke 8 | Genesis 20-22; Luke 8 |
| 9 | Luke 9:1-20 | Genesis 24; Luke 9 | Genesis 23-24; Luke 9 |
| 10 | Luke 10:1-29 | Genesis 25; Luke 10 | Genesis 25-26; Psalms 6; Luke 10 |
| 11 | Luke 11:1-13 | Genesis 28; Psalms 4; Luke 11 | Genesis 27-28; Psalms 4; Luke 11 |
| 12 | Luke 12:35-48 | Genesis 29; Luke 12 | Genesis 29-30; Luke 12 |
| 13 | Genesis 33 | Genesis 33; Luke 13 | Genesis 31-33; Luke 13 |
| 14 | Luke 14:25-35 | Genesis 35; Luke 14 | Genesis 34-36; Luke 14 |
| 15 | Luke 15:11-31 | Psalms 7; Luke 15 | Genesis 37-38; Psalms 7; Luke 15 |
| 16 | Genesis 41:37-57 | Genesis 41; Luke 16 | Genesis 39-41; Luke 16 |
| 17 | Psalms 5 | Psalms 5; Luke 17 | Genesis 42-43; Psalms 5; Luke 17 |
| 18 | Luke 18:1-17 | Genesis 45; Luke 18 | Genesis 44-46; Luke 18 |
| 19 | Luke 19:28-48 | Genesis 48; Luke 19 | Genesis 47-48; Psalms 10; Luke 19 |
| 20 | Genesis 50:1-21 | Genesis 50; Luke 20 | Genesis 49-50; Psalms 8; Luke 20 |
| 21 | Exodus 2:1-10 | Exodus 2; Luke 21 | Exodus 1-2; Psalms 88; Luke 21 |
| 22 | Exodus 3:1-18 | Exodus 3; Luke 22 | Exodus 3-5; Luke 22 |
| 23 | Exodus 6:1-13 | Exodus 6; Luke 23 | Exodus 6-8; Luke 23 |
| 24 | Exodus 9:13-35 | Exodus 9; Luke 24 | Exodus 9-11; Luke 24 |
| 25 | Exodus 12:1-30 | Exodus 12; Psalms 21 | Exodus 12-13; Psalms 21; Acts 1 |
| 26 | Acts 2:1-21; 43-47 | Exodus 15; Acts 2 | Exodus 14-16; Acts 2 |
| 27 | Exodus 18:13-27 | Exodus 18; Acts 3 | Exodus 17-20; Acts 3 |
| 28 | Acts 4:1-22 | Psalms 12; Acts 4 | Exodus 21-22; Psalms 12; Acts 4 |
| 29 | Exodus 23:20-33 | Exodus 23; Psalms 14 | Exodus 23-24; Psalms 14; Acts 5 |
| 30 | Acts 6 | Exodus 27; Acts 6 | Exodus 25-27; Acts 6 |
| 31 | Acts 7:20-43 | Exodus 29; Acts 7 | Exodus 28-29; Acts 7 |

Adapted and used with permission from Life Resources

# BIBLE READING GUIDE

# FEBRUARY

| | MILESTONE 1 | MILESTONE 2 | MILESTONE 3 |
|---|---|---|---|
| 1 | Acts 8:26-40 | Exodus 32; Acts 8 | Exodus 30-32; Acts 8 |
| 2 | Acts 9:1-20 | Exodus 33; Acts 9 | Exodus 33-34; Psalms 16; Acts 9 |
| 3 | Acts 10:1-33 | Exodus 36; Acts 10 | Exodus 35-36; Acts 10 |
| 4 | Psalms 19 | Psalms 19; Acts 11 | Exodus 37-38; Psalms 19; Acts 11 |
| 5 | Exodus 39:32-43 | Exodus 39; Psalms 15 | Exodus 39-40; Psalms 15; Acts 12 |
| 6 | Acts 13:1-12 | Leviticus 1; Acts 13 | Leviticus 1-3; Acts 13 |
| 7 | Acts 14:8-20 | Leviticus 6; Acts 14 | Leviticus 4-6; Acts 14 |
| 8 | Acts 15:1-21 | Leviticus 9; Acts 15 | Leviticus 7-9; Acts 15 |
| 9 | Acts 16:16-40 | Leviticus 10; Acts 16 | Leviticus 10-12; Acts 16 |
| 10 | Acts 17:1-15 | Acts 17 | Leviticus 13-14; Acts 17 |
| 11 | Acts 18:1-17 | Leviticus 16; Acts 18 | Leviticus 15-17; Acts 18 |
| 12 | Acts 19:8-20 | Leviticus 19; Acts 19 | Leviticus 18-19; Psalms 13; Acts 19 |
| 13 | Acts 20:13-38 | Leviticus 22; Acts 20 | Leviticus 20-22; Acts 20 |
| 14 | Psalms 24 | Leviticus 24; Psalms 24 | Leviticus 23-24; Psalms 24; Acts 21 |
| 15 | Psalms 25 | Psalms 25; Acts 22 | Leviticus 25; Psalms 25-26; Acts 22 |
| 16 | Leviticus 26:1-13 | Leviticus 26; Acts 23 | Leviticus 26-27; Acts 23 |
| 17 | Acts 24 | Numbers 1; Acts 24 | Numbers 1-2; Acts 24 |
| 18 | Acts 25:1-22 | Numbers 4; Acts 25 | Numbers 3-4; Acts 25 |
| 19 | Acts 26 | Psalms 22; Acts 26 | Numbers 5-6; Psalms 22; Acts 26 |
| 20 | Psalms 23 | Psalms 23; Acts 27 | Numbers 7; Psalms 23; Acts 27 |
| 21 | Numbers 9:15-23 | Numbers 9; Acts 28 | Numbers 8-9; Acts 28 |
| 22 | Mark 1:29-45 | Psalms 27; Mark 1 | Numbers 10-11; Psalms 27; Mark 1 |
| 23 | Mark 2:1-17 | Psalms 90; Mark 2 | Numbers 12-13; Psalms 90; Mark 2 |
| 24 | Mark 3:13-35 | Numbers 16; Mark 3 | Numbers 14-16; Mark 3 |
| 25 | Numbers 17 | Numbers 17; Mark 4 | Numbers 17-18; Psalms 29; Mark 4 |
| 26 | Mark 5:21-43 | Psalms 28; Mark 5 | Numbers 19-20; Psalms 28; Mark 5 |
| 27 | Mark 6:30-56 | Numbers 23; Mark 6 | Numbers 21-23; Mark 6 |
| 28 | Mark 7:1-23 | Numbers 27; Mark 7 | Numbers 24-27; Mark 7 |

Adapted and used with permission from Life Resources

# BIBLE READING GUIDE

## MARCH

| | MILESTONE 1 | MILESTONE 2 | MILESTONE 3 |
|---|---|---|---|
| 1 | Mark 8:27-38 | Numbers 26; Mark 8 | Numbers 28-29; Mark 8 |
| 2 | Mark 9:14-29 | Numbers 30; Mark 9 | Numbers 30-31; Mark 9 |
| 3 | Mark 10:13-31 | Exodus 32; Mark 10 | Numbers 32-33; Mark 10 |
| 4 | Numbers 36 | Numbers 36; Mark 11 | Numbers 34-36; Mark 11 |
| 5 | Deuteronomy 1: 26-46 | Deuteronomy 1; Mark 12 | Deuteronomy 1-2; Mark 12 |
| 6 | Deuteronomy 4: 1-14 | Deuteronomy 4: Psalms 36; Mark 13 | Deuteronomy 3-4; Psalms 36; Mark 13 |
| 7 | Deuteronomy 6 | Deuteronomy 6; Mark 14 | Deuteronomy 5-6; Psalms 43; Mark 14 |
| 8 | Deuteronomy 7:1-15 | Deuteronomy 7; Mark 15 | Deuteronomy 7-9; Mark 15 |
| 9 | Deuteronomy 10:12-22 | Deuteronomy 10; Mark 16 | Deuteronomy 10-12; Mark 16 |
| 10 | Galatians 1:11-24 | Deuteronomy 14; Galatians 1 | Deuteronomy 13-15; Galatians 1 |
| 11 | Deuteronomy 17:14-20 | Deuteronomy 17; Galatians 2 | Deuteronomy 16-18; Psalms 38; Galatians 2 |
| 12 | Galatians 3:15-29 | Deuteronomy 19; Galatians 3 | Deuteronomy 19-21; Galatians 3 |
| 13 | Galatians 4:8-31 | Deuteronomy 23; Galatians 4 | Deuteronomy 22-24; Galatians 4 |
| 14 | Galatians 5:1-15 | Deuteronomy 27; Galatians 5 | Deuteronomy 25-27; Galatians 5 |
| 15 | Galatians 6 | Deuteronomy 28; Galatians 6 | Deuteronomy 28-29; Galatians 6 |
| 16 | Psalms 40 | Deuteronomy 30; Psalms 40; 1 Corinthians 1 | Deuteronomy 30-31; Psalms 40; 1 Corinthians 1 |
| 17 | Deuteronomy 34 | Deuteronomy 34; 1 Corinthians 2 | Deuteronomy 32-34; 1 Corinthians 2 |
| 18 | Joshua 1 | Joshua 1; 1 Corinthians 3 | Joshua 1-2; Psalms 37; 1 Corinthians 3 |
| 19 | 1 Corinthians 4:1-13 | Joshua 6; 1 Corinthians 4 | Joshua 3-6; 1 Corinthians 4 |
| 20 | 1 Corinthians 5 | Psalms 69; 1 Corinthians 5 | Joshua 7-8; Psalms 69; 1 Corinthians 5 |
| 21 | Joshua 9:3-25 | Joshua 9; 1 Corinthians 6 | Joshua 9-11; 1 Corinthians 6 |
| 22 | Joshua 14:6-15 | Joshua 14; 1 Corinthians 7 | Joshua 12-14; 1 Corinthians 7 |
| 23 | 1 Corinthians 8 | Joshua 17; 1 Corinthians 8 | Joshua 15-17; 1 Corinthians 8 |
| 24 | Joshua 20 | Joshua 20; 1 Corinthians 9 | Joshua 18-20; 1 Corinthians 9 |
| 25 | 1 Corinthians 10:12-33 | Psalms 47; 1 Corinthians 10 | Joshua 21-22; Psalms 47; 1 Corinthians 10 |
| 26 | Joshua 24:11-28 | Joshua 24; Psalms 44 | Joshua 23-24; Psalms 44; 1 Corinthians 11 |
| 27 | 1 Corinthians 12:12-31 | Judges 2; 1 Corinthians 12 | Judges 1-3; 1 Corinthians 12 |
| 28 | 1 Corinthians 13 | Psalms 39, 41; 1 Corinthians 13 | Judges 4-5; Psalms 39, 41; 1 Corinthians 13 |
| 29 | Judges 6:1-21 | Judges 6; Psalms 52; 1 Corinthians 14 | Judges 6-7; Psalms 52; 1 Corinthians 14 |
| 30 | 1 Corinthians 15:35-58 | Psalms 42; 1 Corinthians 15 | Judges 8; Psalms 42; 1 Corinthians 15 |
| 31 | 1 Corinthians 16:5-18 | Psalms 49; 1 Corinthians 16 | Judges 9-10; Psalms 49; 1 Corinthians 16 |

Adapted and used with permission from Life Resources

# BIBLE READING GUIDE

# APRIL

| | MILESTONE 1 | MILESTONE 2 | MILESTONE 3 |
|---|---|---|---|
| 1 | Psalms 50 | Psalms 50; 2 Corinthians 1 | Judges 11-12; Psalms 50; 2 Corinthians 1 |
| 2 | Judges 13 | Judges 13; 2 Corinthians 2 | Judges 13-16; 2 Corinthians 2 |
| 3 | 2 Corinthians 3:7-18 | Psalms 89; 2 Corinthians 3 | Judges 17-18; Psalms 89; 2 Corinthians 3 |
| 4 | 2 Corinthians 4 | Judges 21; 2 Corinthians 4 | Judges 19-21; 2 Corinthians 4 |
| 5 | Ruth 2 | Ruth 2; Psalms 61; 2 Corinthians 5 | Ruth 1-2; Psalms 53, 61; 2 Corinthians 5 |
| 6 | 2 Corinthians 6:1-13 | Ruth 3-4; 2 Corinthians 6 | Ruth 3-4; Psalms 64-65; 2 Corinthians 6 |
| 7 | 1 Samuel 1:1-18 | 1 Samuel 1; Psalms 66 | 1 Samuel 1-2; Psalms 66; 2 Corinthians 7 |
| 8 | 2 Corinthians 8:1-15 | 1 Samuel 3; 2 Corinthians 8 | 1 Samuel 3-5; Psalms 77; 2 Corinthians 8 |
| 9 | 2 Corinthians 9 | Psalms 72; 2 Corinthians 9 | 1 Samuel 6-7; Psalms 72; 2 Corinthians 9 |
| 10 | 2 Corinthians 10 | 1 Samuel 8; 2 Corinthians 10 | 1 Samuel 8-10; 2 Corinthians 10 |
| 11 | 1 Samuel 12:13-25 | 1 Samuel 12; 2 Corinthians 11 | 1 Samuel 11-12; 1 Chronicles 1; 2 Corinthians 11 |
| 12 | 2 Corinthians 12:1-10 | 1 Samuel 13; 2 Corinthians 12 | 1 Samuel 13; 1 Chronicles 2-3; 2 Corinthians 12 |
| 13 | 1 Samuel 14:1-15 | 1 Samuel 14; 2 Corinthians 13 | 1 Samuel 14; 1 Chronicles 4; 2 Corinthians 13 |
| 14 | 1 Samuel 15:10-23 | 1 Samuel 15; Matthew 1 | 1 Samuel 15-16; 1 Chronicles 5; Matthew 1 |
| 15 | 1 Samuel 17:32-51 | 1 Samuel 17; Psalms 9 | 1 Samuel 17; Psalms 9; Matthew 2 |
| 16 | Matthew 3 | 1 Samuel 18; Psalms 11; Matthew 3 | 1 Samuel 18; 1 Chronicles 6; Psalms 11; Matthew 3 |
| 17 | 1 Samuel 19:11-23 | 1 Samuel 19; Matthew 4 | 1 Samuel 19; 1 Chronicles 7; Psalms 59; Matthew 4 |
| 18 | Psalms 34 | 1 Samuel 21; Psalms 34; Matthew 5 | 1 Samuel 20-21; Psalms 34; Matthew 5 |
| 19 | Matthew 6:5-18 | 1 Samuel 22; Matthew 6 | 1 Samuel 22; Psalms 17; Matthew 6 |
| 20 | Psalms 31 | Psalms 31; Matthew 7 | 1 Samuel 23; Psalms 31, 54; Matthew 7 |
| 21 | Matthew 8:5-22 | 1 Samuel 24; Matthew 8 | 1 Samuel 24; Psalms 57-58; 1 Chronicles 8; Matthew 8 |
| 22 | 1 Samuel 25:23-44 | 1 Samuel 24; Matthew 8 | 1 Samuel 25-26; Psalms 63; Matthew 9 |
| 23 | Matthew 10:5-42 | Psalms 141; Matthew 10 | 1 Samuel 27; Psalms 141; 1 Chronicles 9; Matthew 10 |
| 24 | Matthew 11:1-19 | Psalms 109; Matthew 11 | 1 Samuel 28-29; Psalms 109; Matthew 11 |
| 25 | 1 Samuel 31 | 1 Samuel 31; Matthew 12 | 1 Samuel 30-31; 1 Chronicles 10; Matthew 12 |
| 26 | Matthew 13:1-23 | 2 Samuel 1; Matthew 13 | 2 Samuel 1; Psalms 140; Matthew 13 |
| 27 | Matthew 14:22-36 | 2 Samuel 2; Matthew 14 | 2 Samuel 2; 1 Chronicles 11; Psalms 142; Matthew 14 |
| 28 | Matthew 15:21-39 | 1 Chronicles 12; Matthew 15 | 2 Samuel 3; 1 Chronicles 12; Matthew 15 |
| 29 | 2 Samuel 5:1-16 | 2 Samuel 5; Psalms 139 | 2 Samuel 4-5; Psalms 139; Matthew 16 |
| 30 | 2 Samuel 6:1-15 | 2 Samuel 6; 1 Chroncile 13; Psalms 139 | 2 Samuel 6; 1 Chronicles 13; Psalms 68; Matthew 17 |

Adapted and used with permission from Life Resources

# BIBLE READING GUIDE

## MAY

| | MILESTONE 1 | MILESTONE 2 | MILESTONE 3 |
|---|---|---|---|
| 1 | 1 Chronicles 15:1-24 | 1 Chronicles 15; Matthew 18 | 1 Chronicles 14-15; Psalms 132; Matthew 18 |
| 2 | 1 Chronicles 16:7-36 | 1 Chronicles 16; Psalms 106 | 1 Chronicles 16; Psalms 106; Matthew 19 |
| 3 | 1 Chronicles 17:1-15 | 1 Chronicles 17; Matthew 20 | 2 Samuel 7; 1 Chronicles 17; Psalms 2; Matthew 20 |
| 4 | 2 Samuel 9 | 2 Samuel 9; Matthew 21 | 2 Samuel 8-9; 1 Chronicles 18-19; Matthew 21 |
| 5 | Matthew 22:34-46 | 2 Samuel 10; Matthew 22 | 2 Samuel 10; 1 Chronicles 19-20; Psalms 20; Matthew 22 |
| 6 | 2 Samuel 12:1-12 | 2 Samuel 12; Psalms 51 | 2 Samuel 11-12; Psalms 51; Matthew 23 |
| 7 | Matthew 24:1-22 | 2 Samuel 14; Matthew 24 | 2 Samuel 13-14; Matthew 24 |
| 8 | 2 Samuel 15:1-14 | 2 Samuel 15; Matthew 25 | 2 Samuel 15-16; Psalms 32; Matthew 25 |
| 9 | Psalms 71 | Psalms 71; Matthew 26 | 2 Samuel 17; Psalms 71; Matthew 26 |
| 10 | Matthew 27:32-56 | 2 Samuel 18; Matthew 27 | 2 Samuel 18; Psalms 56; Matthew 27 |
| 11 | 2 Samuel 19:24-40 | 2 Samuel 19; Matthew 28 | 2 Samuel 19-20; Psalms 55; Matthew 28 |
| 12 | 2 Samuel 22 | 2 Samuel 22; 1 Thessalonians 1 | 2 Samuel 21-23; 1 Thessalonians 1 |
| 13 | 1 Chronicles 21:18-22:1 | 1 Chronicles 21; 1 Thessalonians 2 | 2 Samuel 24; 1 Chronicles 21; Psalms 30; 1 Thessalonians 2 |
| 14 | 1 Thessalonians 3 | 1 Chronicles 22; 1 Thessalonians 3 | 1 Chronicles 22-24; 1 Thessalonians 3 |
| 15 | 1 Thessalonians 4:1-12 | 1 Chronicles 25; 1 Thessalonians 4 | 1 Chronicles 25-27; 1 Thessalonians 4 |
| 16 | 1 Chronicles 28:8-21 | 1 Chronicles 28; Psalms 91; 1 Thessalonians 5 | 1 Kings 1; 1 Chronicles 28; Psalms 91; 1 Thessalonians 5 |
| 17 | 1 Chronicles 29:10-25 | 1 Chronicles 29; Psalms 95 | 1 Kings 2; 1 Chronicles 29; Psalms 95; 2 Thessalonians 1 |
| 18 | 1 Kings 3:1-15 | 1 Kings 3; Psalms 78; 2 Thessalonians 2 | 1 Kings 3; 2 Chronicles 1; Psalms 78; 2 Thessalonians 2 |
| 19 | 2 Thessalonians 3 | 2 Chronicles 2; 2 Thessalonians 3 | 1 Kings 4-5; 2 Chronicles 2; Psalms 101; 2 Thessalonians 3 |
| 20 | Romans 1:18-32 | 2 Chronicles 3; Romans 1 | 1 Kings 6; 2 Chronicles 3; Psalms 97; Romans 1 |
| 21 | Romans 2:17-29 | 1 Kings 7; Romans 2 | 1 Kings 7; 2 Chronicles 4; Psalms 98; Romans 2 |
| 22 | Romans 3:21-31 | 1 Kings 8; Romans 3 | 1 Kings 8; 2 Chronicles 5; Psalms 99; Romans 3 |
| 23 | Psalms 135 | Psalms 135; Romans 4 | 2 Chronicles 6-7; Psalms 135; Romans 4 |
| 24 | Romans 5:1-11 | 1 Kings 9; Romans 5 | 1 Kings 9; 2 Chronicles 8; Psalms 136; Romans 5 |
| 25 | Romans 6:15-23 | 1 Kings 10; Romans 6 | 1 Kings 10-11; 2 Chronicles 9; Romans 6 |
| 26 | Proverbs 2 | Proverbs 2; Romans 7 | Proverbs 1-3; Romans 7 |
| 27 | Romans 8:1-17 | Proverbs 6; Romans 8 | Proverbs 4-6; Romans 8 |
| 28 | Proverbs 7 | Proverbs 7; Romans 9 | Proverbs 7-9; Romans 9 |
| 29 | Romans 10:5-21 | Proverbs 12; Romans 10 | Proverbs 10-12; Romans 10 |
| 30 | Romans 11:25-36 | Proverbs 14; Romans 11 | Proverbs 13-15; Romans 11 |
| 31 | Proverbs 16 | Proverbs 16; Romans 12 | Proverbs 16-18; Romans 12 |

Adapted and used with permission from Life Resources

# BIBLE READING GUIDE

# JUNE

|  | MILESTONE 1 | MILESTONE 2 | MILESTONE 3 |
|---|---|---|---|
| 1 | Romans 13 | Proverbs 20; Romans 13 | Proverbs 19-21; Romans 13 |
| 2 | Romans 14 | Proverbs 24; Romans 14 | Proverbs 22-24; Romans 14 |
| 3 | Romans 15:1-13 | Proverbs 27; Romans 15 | Proverbs 25-27; Romans 15 |
| 4 | Proverbs 29 | Proverbs 29; Romans 16 | Proverbs 28-29; Psalms 60; Romans 16 |
| 5 | Ephesians 1:14-23 | Proverbs 31; Psalms 33; Ephesians 1 | Proverbs 30-31; Psalms 33; Ephesians 1 |
| 6 | Ephesians 2:11-22 | Ecclesiastes 3; Ephesians 2 | Ecclesiastes 1-3; Psalms 45; Ephesians 2 |
| 7 | Ephesians 3 | Psalms 18; Ephesians 3 | Ecclesiastes 4-6; Psalms 18; Ephesians 3 |
| 8 | Ephesians 4:17-32 | Ecclesiastes 7; Ephesians 4 | Ecclesiastes 7-9; Ephesians 4 |
| 9 | Ephesians 5:1-20 | Ecclesiastes 12; Ephesians 5 | Ecclesiastes 10-12; Psalms 94; Ephesians 5 |
| 10 | Ephesians 6:10-23 | Song of Songs 1-2; Ephesians 6 | Song of Songs 1-4; Ephesians 6 |
| 11 | Philippians 1:12-26 | Song of Songs 8; Philippians 1 | Song of Songs 5-8; Philippians 1 |
| 12 | Philippians 2:1-18 | 1 Kings 12; Philippians 2 | 1 Kings 12; 2 Chronicles 10-11; Philippians 2 |
| 13 | Philippians 3:1-11 | 1 Kings 14; Philippians 3 | 1 Kings 13-14; 2 Chronicles 12; Philippians 3 |
| 14 | Philippians 4 | 1 Kings 15; Philippians 4 | 1 Kings 15; 2 Chronicles 13-14; Philippians 4 |
| 15 | Colossians 1:1-14 | 1 Kings 16; Colossians 1 | 1 Kings 16; 2 Chronicles 15-16; Colossians 1 |
| 16 | Colossians 2:6-23 | 1 Kings 18; Colossians 2 | 1 Kings 17-19; Colossians 2 |
| 17 | 2 Chronicles 17 | 2 Chronicles 17; Colossians 3 | 1 Kings 20-21; 2 Chronicles 17; Colossians 3 |
| 18 | Colossians 4:2-18 | 2 Chronicles 19; Colossians 4 | 1 Kings 22; 2 Chronicles 18-19; Colossians 4 |
| 19 | 2 Kings 2:1-18 | 2 Kings 2; Psalms 82; 1 Timothy 1 | 2 Kings 1-3; Psalms 82; 1 Timothy 1 |
| 20 | 1 Timothy 2 | 2 Kings 4; 1 Timothy 2 | 2 Kings 4-5; Psalms 83; 1 Timothy 2 |
| 21 | 2 Chronicles 20:1-30 | 2 Chronicles 20; 1 Timothy 3 | 2 Kings 6-7; 2 Chronicles 20; 1 Timothy 3 |
| 22 | 1 Timothy 4:6-16 | 2 Chronicles 21; 1 Timothy 4 | 2 Kings 8-9; 2 Chronicles 21; 1 Timothy 4 |
| 23 | 1 Timothy 5:3-25 | 2 Chronicles 22; 1 Timothy 5 | 2 Kings 10; 2 Chronicles 22-23; 1 Timothy 5 |
| 24 | 1 Timothy 6:1-10 | 2 Chronicles 24; 1 Timothy 6 | 2 Kings 11-12; 2 Chronicles 24; 1 Timothy 6 |
| 25 | Joel 2:12-32 | Joel 2; 2 Timothy 1 | Joel 1-3; 2 Timothy 1 |
| 26 | 2 Timothy 2:1-13 | Jonah 2-3; 2 Timothy 2 | Jonah 1-4; 2 Timothy 2 |
| 27 | 2 Timothy 3 | 2 Chronicles 25; 2 Timothy 3 | 2 Kings 13-14; 2 Chronicles 25; 2 Timothy 3 |
| 28 | 2 Timothy 4 | Psalms 80; 2 Timothy 4 | Amos 1-3; Psalms 80; 2 Timothy 4 |
| 29 | Amos 5:1-17 | Amos 5; Titus 1 | Amos 4-6; Psalms 86; Titus 1 |
| 30 | Titus 2 | Psalms 104; Titus 2 | Amos 7-9; Psalms 104; Titus 2 |

Adapted and used with permission from Life Resources

# BIBLE READING GUIDE

# JULY

| | MILESTONE 1 | MILESTONE 2 | MILESTONE 3 |
|---|---|---|---|
| 1 | Isaiah 1:2-20 | Isaiah 1; Titus 3 | Isaiah 1-3; Titus 3 |
| 2 | Isaiah 5:1-7 | Isaiah 5; Jude | Isaiah 4-5; Psalms 115-116; Jude |
| 3 | Isaiah 6 | Isaiah 6; 2 Chronicles 26 | Isaiah 6-7; 2 Chronicles 26-27; Philemon |
| 4 | Hebrews 1 | Hosea 1; Hebrews 1 | 2 Kings 15-16; Hosea 1; Hebrews 1 |
| 5 | Hosea 2:14-23 | Hosea 2; Hebrews 2 | Hosea 2-5; Hebrews 2 |
| 6 | Hebrews 3 | Hosea 6; Hebrews 3 | Hosea 6-9; Hebrews 3 |
| 7 | Hosea 12 | Hosea 12; Psalms 73; Hebrews 4 | Hosea 10-12; Psalms 73; Hebrews 4 |
| 8 | Hosea 14; Hebrews 5 | Hosea 14; Psalms 102; Hebrews 5 | Hosea 13-14; Psalms 100,102; Hebrews 5 |
| 9 | Hebrews 6:1-12 | Micah 4; Hebrews 6 | Micah 1-4; Hebrews 6 |
| 10 | Hebrews 7:15-28 | Micah 7; Hebrews 7 | Micah 5-7; Hebrews 7 |
| 11 | Isaiah 8:11-22 | Isaiah 8; Hebrews 8 | Isaiah 8-10; Hebrews 8 |
| 12 | Hebrews 9:11-28 | Isaiah 11; Hebrews 9 | Isaiah 11-14; Hebrews 9 |
| 13 | Hebrews 10:1-18 | Isaiah 15-16; Hebrews 10 | Isaiah 15-18; Hebrews 10 |
| 14 | Hebrews 11 | Isaiah 21; Hebrews 11 | Isaiah 19-21; Hebrews 11 |
| 15 | Hebrews 12:14-29 | Isaiah 24; Hebrews 12 | Isaiah 22-24; Hebrews 12 |
| 16 | Isaiah 26:1-19 | Isaiah 26; Hebrews 13 | Isaiah 25-28; Hebrews 13 |
| 17 | James 1 | Isaiah 31; James 1 | Isaiah 29-31; James 1 |
| 18 | James 2:14-26 | Isaiah 32; James 2 | Isaiah 32-35; James 2 |
| 19 | James 3:13-18; Psalms 46 | 2 Chronicles 28; Psalms 46; James 3 | 2 Kings 17; 2 Chronicles 28; Psalms 46; James 3 |
| 20 | James 4:1-10 | 2 Chronicles 30; James 4 | 2 Chronicles 29-31; James 4 |
| 21 | 2 Kings 19:1-19 | 2 Kings 19; James 5 | 2 Kings 18-19; 2 Chronicles 32; James 5 |
| 22 | 1 Peter 1:13-25 | Psalms 76; 1 Peter 1 | Isaiah 36-37; Psalms 76; 1 Peter 1 |
| 23 | 1 Peter 2:4-17 | Isaiah 38; 1 Peter 2 | 2 Kings 20; Isaiah 38-39; Psalms 75; 1 Peter 2 |
| 24 | 1 Peter 3:1-12 | Isaiah 40; 1 Peter 3 | Isaiah 40-42; 1 Peter 3 |
| 25 | 1 Peter 4:1-11 | Isaiah 43; 1 Peter 4 | Isaiah 43-45; 1 Peter 4 |
| 26 | Isaiah 49:8-26 | Isaiah 49; 1 Peter 5 | Isaiah 46-49; 1 Peter 5 |
| 27 | 2 Peter 1:1-11 | Isaiah 51; Psalms 92; 2 Peter 1 | Isaiah 50-52; Psalms 92; 2 Peter 1 |
| 28 | 2 Peter 2 | Isaiah 55; 2 Peter 2 | Isaiah 53-56; 2 Peter 2 |
| 29 | Psalms 103 | Psalms 103; 2 Peter 3 | Isaiah 57-59; Psalms 103; 2 Peter 3 |
| 30 | John 1:1-28 | Isaiah 62; John 1 | Isaiah 60-62; John 1 |
| 31 | John 2:1-12 | Psalms 107; John 2 | Isaiah 63-64; Psalms 107; John 2 |

Adapted and used with permission from Life Resources

# BIBLE READING GUIDE

## AUGUST

| | MILESTONE 1 | MILESTONE 2 | MILESTONE 3 |
|---|---|---|---|
| 1 | John 3:1-21 | Isaiah 66; John 3 | Isaiah 65-66; Psalms 62; John 3 |
| 2 | John 4:1-42 | 2 Chronicles 33; John 4 | 2 King 21; 2 Chronicles 33; John 4 |
| 3 | John 5:16-47 | Nahum 2; John 5 | Nahum 1-3; John 5 |
| 4 | John 6:22-59 | 2 Chronicles 34; John 6 | 2 Kings 22; 2 Chronicles 34; John 6 |
| 5 | John 7:25-52 | 2 Kings 23; John 7 | 2 Kings 23; 2 Chronicles 35; John 7 |
| 6 | John 8:31-59 | Habakkuk 3; John 8 | Habakkuk 1-3; John 8 |
| 7 | John 9:1-34 | Zephaniah 2; John 9 | Zephaniah 1-3; John 9 |
| 8 | John 10:1-21 | Jeremiah 2; John 10 | Jeremiah 1-3; John 10 |
| 9 | Jeremiah 4:1-18 | Jeremiah 4; John 11 | Jeremiah 3-4; John 11 |
| 10 | John 12:1-19 | Jeremiah 5; John 12 | Jeremiah 5-6; John 12 |
| 11 | John 13:1-17 | Jeremiah 9; John 13 | Jeremiah 7-9; John 13 |
| 12 | John 14:15-31 | Jeremiah 10; John 14 | Jeremiah 10-12; John 14 |
| 13 | John 15:1-17 | Jeremiah 13; John 15 | Jeremiah 13-15; John 15 |
| 14 | John 16:16-33 | Psalms 96; John 16 | Jeremiah 16-17; Psalms 96; John 16 |
| 15 | John 17 | Jeremiah 18; Psalms 93; John 17 | Jeremiah 18-20; Psalms 93; John 17 |
| 16 | John 18:19-40 | Jeremiah 22; John 18 | 2 Kings 24; Jeremiah 22; Psalms 112; John 18 |
| 17 | Jeremiah 25:1-14 | Jeremiah 25; John 19 | Jeremiah 23-25; John 19 |
| 18 | John 20:11-29 | Jeremiah 36; John 20 | Jeremiah 26, 35-36; John 20 |
| 19 | John 21:15-23 | Psalms 105; John 21 | Jeremiah 45-47; Psalms 105; John 21 |
| 20 | 1 John 1 | Jeremiah 48; Psalms 67; 1 John 1 | Jeremiah 48-49; Psalms 67; 1 John 1 |
| 21 | 1 John 2:7-29 | Psalms 118; 1 John 2 | Jeremiah 21, 24, 27; Psalms 118; 1 John 2 |
| 22 | Jeremiah 29:1-23 | Jeremiah 29; 1 John 3 | Jeremiah 28-30; 1 John 3 |
| 23 | 1 John 4:7-21 | Jeremiah 32; 1 John 4 | Jeremiah 31-32; 1 John 4 |
| 24 | Jeremiah 33 | Jeremiah 33; 1 John 5 | Jeremiah 33-34; Psalms 74; 1 John 5 |
| 25 | 2 John | Psalms 79; 2 John | Jeremiah 37-39; Psalms 79; 2 John |
| 26 | Jeremiah 51:1-19 | Jeremiah 51; 3 John | Jeremiah 50-51; 3 John |
| 27 | Psalms 144 | Psalms 144; Revelation 1 | Jeremiah 52; Psalms 143-144; Revelation 1 |
| 28 | Ezekiel 3:1-15 | Ezekiel 3; Revelation 2 | Ezekiel 1-3; Revelation 2 |
| 29 | Revelation 3:7-22 | Ezekiel 5; Revelation 3 | Ezekiel 4-7; Revelation 3 |
| 30 | Revelation 4 | Ezekiel 11; Revelation 4 | Ezekiel 8-11; Revelation 4 |
| 31 | Revelation 5 | Ezekiel 14; Revelation 5 | Ezekiel 12-14; Revelation 5 |

Adapted and used with permission from Life Resources

# BIBLE READING GUIDE

# SEPTEMBER

| | MILESTONE 1 | MILESTONE 2 | MILESTONE 3 |
|---|---|---|---|
| 1 | Ezekiel 16:1-34 | Ezekiel 16; Psalms 70; Revelation 6 | Ezekiel 15-16; Psalms 70; Revelation 6 |
| 2 | Ezekiel 18 | Ezekiel 18; Revelation 7 | Ezekiel 17-19; Revelation 7 |
| 3 | Revelation 8 | Psalms 111; Revelation 8 | Ezekiel 20-21; Psalms 111; Revelation 8 |
| 4 | Ezekiel 22:23-31 | Ezekiel 22; Revelation 9 | Ezekiel 22-24; Revelation 9 |
| 5 | Revelation 10 | Ezekiel 28; Revelation 10 | Ezekiel 25-28; Revelation 10 |
| 6 | Revelation 11:1-14 | Ezekiel 31; Revelation 11 | Ezekiel 29-32; Revelation 11 |
| 7 | Revelation 12 | 2 Chronicles 36; Revelation 12 | 2 Kings 25; 2 Chronicles 36; Jeremiah 40-41; Revelation 12 |
| 8 | Psalms 48 | Psalms 48; Revelation 13 | Jeremiah 42-44; Psalms 48; Revelation 13 |
| 9 | Revelation 14:6-20 | Lamentations 2; Revelation 14 | Lamentations 1-2; Obadiah; Revelation 14 |
| 10 | Revelation 15 | Lamentations 3; Revelation 15 | Lamentations 3-5; Revelation 15 |
| 11 | Daniel 2:24-44 | Daniel 2; Revelation 16 | Daniel 1-2; Revelation 16 |
| 12 | Daniel 4:19-37 | Daniel 4; Psalms 81 | Daniel 3-4; Psalms 81; Revelation 17 |
| 13 | Ezekiel 34:1-24 | Ezekiel 34; Revelation 18 | Ezekiel 33-35; Revelation 18 |
| 14 | Revelation 19 | Ezekiel 36; Revelation 19 | Ezekiel 36-37; Psalms 110; Revelation 19 |
| 15 | Psalms 145 | Psalms 145; Revelation 20 | Ezekiel 38-39; Psalms 145; Revelation 20 |
| 16 | Revelation 21 | Ezekiel 41; Revelation 21 | Ezekiel 40-41; Psalms 128; Revelation 21 |
| 17 | Revelation 22:7-21 | Ezekiel 43; Revelation 22 | Ezekiel 42-44; Revelation 22 |
| 18 | Luke 1:26-56 | Ezekiel 45; Luke 1 | Ezekiel 45-46; Luke 1 |
| 19 | Luke 2:1-20 | Ezekiel 47; Luke 2 | Ezekiel 47-48; Luke 2 |
| 20 | Daniel 6 | Daniel 6; Psalms 130; Luke 3 | Daniel 5-6; Psalms 130; Luke 3 |
| 21 | Luke 4:1-13 | Daniel 8; Luke 4 | Daniel 7-8; Psalms 137; Luke 4 |
| 22 | Daniel 9:1-19 | Daniel 9; Psalms 123; Luke 5 | Daniel 9-10; Psalms 123; Luke 5 |
| 23 | Luke 6:27-49 | Daniel 12; Luke 6 | Daniel 11-12; Luke 6 |
| 24 | Psalms 84 | Psalms 84-85; Luke 7 | Ezra 1; Psalms 84-85; Luke 7 |
| 25 | Ezra 3:7-13 | Ezra 3; Luke 8 | Ezra 2-3; Luke 8 |
| 26 | Luke 9:46-62 | Psalms 127; Luke 9 | Ezra 4; Psalms 113,127; Luke 9 |
| 27 | Luke 10:21-37 | Haggai 2; Luke 10 | Haggai 1-2; Psalms 129; Luke 10 |
| 28 | Luke 11:1-13 | Zechariah 2; Luke 11 | Zechariah 1-3; Luke 11 |
| 29 | Luke 12:13-34 | Zechariah 4; Luke 12 | Zechariah 4-6; Luke 12 |
| 30 | Luke 13:1-17 | Zechariah 8; Luke 13 | Zechariah 7-9; Luke 13 |

Adapted and used with permission from Life Resources

# BIBLE READING GUIDE

# OCTOBER

| | MILESTONE 1 | MILESTONE 2 | MILESTONE 3 |
|---|---|---|---|
| 1 | Luke 14:25-35 | Zechariah 12; Psalms 126; Luke 14 | Zechariah 10-12; Psalms 126; Luke 14 |
| 2 | Luke 15:11-32 | Zechariah 14; Psalms 147; Luke 15 | Zechariah 13-14; Psalms 147; Luke 15 |
| 3 | Luke 16:1-18 | Ezra 6; Psalms 138; Luke 16 | Ezra 5-6; Psalms 138; Luke 16 |
| 4 | Luke 17:20-37 | Esther 1; Luke 17 | Esther 1-2; Psalms 150; Luke 17 |
| 5 | Esther 4 | Esther 4; Luke 18 | Esther 3-8; Luke 18 |
| 6 | Luke 19:11-27 | Esther 9; Luke 19 | Esther 9-10; Luke 19 |
| 7 | Luke 20:9-19 | Ezra 7; Luke 20 | Ezra 7-8; Luke 20 |
| 8 | Ezra 10:1-17 | Ezra 10; Psalms 131; Luke 21 | Ezra 9-10; Psalms 131; Luke 21 |
| 9 | Luke 22:7-46 | Nehemiah 1; Psalms 133; Luke 22 | Nehemiah 1-2; Psalms 133; Luke 22 |
| 10 | Luke 23; 26-43 | Nehemiah 3; Luke 23 | Nehemiah 3-4; Luke 23 |
| 11 | Psalms 146 | Psalms 146; Luke 24 | Nehemiah 5-6; Psalms 146; Luke 24 |
| 12 | Nehemiah 8:1-12 | Nehemiah 8; Acts 1 | Nehemiah 7-8; Acts 1 |
| 13 | Acts 2:14-42 | Nehemiah 10; Acts 2 | Nehemiah 9-10; Acts 2 |
| 14 | Acts 3:12-26 | Nehemiah 12; Psalms 1; Acts 3 | Nehemiah 11-12; Psalms 1; Acts 3 |
| 15 | Acts 4:23-37 | Malachi 2; Acts 4 | Nehemiah 13; Malachi 1-2; Acts 4 |
| 16 | Malachi 3:6-18 | Malachi 3; Acts 5 | Malachi 3-4; Psalms 148; Acts 5 |
| 17 | Acts 6 | Job 2; Acts 6 | Job 1-2; Acts 6-7 |
| 18 | Acts 8:26-40 | Job 3; Acts 8 | Job 3; Acts 8-9 |
| 19 | Acts 10:9-33 | Job 4; Psalms 108; Acts 10 | Job 4-5; Psalms 108; Acts 10-11 |
| 20 | Acts 12:6-19 | Job 7; Acts 12 | Job 6-7; Acts 12 |
| 21 | Acts 14; 8-28 | Job 8; Acts 14 | Job 8; Acts 13-14 |
| 22 | Job 10 | Job 10; Acts 15-16 | Job 9-10; Acts 15-16 |
| 23 | Acts 18:1-17 | Job 11; Acts 18 | Job 11; Acts 17-18 |
| 24 | Acts 20:13-38 | Job 13; Acts 20 | Job 12-14; Acts 19-20 |
| 25 | Acts 23:12-35 | Job 15; Acts 23 | Job 15; Acts 21-23 |
| 26 | Job 17 | Job 17; Acts 26 | Job 16-17; Acts 24-26 |
| 27 | Acts 28:17-31 | Psalms 114; Acts 28 | Job 18; Psalms 114; Acts 27-28 |
| 28 | Job 19 | Job 19; Mark 1 | Job 19; Mark 1-2 |
| 29 | Mark 4:1-20 | Job 20; Mark 4 | Job 20; Mark 3-4 |
| 30 | Mark 6:1-13 | Job 21; Mark 6 | Job 21; Mark 5-6 |
| 31 | Mark 8:27-37 | Job 22; Mark 8 | Job 22; Mark 7-8 |

Adapted and used with permission from Life Resources

# Grow - Bibliography

1.  C.S. Lewis, *Mere Christianity* (New York: Macmillan, 1952)

2.  Wayne Cordeiro, *The Divine Mentor* (Bloomington: Bethany House, 2007)

3.  Erik Rees, *S.H.A.P.E. Purpose Driven* (Grand Rapids: Zondervan, 2006)

4.  John Bevere, *The Bait of Satan* (Lake Mary: Charisma, 1994, 1997, 2004)

5.  Andy Stanley, *Dallas Theological Seminary Talk* (Dallas: You Tube, 2015)

6.  Tyler VanderWeele, *Harvard T.H. Chan School Religious Service Study* 1992-2012

7.  *Grant & Glueck Study* - Harvard University 1939 to 2014 (Cambridge)

8.  John Ortberg, *If You Want to Walk on Water, You've Got to Get Out of The Boat* (Grand Rapids: Zondervan, 2001)

9.  Dixon Murrah, *Stress In The Ministry* (Houston: Self Published, 1989)

10. Peter Scazzero, *The Emotionally Healthy Church* (Grand Rapids: Zondervan, 2003)

11. *Alcoholic Anonymous* (Alcoholics Anonymous World Services, Inc. 1939, 1955, 1976, 2001)

12. D.A. Carson, R.T. France, *J.A. Motyer & G.J. Wenham, New Bible Commentary* (Downers Grove: InterVarsity Press, USA, 1994)

CPSIA information can be obtained
at www.ICGtesting.com
Printed in the USA
FSOW02n1540200417
33360FS